D1714612

**SAGE** was founded in 1965 by Sara Miller McCune to support the dissemination of usable knowledge by publishing innovative and high-quality research and teaching content. Today, we publish over 900 journals, including those of more than 400 learned societies, more than 800 new books per year, and a growing range of library products including archives, data, case studies, reports, and video. SAGE remains majority-owned by our founder, and after Sara's lifetime will become owned by a charitable trust that secures our continued independence.

Los Angeles | London | New Delhi | Singapore | Washington DC | Melbourne

# Advance Praise

In this book, Arnab Chatterjee attempts the difficult task of describing the place of the personal in the public/private divide that is supposed to form the basis of modern institutions in Indian society. His methods are both phenomenological and historical. Of particular interest is his treatment of the little-known works of Indian Hegelians such as Brajendranath Seal and Hiralal Haldar. This book promises to draw the attention of scholars of everyday practices in modern Indian life.

**Partha Chatterjee,** *Professor of Anthropology*
*Columbia University*

The book is very engaging.

**Dipesh Chakrabarty,** *Lawrence A. Kimpton Distinguished Service Professor of History, The University of Chicago*

This book crosses the boundaries of philosophy and social theory in very interesting ways and is a great contribution to the development of the ideas of discourse, criticism, and subjectivity.

**Veena Das,** *Krieger-Eisenhower Professor of Anthropology, Johns Hopkins University*

# Is the
# Personal
## beyond
# PRIVATE
## and
# Public?

# Is the
# Personal
## beyond
# PRIVATE
## and
# Public?

## New Perspectives in
## Social Theory and Practice

# Arnab
# Chatterjee

Los Angeles I London I New Delhi
Singapore I Washington DC I Melbourne

First published in 2018 by

**SAGE Publications India Pvt Ltd**
B1/I-1 Mohan Cooperative Industrial Area
Mathura Road, New Delhi 110 044, India
www.sagepub.in

**SAGE Publications Inc**
2455 Teller Road
Thousand Oaks, California 91320, USA

**SAGE Publications Ltd**
1 Oliver's Yard, 55 City Road
London EC1Y 1SP, United Kingdom

**SAGE Publications Asia-Pacific Pte Ltd**
3 Church Street
#10-04 Samsung Hub
Singapore 049483

Published by Vivek Mehra for SAGE Publications India Pvt Ltd, typeset in 10/12 pt Times New Roman by Fidus Design Pvt. Ltd., Chandigarh and printed at Chaman Enterprises, New Delhi.

**Library of Congress Cataloging-in-Publication Data**
Names: Chatterjee, Arnab, author.
Title: Is the personal beyond private and public?: new perspectives in social theory and practice/
    Arnab Chatterjee.
Description: Thousand Oaks, CA: SAGE Publications India Pvt Ltd, [2018] | Includes bibliographical
    references and index.
Identifiers: LCCN 2017055386 | ISBN 9789352805204 (print (hb): alk. paper) | ISBN 9789352805211
    (e pub 2.0) | ISBN 9789352805228 (e book)
Subjects: LCSH: Privacy. | Social interaction.
Classification: LCC BF637.P74 C43 2018 | DDC 302.5/4—dc23
LC record available at https://lccn.loc.gov/2017055386


**ISBN:** 978-93-528-0520-4 (HB)

**SAGE Team:** Rajesh Dey, Guneet Kaur Gulati and Shobana Paul

*To my (late)* ma, mejdi, bacchiya, *Chotu Singh,*
*and lately, Anuradha*

*Those who deeply mourned my slowness and*
*the non-being of this work—over a*
*long time; now, finally...*

Thank you for choosing a SAGE product!
If you have any comment, observation or feedback,
I would like to personally hear from you.

*Please write to me at* **contactceo@sagepub.in**

**Vivek Mehra,** Managing Director and CEO, SAGE India.

## Bulk Sales

SAGE India offers special discounts
for purchase of books in bulk.
We also make available special imprints
and excerpts from our books on demand.

*For orders and enquiries, write to us at*

Marketing Department
SAGE Publications India Pvt Ltd
B1/I-1, Mohan Cooperative Industrial Area
Mathura Road, Post Bag 7
New Delhi 110044, India

*E-mail us at* **marketing@sagepub.in**

## Get to know more about SAGE

Be invited to SAGE events, get on our mailing list.
*Write today to* **marketing@sagepub.in**

This book is also available as an e-book.

# Contents

# Contents

# Prologue

## I

Unlike Lyotard who wanted to "stroke his [Marx's] beard as a complex libidinal volume, reawakening his hidden desire and ours along with it,"[1] we must be serious enough and consider that when such an energetic and forceful theorist as Marx wrote "the [modern] state is founded upon the contradiction between public and private life,"[2] it rehearsed in one breath as if the taxonomic key to understanding modernity—which is the public/private divide; and notwithstanding Marx's own resolution (i.e., the abolition of private property), a corresponding failure (of thinkers including Marx) to find a way beyond the conflictual binary of the public and private, could be said to have been, pace Marx's own words, momentously, unboxed. Marx's agenda and resolution are well-known, but while Marx had an effective concern with smashing the liberal divide, there is a long list of other thinkers who have grappled—being imbibed with an unputdownable "interpretive" interest—with the problem of finding a way beyond the binary. For the great, canonical thinkers of the public sphere, Hannah Arendt had previously rejected intimacy as a "deep private;" for Habermas, it reappeared as the beyond of private and public. The personal remains manifestly and immanently under-theorized in the works of both the thinkers, and this book steps in with caution to fill this gap. Recent researches—while tracing "the ongoing struggle [since two hundred years ago] in Locke, Shafetusbury, Hutcheson, Hume, and Smith to find a framework to mediate between the public and private,"—in order to grasp our own times, switch over to—"Levinas's belief that a certain mediation between the public and private is possible and in Derrida's insistence that a discourse predicated on a clear and

---

[1] Jean-Francois Lyotard, "The Desire Named Marx" in *Libidinal Economy*, transl. I. H. Grant (1994; repr., London: Continuum, 2005), 94–150.

[2] Karl Marx, *Selected Writings in Sociology and Social Philosophy,* eds. T. B. Bottomore and M. Rubel (Harmondsworth: Penguin Books, 1961), 222.

absolute distinction between the public and the private can only fall into ruins."[3] Now, what is the register of this crucial, mediating mark? These researches—of which Gaston's book is the most competent and poignant example—advocate (albeit erroneously) the "secret"[4] in Derrida's (and Levinas's) works to have been the tempting solution. Death ("language about death is nothing but the long history of a secret society, neither public nor private, semi-private, semi-public, on the border between the two"), the postcard ("half-private half-public neither the one nor the other"), and the telephone are Derrida's three examples of the secret meant to solve the liberal dichotomy.

All this is to make a single point: those thinkers who have been pivotal in finding (Western) modernity and continue to engage with its gestures through their breathing apostles, and also those who were prophets of colonial (and now postcolonial) modernities, could be seen to have been—though not always in an informed manner—struggling to solve the public/private riddle with an answer of their own. This has been the story since 1767, and it runs amok till 2017. The public/private riddle is one of the strongest unsolved puzzles in the history of ideas. Strongest all the more because the dissenting strands always ran up to alternative versions or weak synonyms of either the private or the public (a classical example is the personal that appeared/and still appears as another version of the private being used as a moment of parole, that is, speech, particularly in everyday life and language). The mix-up between the private and the personal has been naturalized to the extent that their doubtful assonance within texts and discourses go un-problematically, and dangerously, unheeded. Are the personal and the private the same and thus interchangeable? If not, in what ways could they be said to have been different? When did this confusion set in? Now, if it is possible to distance and distinguish them, then what are the results of such a revision? In this work, these issues will be broached to argue in favor of a trichotomy (personal, public, and private) to consequently arrive at a point beyond the debated dichotomy (where the personal and the private serve as a single algorithm and that has been conveniently pitted against the public).

This work, in an attempt to grapple with this dilemma in a new way, if not to resolve it altogether, argues the personal as a beyond of the private/public binary and distinguishes it from the private vis-à-vis

---

[3] Sean Gaston, *Derrida and Disinterest* (London: Continuum, 2005), vii–viii.

[4] How a "secret" as the "deep private" fails in its mediation has been discussed in Chapters 3 and 4.

the public. The private is opposed to the public and resists public scrutiny and publicity—the stuff of which the public is made. The way we do not know what a person is, what his/her real/final intentions are, or whether somebody is genuinely aggrieved or not—makes the personal largely unpredictable and indeterminate in the final instance, and not necessarily opposed to the public. Originally being legal-juridical categories, private and public have specific indicators. Personal relationships such as love or friendship remain outside legislation.

For the second moot point in this work, I shall show, schematically though, how the journey—at least in colonial modernity, and its aftermath—has not been from personality to impersonality, as has often been assumed, but from the realm of the natural personal to that of the juridical/group/collective personality of organizations. This will be pursued specifically in Part 2 of the work: the inviting emptiness of legal fictions—plausible even in the wake of contemporary, originary capitalism, as Rose states, "The concept of capital brings the relation of person and thing to the crunch. Capital acts like a person [and] not a thing. The illusion of natural personality is destroyed by this personification."[5] This could be provocative for many, particularly for the specialists dedicated to postcolonial theory, but, given the volume and span of the present work, I could not assuage their hunger by delving into the burgeoning literature of legal personality and legal fictions—more than that was minimally required—excluding even the exciting oeuvre that engages with neo–Kantian jurisprudence, particularly Emile Lask, Radbruch, Stammler, and Dabin.[6] But while this is trapped by and in law, the root metaphors of love and friendship–(stated before), again when instituted, escape the law as event. Finally, I intend to show that all the helping structures including the welfare state and social work—which raided by the whimsical and arbitrary metaphors of "personal" relational filiations, admittedly, with or against their own intended grain—cannot be grasped by the public/private motors.

# II

Personalism (which posits that the person is of the supreme value) forms the primary theoretical fillip to this study. Classic treatises in this tradition

[5] Gillian Rose, *Dialectic of Nihilism: Post-structuralism and Law* (England: Basil Blackwell, 1984), 46.
[6] Rose's book is perhaps the only classic on this (in English) which is neither used nor cited extensively.

tend to trace the lineage back to medievalism and then to the interlocution recovered from the philosophic tracts of Lotze, Fichte, Jacobi, Scheler, Feuerbach, etc. And then the neo-Hegelians turned the world of the God-based personalism upside down when Marx came with a warrant: God also became radical and worn. Putting aside the various versions of personalism, I have tended to rely on the German version (against the view that "the American school [only] ... is perceived by scholars to define personalism"[7]); here the person is irreducible—which I think relies on and, in turn, refers to the essence of personalism. An initial note of caution here (since there is a huge literature in analytical philosophy on personal identity): this work is not inspired by nor does it intend to contribute to the debate on "who is a person" or "what is personal identity" as such, though tangentially these notions do crop up as flowers by the wayside,[8] but only as much as or as many times as they are relevant to the concept-metaphor "personal" as against that of the private vis-à-vis the public. If we are to go by the definition of persons as rational beings with rights (as the legal definition purportedly goes) or of intrinsic worth and dignity "not equaled by nonpersons"[9] (as goes in moral theory, too), we are in for further dismay, since the nonpersons being the self-servicing, categorical constructions of the persons themselves is out-and-out discriminatory, solipsistic, and ideological (recall the nonperson status of women, children, and slaves to understand this detestable historical logos); they were (or are) nonpersons as they have been deprived of the rights that could be accrued to them when rightfully considered. Though the general, running paradigms of all schools of personalism, regardless of their origins, believe in the "personal reason and impersonal understanding," the "personal absolute," and the "personal unity in diversity,"[10] all are treated in this work with a defamiliarizing effect, and thereby, the orthodox personalists will find their categories being addressed after all. It is to this German tradition, where what goes by the name of personalism in a phenomenological mode, that my debt is the most; Max Scheler (a dark disciple of Husserl, and whom the latter distinctly disliked) should be named as an inspiring instance here. While personalism informs this work, in the tradition of Hegel and Alasdair MacIntyre—as they practiced it—the methodological approach

[7] Jan Olof Bengtsson, *The Worldview of Personalism: Origin and Early Development* (New York, NY: Oxford University Press, 2006), 271.
[8] For example see the discussion on personal agency and identity contra Amartya Sen in Chapter 4.
[9] Bengston, *The Worldview of Personalism*, 31.
[10] Ibid., 272.

to be borne by this work can be called philosophical history (when the proposal was first mooted), that is, a history of concepts, ideas, and so on. After many years, in hindsight, I still find the recommendation useful. A philosophical history is necessary to interrupt the self-complicity of concepts, which would have paraded—if it were only a philosophical study—as atemporal and uniquely essential. Therefore, philosophical history, simply put, is generated when we tend to philosophize history and historicize philosophy. Hegel thinks that these binaries (history and philosophy) are sometimes "necessary dichotomies" and "one factor in life,"[11] necessary because "life eternally forms itself by setting up opposition[s]."[12] But he perceives that when the might of unity "vanishes from the life of men and the antitheses lose their living connection and reciprocity and gain independence, the need of philosophy arises."[13] This gaining of independence is important: as if history and philosophy become two independent autonomous sectors of a single thought. And we must also mark the moment that it is in modernity that such oppositions take an objective form: faith versus knowledge, objectivity versus subjectivity, rational versus speculative, critical versus dogmatic, and lastly history versus philosophy. Reason unites what intellect has divided—history and philosophy. The task of reason is the task of philosophy.

Similarly, the person and the personal are not reducible to history and philosophy, too! But while transcendental phenomenology teaches us the irreducibility of the person to an act or agency (I extend it in this study to mean that the person is irreducible to the private or the public), it rarely engages with other discourses to see the consequences this view entails. The theological gloss often attributed to personalism derives, I guess, from this not-so-unclear apathy. This is abandoned in the present study to engage in a pluridisciplinary feat. This work is at the cusp of social and political philosophy, welfare sociology, social work, moral and legal theory, and philosophical history—and that too in the continental tradition. Not that the analytic tradition—as I have hinted at before—cannot offer intriguing thought forms or insights into the personal and personal identity and others, but there is a hunch that it can rarely explicate, self-reflexively, its own politics and bring back in politics, history, law, or literature in the style of cultural formations in which they occur in

---

[11] G. W. F. Hegel, "*The Difference Between Fichte's and Schelling's System of Philosophy: The Need of Philosophy*" in *The Hegel Reader*, ed. Stephen Houlgate (Blackwell Publishers: UK, 1998), 40–43.

[12] Ibid.

[13] Ibid.

terribly mixed moorings, in the practice of everyday life.[14] This dawned on Husserl, who brooked the life-world, and Heidegger, who pushed it to extremes. Consider, for instance, when Derek Parfit concludes, "our reasons for acting should become more impersonal...it would often be better for everyone,"[15] he chooses to be unaware (in fact, he could very well be) of the very fact that this is a political proposition, and public, political modernity appeared with such an axiom to be maintained and administered for its rational regime of technology; but the immanent reality of it, as I unravel it, could be examined for its truth in Chapter 1.[16] But this investment does not come from nowhere. "It results as well from a kind of double censorship which the philosophy of language exercises as it sets the stage for thinking about language: Anglo-American philosophy of language not only censors the personal, it also obliterates all signs of this censorship."[17] It was incumbent upon us to restore the personal when it is seen to have been silenced in the classical continental tradition; at least, that is the complaint of Nietzsche—the first philosopher of the personal.[18]

# III

Then, the present task—the task at hand—in all its homelessness in the present work, expands along the following registers and could be

---

[14] In endorsement, consider the following from Habermas:

> Since analytic philosophy of language more or less confines itself to issues it has inherited from the epistemological tradition, it lacks a certain sensibility for as well as the tools for dealing with the looser and larger issues of a diagnostics of an era. Since Hegel, the philosophical discourse of modernity has, therefore, been the domain of so-called continental philosophy. In this regard, the opposition between analytic and continental currents, which has otherwise become obsolete, still somewhat makes sense.

See Jürgen Habermas, *Truth and Justification*, ed. and trans. Barbara Fultner (Cambridge, MA: The MIT Press, 2003), 79.

[15] Derek Parfit, *Reasons and Persons* (Oxford: Clarendon Press, 1986), 442.

[16] So far as Parfit's augmentation of a "rational altruism" [we should "give no priority to our own children, this would be better for all our children" (Ibid., 444)] is considered, my discussion of altruism in Chapter 6 critiquing Nagel and others could be considered a beginning. I pick up the analytic tradition on the person in a separate study.

[17] Hagi Kenaan, *The Present Personal: Philosophy and the Hidden Face of Language* (New York, NY: Columbia University Press, 2005), 6.

[18] See Chapter 4 for more on Nietzsche as the first philosopher of the personal.

delineated as follows in an attempt to describe the thematic matrix of the chapters.

Chapter 1 theoretically narrates how modernity arrives with a burgeoning impersonality and a formal rationality spread to life-spheres. A separation of the private and the public and the constraints of formal law are idealized. But the person with his/her "politics of dirty hands" overwhelms this disjunction and projects a peculiar crisis. In response, "personal attacks," with their Greek origins and reaching their heights in 18th century political pornography, are such iconic examples, pointing out at the underbelly of objective events, ethics, and their symbolic dressing. The first signs of the person standing apart and standing out of the judicious separation of the public and the private, then, spill over. The person is the one, then, who can manipulate the private and the public.

Now, if Chapter 1 delineated how the person is capable of deceiving and escaping the limits set out by both the private and the public realms, the call for integrating them have been enormous and stifling, (as if) the public preacher and the private practitioner have to be reconciled in the same person and at some level of virtue! But how is it possible to integrate the private and the public at the site of an "echo" without dissolving the differences on which they are found? Taking cue from a neglected exchange between Mahatma Gandhi and Motilal Nehru, Chapter 2 brings out the dilemmas inherent in such an experiment and opens up the personal to its own prehistory. The monarch and the dictator unite the private and the public in the same, sovereign person. This chapter prefaces the prehistory of the person and the personal.

Having made in Chapter 2 a short detour into charting the pre-history of the personal in telegraphic terms—from the monarch to the dictator—we took Gandhi's desire as drive. In Chapter 3, we delve deeper into this prehistory—which because of its unavailability has to be reconstructed from disparate and disseminated sources and is bound to be episodic, while subsequently being the inscription of cultural history—which, as will be evident, could be reconstructed willfully in its sutured adequation.

After hinting at a historical and a subsequent cultural historical reconstruction of the personal in Chapter 3, it was necessary to examine if the distinction could be sustained theoretically as well. In Chapter 4, we pursue it in a short and sharp—albeit simple—manner. In concurrence with the definitive part of our book, this chapter tends to deploy the personal as recovered in history and tested in theory where the personal seems to have been problematized—matching the impersonal essence of modernity—and ought to have been expelled from the public sphere.

Chapter 5 shows how the indeterminate, whimsical personal subverts all rationally determinate welfare schemes in modern civil society, and how, against its well-honed intentions, it is a journey from personality to personality. The chapter charts how the affirmation of ordinary life generated a secular ethic of social virtue. Through this, helping (among other actions) and a helping canon (social work) was to be emancipated from the personal character of an individual and his/her idiosyncratic virtues of whimsical giving. The chapter documents how Hegel—appreciating the universal aspects of poverty—had proposed the mediating institutions of civil society to order this transition. The fate of such a hunt for the universal in 19th century Bengal is examined through the texts of a Bengali neo-Hegelian, Brajendranath Seal. Part 2 (on Hiralal Haldar) of this chapter takes cue from the preceding part and expands on the journey of our modernity from natural personality to the personality of organizations. To graph this journey is fairly straight: we've deployed the personal in mirroring how the Western universal forms of impersonal civil-social helping has been smeared with the whimsical and arbitrary forms of personalistic polemic, finally, coalescing in the personality of organizations or group personalities—evident even in postcolonial India.

The last chapter (6) tries to weigh the analytical use the category personal could have in laying bare the similarities and differences between various informal helping modalities and social work—the disciplinary helping canon. The perusal—selectively—has been dispersed along the essential registers of etymology and genealogy.

# IV

The impact of this study may be conjectured along the following lines. Apart from re-invoking a long-lost philosophical history, the substantive content of this work—if persuasive enough—will correct and contribute to a long overdue lack in social theory and social philosophy, which—being trapped and allegedly engaged in the act of sacrificing either the private to the public or the public to the private (i.e., either domesticate the public or submit the private to public scrutiny)—went on, in an act of mourning, as if to discover alternative privacies or proletarian counter publics. The personal emerges in this book, as a distinct first, neither incorporated nor "assimilable" in either the private or the public.

As it is evident, this might entail—in future—via the domestication through research of those forgotten comportments (those institutions, people and their work as social texts) a large-scale theoretical revision of the present history of modernity, philosophy of helping, and the ethics of care; it would be interesting to watch how disciplinary social sexual and legal-ethical care try to thematize this disturbance through the narrative management of historical differences.

# Acknowledgments

This book is not "an accident of chapters" as some would like to fashion the print-orientation that is inscribed here; this goes back to an investment of a decade and more than six years of labored, active imagination.

In fact, throughout these years, an array of publications and seminars sustained my interest in the work and even authenticated its place among the learned (the "warm fraternity of useless erudition")—where a paradigm is performed co-constitutively. For instance, the thesis of this book (which was sent as a paper to Sandra Harding and she was kind enough to confirm it in a letter on February 23, 2005) was first published in the year 2006 in the *Indian Journal of Social Work* as an article. It is indexed—as a student working on it informed me—with the US Library of Congress; London School of Economics (Sarah Hayward, Library Assistant, LSE Library, was kind enough to correspond with me on this [beginning May 8, 2016]), Sociological Abstracts, Inc. with International Sociological Association, US; Social Science Citation Index with the Institute for Scientific Information, USA; etc. I gratefully remember the gesture of scholars such as Professor Sharmila Rege who made the article a reference reading material in the Women's Studies Center at the University of Pune in 2007; I mourn her untimely demise.

I will cite the reason for rememorating all these with the help of an apparent, and immediate, hypothetical imperative. In the Prologue, I had deployed Paul Halmos who proposed a transition from pastoral social work (comprising pre-social work forms of helping) to professional social work (scientific, institutionalized disciplinary and paid form of helping). My spin on it will be available in Chapter 6 and also in others. What, however, is ridiculous—even scandalous—is to have someone who claims to have been "proposing" a pre-social work indigenous form (whose translation is even erroneous with him) as pastoral. In terms of an episodic and periodic history, too (Chapter 5 here, in longer version) while holding onto a few neo-Hegelian 19th century philosophers of colonial Bengal, I arrived at the distinction that marks and remarks [on] modern and premodern helping forms, and learnt how the personal not only invades the impersonal-rational universal modern motors of helping but contaminates and nearly destroys them (referred to in Chatterjee 2008 and published differently in 2010). I have not moved an inch away from that observation. Therefore, if any activist-scholar of the nationalist phase of a helping form bribes him/herself with the new found *relata* of modernity and in trying to forge an unacknowledged but inspired, labored linkage fails to match his/her otherwise empirical stuff, few would empathize. So keenly I remember (my wife's favorite) Thoreau here:

> Shall I not have words as fresh as my thoughts? Shall I use any other man's word? A genuine thought or feeling can find expression for itself, if it have to invent hieroglyphics. It has the universe for type-metal. It is for want of original thought that one man's style is like another's.

Grateful thanks to Ms Nandita Bhattacharya, Professor Gautam Gupta, Professor Nilanjana Gupta, Professor Sadhan Chakraborti, Professor Soumitra Basu, Professor Gautam Bhadra, and the Governor of West Bengal, Shri Kesari Nath Tripathi.

My tryst at the Indian Institute of Advanced Study (IIAS), Shimla, during 2013–15 will always remain memorable—with Professor D. N. Dhanagare, Professor Radhaballav Tripathi, Professor Udayan Mishra, Sri Rajesh Joshi, Professor Kunal Chakraborty, Shri Sumanta Banerjee—a constellation of academic and creative stalwarts. Professor Chetan Singh, the Director, and Mr Premchand, Secretary and Librarian, are the best of peoples I have ever met. Moidul Islam, Rahul Govind, Amitranjan Basu, and Enakshi Mitra were excellent academic partners and interlocutors. Dr Moidul Islam—especially—combines in him the highest standards of academic excellence, competence with a down to earth, helpful generosity and intellectual honesty that is seemingly without a parallel.

Professor Nasrin Siddiqui of Yashwantrao Chavan Academy of Development Administration (YASHADA), Pune (in 2008), Shuddhabrata, Jeebesh, Monica, Sadan Jha, and Vivek Narayanan (in 2007)—the poet—besides Professor Pratiksha Baxi, Professor Lawrence Liang, and V. Sanal Mohan who remain as the Delhi-based authors whom I admire, acknowledge, and keenly follow.

At the Centre for Studies in Social Sciences, Calcutta (CSSSC) in Kolkata, my past, elective affinities with Shri Prabir Basu (whose non-administrative poetics—he being a great translator of Jibanananda Das) relieves and robs me of any nightmares; Professor Partha Chatterjee, Professor Pradip Bose, Professor Tapati Guhathakurta, and Professor Rosinka Chaudhury contributed to my work with longstanding empathy, at times deliberate pity due to the prolong, era-taking attitude of mine (in response, my shy answer was always Walter Benjamin: "under the shadow of Saturn, I'm slow.")

Dr Debarshi Sen—a perfect academic administrator at IIAS first and then at CSSSC, Kolkata—sets a standard too high for any bureaucrat, but is an absolute well-wisher. Only Sandip Chatterjee, the ex-registrar of TISS and JNU, gloriously matches the level set by Prabir Basu and Debarshi Sen and is with force an honorable exception.

Dr Palash Mandal, Professor Arya Ghosh, Arunangsu Guhathakurta, Mohid Hyder, Sanjib Ganguly, and Ranjan Banerjee bear the remnants of the Deoghar and the Santiniketan gang. Professor Rajsekhar Basu, Professor Sanjeeb Mukherjee, Professor Someswar Bhowmik, Dr Abhijit Roy, and Shri Bibhas Bagchi are all stars of the Kolkata academia. Subodh Sarkar, Roro Sarkar are superstars. I owe each of them a mental nail. Professor Manas Roy, Professor Dipankar Gupta, Professor Mahendra Pal Singh, Professor Surinder Singh Jodhka, Professor Abha Chauhan, Professor Aditya Nigam, and Professor Rajeev Bhargava, with their distant presence, do not always know that they epistemically excite me and I have an inheritance of gain. The same goes for Soumyabrata Choudhury and Prasenjit Biswas—two continental stars, besides our own Aniruddha Choudhury and Rahul Govind—in the Indian and international philosophical space.

Also, the late Niranjan Chatterjee, Atonu Chatterjee (who introduced me to the Subaltern Studies when I was in higher secondary), Manisha Chatterjee, Paramita Chatterjee, Tathagata (Nanda) Ray, Sushmita (Minti) Chatterjee, Sujit and Srirup Kanjilal—as my immediate and extended family—suspect that even in social intercourse, I'm engaged in "fake encounters," but the kinship—they know—is too real, even if materially absent at times.

My wife, Anuradha Chatterjee, came from nearly nowhere in 2016 and has defamiliarized my life to the extent it is not recognizably the same anymore. Having worked on Emerson and Thoreau and American neo-transcendentalism, she is equally eloquent about poets who were auto-destructive and often killed themselves. That is a (mis)match with her conservatist orthodoxy and hides the immense duties she caps and carries on her lean shoulders.

Finally, the book is dedicated to my mother Dipali Chatterjee (among other fellow tragedians) who even months before her death on October 30, 2006 was scared about my tryst with obscure and sometimes scandalous thinkers and writers and urged me to come to terms with acceptable academia in Kolkata and India. She wished me to put to rest my habit of "polemicizing," which has earned me a team of fierce and active "well-wishers." Her unforgettable concern will always remain higher than my unforgivable stubbornness. Higher all the more because she, apart from Guddie, would have been the happiest to know that my work has had such a large and informed audience that goes with the prestige and stardom of SAGE.

And I must confess now, "particularly" before you "actually" read the book, that my fiancé and companion Chotu-Chotu Singh—whom some erroneously call a parakeet—dug her heels and nails in every letter and ate some of them too. It is Chotu who screamed in her shrill voice once, "You can read nothing except through appetite" and thereby obliged me to be in a frozen standstill. And I'm still standing there, here and nowhere, only to later find Chotu sitting on my shoulder, wings bare.

Grateful thanks to all!

# Part One

# Recovering the Personal in Politics, Ethics, Culture, Law, History, and Theory

# 1

# Personal in the Public Sphere: The Politics of Modernity

*How poisonous, how crafty, how bad, does every long war make one, that cannot be waged openly by means of force! How personal does a long fear make one, a long watching of enemies, of possible enemies!*
—Nietzsche (2000: 226)

*From now on conditions will favour more extensive structures of mastery, the like of which have never yet been seen. And there's something even more important: ... a new, tremendous aristocracy built upon the harshest self-legislation, in which the will of philosophical men of violence and artist tyrants is made to last for thousands of years: ... to take the destinies of the earth in hand, to sculpt at "man" himself as artists. In short: the time is coming where we will learn to think differently about politics.*
Nietzsche (2003: 71)

Inspired by Nietzsche's indictment and Immanuel Kant's immortal, controversial maxim, "He who openly declares himself an enemy can be relied upon, but the treachery of secret malice ... is more detestable than violence,"[1] this chapter looks at some of the "wicked," malicious, and dirty everyday ways of experiencing the political where violence and nonviolence could rarely be distinguished, because, as we notice, the public/private division is transgressed by the maneuvering person and his/her cunning of reason. In other words, this chapter is about something

---

[1] Immanuel Kant, *Lectures on Ethics*, trans. Louis Infield (New York: Harper and Row, 1963), 215.

worse than violence. (And because these everyday binaries are transcended in this form of politics, it is also called "pure.")

This pure politics of dirty hands is made up of persons being subjected to negative gossiping, malice, backstabbing, lying, treachery, deception, taking undue advantage, subtle—nearly invisible—forms of discrimination, exploitation, etc. These examples recover, one might hazard, mythical forms of punishment. This chapter, in order to reckon with this genuinely real, "pure" politics of dirty hands with a distinct Machiavellian dig, comments on narratives of manipulations, machinations, intrigues, and malice—all blossoming in nonviolent peace where peace is also a product of leisure. (In Aristotlean terms, peace is a virtue derived from leisure.)

In the discourse of pure politics, lying is the first personal political act by which persons govern each other; coercion or domination, thus, comes always in personal forms of brute factuality (being exploited in this discourse is a matter of political feeling) and, thereby, personal attacks are often its primary raw materials. But there is a lack of causality and diagnostic scientificity in such events too; in fact, they are always marked by an empty, nonhistorical circularity, a lack of distinct teleology. An illustration is given in Kant when he discusses malice: "Men prone to this vice will seek, for instance, to make mischief between husband and wife, or between friends, and then enjoy the misery they have produced."[2] Thereby, our interrogation, in its impact, could entail even the lost history of conjugal quarrels incited by unknown others for nothing, or envious accounts of jilted lovers or friends.

But is there not a counter discourse? How were such pure political experiences handled—then and now? When we refer to experiencing the political, no form of theory or practical political activity, public/private defenses could have worked. Kant again states: "The defence against such mischief makers is upright conduct. Not by words but by our lives we should confute them."[3] Personal attacks apart, they are essentialized now as real life problems (those agony columns abound with the proliferation of false auto-suggestions inscribed by an ever increasing number of urban agony aunts) and, thus, excluded from political discourse or theories of violence—undercoding, thus, the fact that they are distinctly related to a certain form of governance.

---

[2] Ibid.
[3] Ibid. 219.

So far as the impact of this chapter is concerned, we shall see that it discovers, vis-à-vis pure politics or politics of dirty hands, a third form of governance: besides governance by force and consent—two established modes—this is governance by fraud, which parasitically feeds on the other two so much so that force and consent, coercion and persuasion, and violence and nonviolence can rarely be distinguished when fraud touches and transforms them. "Fraud thus opens up a space, beyond force and laws, for diverting their existence—a space in which force and laws are substituted for, feigned, deformed, and circumvented."[4]

This chapter is then ultimately about the third, invisible form of governance that is regulated by the person transcending the private and the public by the sheer cunning of reason—even unreason—that is, if unreason has to have an "inner source". And personal invectives travel a long way to meet it and to demonstrate the way the person by his/her personal cunning transcends the public/private divide; personal invectives name the person with the "dirty hands" and are not necessarily attacks upon the person's privacy—as it has often been argued—to denounce and disparage them without a heightened scrutiny.

## "Personal Attacks" from India via the Ancient Greek, the Middle Ages to Modernity: An Excursus

What is the single concept metaphor to hold onto, in order to understand and chart a trajectory, where the personal appears distinctive, yet unsullied through history? It is, arguably, "personal attacks"; we shall come to what personal attacks are about—its telos later—and finally its results.

We shall notice that it is only in the third or modern phase that personal attacks could be seen to have been disapproved in a form that is paradigmatic. This is because the logic of modernity itself, unlike the ancient Greek or medieval predicament, is emphatically moored against the tenor and vehicle of personal attacks, slander, or abuse. Let us, briefly, rehearse the motors of this modernity.

---

[4] Louis Althusser, *Machiavelli and Us*, trans. Gregory Eliott (London: Verso, 1999), 95–96.

## Personal—Against and Within the Impersonal Modern: Weber's Disenchantment

The best description of modernity in terms of politics is available in Max Weber with whom tradition, charisma, and affective forms of patrimonial monarchies (Sultanism for example) receded to the background, and what emerged is, to borrow Owen's brilliant capsule, "the impersonal rationalisation of the social organisation [providing] an impetus towards the regulation of all public spheres of life on the basis of formal legal norm[s]."[5]

The maintenance of this regime is ensured by a strict separation of the public and private spheres, where personal is understood as partial and an offspring of the specific, accidental subjectivity of a person. The formulation that it has had in Weber—to repeat its importance—is something like this:

> Objective discharge of business primarily means a discharge of business according to calculable rules and "without regard for persons." "Without regard for persons," however, is also the watchword of the market and, in general, of all pursuits of naked economic interests. ... Bureaucracy develops the more perfectly ... the more completely it succeeds in eliminating from official business love, hatred, and all purely personal, irrational, and emotional elements which escape calculation. This is appraised as its special virtue by capitalism.[6]

But this operation cannot be limited or short circuited to mean just the response required by a "complicated and specialized modern culture"[7] since, as Weber himself charts, it could be traced to that of Roman law and the late middle ages. Classical natural law evolved into rational natural law, and this rational law was "conceptually systematized on the basis of statutes."[8] Pursuing this line of argument, the first signs of the modern bureaucratized impersonality were evident, according to Weber, in legal administration. We shall get back to this later elsewhere.

Rational economic activity originates from the market and is oriented to money "the most abstract and most 'impersonal' thing in all human

---

[5] David Owen, *Maturity and Modernity: Nietzsche, Weber, Foucault and the Ambivalence of Reason* (New York: Routledge, 1994), 117.

[6] Max Weber, *Economy and Society: An Outline of Interpretive Sociology*, eds. Guenther Roth and Claus Wittich. (1968; repr., Berkley: University of California Press, 1978), 2: 975.

[7] Ibid.

[8] Ibid.

life."[9] The more rational activity there is, the more impersonalization there is of the economy.[10]

> One could regulate the personal relationship of lord and slave in a completely ethical manner, simply because it was personal. This cannot be said of ... the relationship between the changing holders of credit notes and to the (to them) unknown and also changing debtors of a mortgage lending institution, between whom no possible personal relationship could exist.[11]

Now, shifting the burden of this tangle to the domain of current discussion, we see how the public and the public sphere come to be invested with this impersonality. The point is, is "the regulation of all public spheres of life on the basis of formal norms" successful?[12] If it fails, then in what form? In order to examine it, we can limit ourselves to exploring politics as the sanctioned activity of the public sphere. Here it is urged—what to say of political rational action—that politics even at the level of persuasion or political rhetoric, is encouraged to become—in this discourse, ostensibly—

[9] Max Weber, "Intermediate Reflections on the Economic Ethics of the World Religions: Theory of the Stages and Directions of Religious Rejection of the World," in *The Essential Weber: A Reader*, ed. Sam Whimster (London: Routledge: London, 2004), 215–44.

[10] But Weber's critics—particularly Karl Fischer—invoke John Stuart Mill, in order to explain the emerging capitalist attitude, and argue, how money being an impersonal means to achieving things, becomes by a sleight of transference, the loved object-end itself. See Karl Fischer, "Karl Fischer's Review of *The Protestant Ethic, 1907*," in *The Protestant Ethic Debate: Max Weber's Replies to his Critics 1907–10*, eds. David J. Chalcraft and Austin Harrington, trans. Austin Harrington and Mary Shields (Liverpool: Liverpool University Press, 2001), 28–29. Does this personalize the impersonal medium of money? Hardly so. Simmel elaborately shows how the money economy mediates and carpets the hiatus between possession and personality unlike the ancient Germanic law, thereby personality becoming increasingly impotent to possess (the medium) that dispossesses. We shall return to this historical point later. See Georg Simmel, *The Philosophy of Money*, trans. Tom Bottomore and David Frisby (London: Routledge, 1990) 334.

[11] But Weber does note the exception in the attempt to personalize this nearly impossible credit machine in China, which resulted in the two way emergence of formal and material rationality, often, in conflict with each other (Max Weber, "Intermediate Reflections on the Economic Ethics of the World Religions: Theory of the Stages and Directions of Religious Rejection of the World," in *The Essential Weber: A Reader*, ed. Sam Whimster [London: Routledge: London, 2004], 222).

[12] The revision in Weber was evident in some of his later formulations where he seemed to have been stressing on the power of informal networks and personal warranties for the purposes of credit lending imminent in particular sect societies. For a richer discussion see Benjamin Cornwell, "The Protestant Sect Credit Machine: Social Capital and the Rise of Capitalism," *Journal of Classical Sociology* 7, no. 3 (2007): 267–90.

shorn of all personal benefits and burden, personal mention, and personal attacks through our advocacy of issue-based politics. A few more words are in order.

By stating the political, we stand to approach the question of the personal through the disciplinary deployment of the former. To go on with this, we first examine the personally oriented politics as against an impersonal, issue-based politics, followed by that very famous register, and that which is absolutely relevant and rehearsed in eternal negativity is the notion of personal attacks condemned in the wake of such an impersonal, objective, issue-based politics (the question of civility added to it) that could be found to have been neatly tailored to ground the public or public sphere in terms of public reason and so on. And the temptation is understandable in as much as politics in modernity with its concomitant notion of rights, public opinion, and rational will formation imagines a political public—without a personal-irrational investment. Here, we have apparently the classical Weberian paradigm to guide us;[13] further, and later, it was Habermas who refined these arguments at the level of language by rooting this metaphor in a form of systematically undistorted communicative practice. It is with Habermas that we have the normative turn given to political modernity or, in the words of Luhmann, what Habermas did was to show that all rational considerations may be shown to have had a normative content. In later chapters, we shall show that the undertaking to institute modernity in the colonies exhibit much against their intentions the personal-particular core in the public-universal garb. The present exercise will preface this moment in a significant manner.

---

[13] I've already stated the Weberian position. A note on my differences would be a reminder here. Apparently Max Weber did articulate in the wake of an emergent disenchantment of the world a corresponding journey from the personal bonding of informal communities to formal, impersonal bureaucracy marked by the anonymous transit of symbolic movement of the "file" in the office. But first, the personal in Weber is nearly commonsensical and provisional; second, it is the impersonal, which is at the center of the Weberian project; third, he does not distinguish it or relate it to private and public—which are at the core of modernity as I describe it; fourth, his project does not include showing how the personal becomes a pale shadow of the private; fifth and final, if allowed to pursue further, my work will try to prove just the reverse of what Weber has to show. In any case, irrespective of these disagreements, the paradigm of impersonal bureaucracy is a good starting point for all this, and I neatly adhered to it.

# Accommodating Personal Attacks in an Impersonally Modern? Two Arguments

While inspecting the personal in the discourses of politics, we need to address ourselves—even if tangentially—to a personal orientation to politics as against an issue-based, impersonal politics where issues are understood as states of affairs. Subsequent to the completion of identifying the objection which prioritizes a principled, "issue-based politics" over personal issues and personal-attack-based politics, we must reckon with the fact that it also invokes and locates the personal at the level of rhetoric and states that political rhetoric, unless healthy and respectful of the other participant, violates the rules of debate and deliberation. It entails, albeit implicitly, that democracy being a procedure to peacefully and procedurally disagree, personal attacks, abuses, and invectives imply more than disagreement: by trying to impeach the credibility of a democratic witness. It denigrates democracy itself, because what is democracy if not its culture! But within the horizon of our history—connected to the unity of a Western history—this argument was first negotiated in the domain of culture, and then incorporated in the real of political culture.

## Argument One: Disagreement (Democracy) Within Civility and Culture: Personal Attacks in the Times of the Colony and the Post Colony

Let us begin with the here and now so far as our own history is concerned. Subsequent to this subsection, we shall separate three moments: first, the rhetorically Greek; second, against the church; and third, against the state—phases of invectives so far as our Western history is concerned. Prior to that, it is necessary to curve out this history as it featured in a colonial polity and still features in a postcolonial polity, or otherwise we shall be missing the diversity and specificity of historical voices and would be assuming, much against our broad intentions, the univocity of just one imperial reason—a single imperial canon. To do this, we shall hatch on to a representative modern icon, Bankimchandra Chatterjee, since in his writings—it is established by now—the discursive foundations of modernity and modernism are supposed to have been most emphatically drawn.

Bankim, in an attempt to review a book by Rajnarayan Bose—another great Renaissance figure—here, enumerates the intolerance of Bengali writers that emerges in its worst form while they are responding to criticism.

The moment they sense a lack of favour, they feel compelled to object; but in the act of objecting—this class of writers sincerely believe that gentleman's language and gentlity have to be abandoned. In a country where not long ago *kavir larai*[14] was the major entertainment; where still *panchali*[15] is in vogue, and people apart from obscene abuses remain ignorant of other abuses ("onlyo gali"), in such a country it is but obvious that angry writers in their moment of eruption would not budge from exhibiting their true literacy and company. At times I've noticed that highly sophisticated persons with a nationwide reputation, presupposing their dignity had been undermined, had reacted in feats of blind rage and took recourse to the lowest level of sociality ("itarer ashray") and thus contaminated the mother tongue.[16]

Elsewhere, reviewing a collection of poems by Ishwarchandra Gupta—a 19th century Bengali soft satirist—Bankim praises *kabir larai* for staging "abuse without enmity".[17] He seems to hold the view that Gupta, having been brought up in that tradition, has written verses which are free of *bidwesh* (hate or grudge or indignity).[18] Having said that, Bankim now emerges with the grand comparison; he is quick to notice that European satire is full of jealousy, bad blood, and indignation that devastates and depresses people. "Various European bad commodities ('kusamagri') are entering this country; this killing comedy ('narghatini rasikata') has also made its entry."[19] Ishwar Gupta "abuses without 'anger and enmity'; his is a satire without indignation ('biddeshhin byango')." His only

---

[14] A mock fight in lewd verses among folk poets of Bengal.

[15] A song in verses written and recited in praise of local gods.

[16] Bankimchandra Chattopadhyay, "Review of *Hindudharmer Sreshthata* by Rajnarayan Basu," in *Bankim Rachanabali* (Calcutta: Sahitya Samsad, 1384), II: 873, 6th reprint (translation mine).

[17] *Kabir larai* or the mock fight of poets in "lewd" verses was an immensely popular cultural form that continued to remain popular till the middle of the 19th century in Bengal. The *larai* or fight would be staged mostly around the instantly created extempore "obscene" parodies of Gods and goddesses orally presented in a running dialogue. Among several structural phases, the third part of the larai named *lahar* or *khessa* would include what a historian calls "personal attacks." Absolutely "vulgar" attacks involving the opponents' parents, lovers or girls in the families, affairs, and habits would be called names through rhymes and the audience would applaud being absolutely delighted. See Asit Kumar Bandyopadhyaya, *Bangla Sahityer Ittivritta,* (Calcutta: Modern Book Agency Pvt. Ltd, 1973), IV: 86–88.

[18] Ibid., 851.

[19] Bankim, Review, 851.

determination is that he has to defeat the Brahmin in the use of corrupt language (*kubhasay*). Bankim does acknowledge that at times Gupta is obscene, but at a remove and with a qualification: his obscenity is inspired by his genuine anger on artificialness—for instance "artificial politics." "Often Iswar Gupta's obscenity derives from this anger" [which is] "not true obscenity."[20] So this is artificial obscenity in responsible response to a false politics. But then what is real, genuine, or true obscenity according to Bankim? One of the architects of the Obscenity Law in India, Bankim argues that which is aimed at exciting the senses or expresses the nasty robustness of the author[21] is truly obscene—even if it is written in a "pure ... language"; but in cases where it is deployed to condemn or parodize sin and only sin, it is far from being obscene—even if it goes against the apparently standard structures of taste and civilization. A significant discursive resonance in Bankim's oeuvre is the way he captures obscenity as crass sensuality aimed at corrupting the morals of the reader, which nearly coincides, even unites, with the primary and founding definitions of obscenity and pornography in the West.

That "our" disagreement and civility in the event of their joint cultural incorporation is problematic too will have been evident from the foregone discussion. By impersonally grounding civic conversation, we are already without the sure-footing to tell an agent personally not to violate the rules of a moral conversation. Interpersonal rather than impersonal should be the a priori or transcending principle that will found or normatively define the action of dialogue before it actually begins. The denigration and withering of ritual abuses and "personal attacks" through *kheur* and the will to be incorporated within the grand project of modernity in order to civilize[22] dissent summarizes the state of things with us today—here and now.

This question of culture was later translated to become a matter of political culture in the post colony, and the issue of civility soon became a

---

[20] Ibid.

[21] Adopting Meaghan Morris we can identify this obscene as that which makes anything "more visible than the visible" and deals with the secret in a way that exposes its identity as "more hidden than the hidden." Meaghan Morris, *The Pirates's Fiancee* (London: Verso, 1988), 188.

[22] This should not, of course, blind us to the fact that there was always another discourse on civility in the Western narrative too: consider for instance Norbert Ilias when he quotes Erasmus of the 16th century, " ... (Fools who value civility more than health repress natural sounds.) Do not be afraid of vomiting if you must; 'for it is not vomiting but holding the vomit in your throat that is foul'." Norbert Elias, *The Civilizing Process (The History of Manners)*, trans. E. Jephcott (Oxford: Basil Blackwell, 1978), 58.

placeholder for democracy. The paradigm was prefaced by the importation of an impersonal, principle-based politics pitted against personal, interest-based politics as in the West. Here is just one instance; one could recover thousand others.

To historicize, first the dialectic between the so-called principle-based politics and personal (meaning private) interest-based politics here is, therefore, an excerpt from the annals of the nationalist narrative. The report of this debate came out in the *Hindustan Times* and dates back to 1938–39, years before Independence.

It was during the Fazlul Haq ministry in Bengal. Two *praja* parties who had had the reputation of being pro-peasant demanded the removal of as many as five cabinet ministers and wished instead to induct themselves to have a clear majority in the cabinet. A commentator of the paper wrote on the efforts at mediation by Fazlul Haq, "There cannot and should not be any compromise if they really stand on any principle and if the dispute between them and the Ministry was not purely personal, but one of principles and programmes."[23] The commentator ended by suggesting, "How can there be a compromise between the two sides if the differences between them was not purely personal."[24] His principled opinion was that to stick to office at any cost would be to sacrifice principles to personal equations: any compromise would signify such un-democracy; rather, it would be wise to resign and seek re-election to concur "with the legible canons of democratic government."[25] Do we have today a rhetoric of repetition where "compromise" has been transformed into an ineradicable sign of democratic understanding?

Despite having had a taste of a semblance of a principle-dominated, developing political culture, the ritualistic mooring of personal attacks, resembling the colony, is not altogether lost even in the post colony. An essay by the anthropologist Lawrence Cohen titled "Holi in Banaras and the *Mahaland* of Modernity."[26] could be considered in which Cohen documents an interesting cartoon among numerous others showing a

[23] Basudev Chatterjee, ed. *Towards Freedom: Documents on the Movement for Independence in India, 1938* (New Delhi: Indian Council for Historical Research and Oxford University Press), 2417.

[24] Ibid.

[25] Ibid.

[26] Lawrence Cohen, "Holi in Banaras and the Mahaland of Modernity," *GLQ: A Journal of Gay and Lesbian Studies* 2, no. 4 (1999): 399–424. Nearly all the issues like communal peace, etc. and all the national leaders have been picturesquely "addressed" in these books. I'm grateful to Professor Pradip Bose for suggesting and providing me with this reference.

man labeled as the *sikhandin janata* (meaning eunuch or helpless people) having in his mouth the member of a man with a politician's congress cap (labeled as the *gandu neta*) while being sodomized by a man standing behind in police uniform (with the label "*jhandu* police"). The circulation of these thin booklets, particularly during the immensely popular Holi festival in Benaras, exhibits its incorporation within the ritual paradigm of festivity and the element of obscenity in a carnivalesque manner, nearly. But what is remarkable about these are the common motif of condemnation,[27] where the victim is the member of the ordinary public, and which overrides all party lines. The narrative of mobilization in postcolonial India inheres in the structural pre-formation present in the aforementioned and is directed against the whole political class. We could briefly reflect on the foregone section before we move on to the next: the objection of impersonally principled politics against a politics of the personal style was raised only after the colonial, politico-civilizing mission had arrived; what had pre-existed was the realm of personal abuses and attacks within the folk norms of ritualistic more. We could see Bankim—the modernizer—striking a balance with a modern poser. This ritualistic remnant of personal invectives, in the postcolonial predicament, is absorbed in the festive prolongation of Holi in Benaras. Explicitly, and defiantly if it is, the personal is not tolerated as an arm of politics today—in India. There exists only a liminal underworld—the content of which we shall explore later—as a part of universal history.

The question could be rephrased thus: in a democracy that intends to be "deliberative" in nature, that is, wants to see the major issues that have consequences for the public settled by free and rational deliberation of all concerned, could political invectives at all be productive? Let us try in brief to examine the theoretical problems involved. The claim is, of course, made first (and perhaps last) from the standpoint of civility. And a certain reference to the norms of deliberation in a ripening, "developing" democracy is often made too. But is it possible to sustain such a claim? For this, it will suffice to review the position espoused by Gary Shiffman[28]

---

[27] In West Bengal's institutional politics, how such gossips through condemnations and affirmations become sanctioned instruments of mobilization and manipulation and how the image of the leader or parties are created, the village agendas are set within the informal and private realms of gossip, see Arild Engelsen Ruud, *Poetics of Village Politics, The Making of West Bengal's Rural Communism* (New Delhi: Oxford University Press, 2003), 198–200.

[28] Gary Shiffman, "Construing Disagreement: Consensus and Invective in 'Constitutional' Debate," *Political Theory* 30, no. 2 (2002, April): 175–203.

where he forcefully argues with much justification that consensus seeking and civility in constitutional debate cannot be obtained at the same time. He concludes that

> Would be-arbiters of public deliberation like Rawls, who simultaneously insist on consensus seeking and civility in constitutional debate, cannot have it both ways. They can—and should—endorse a norm of consensus to govern constitutional deliberation, but must also not insist that such deliberations be conducted according to norms of civility. Serious public debate of constitutional questions necessarily runs the risk of rhetorical vehemence, of mutual castigation by adversaries. Demanding pursuit of consensus while hewing to civil comportment amounts to insisting on two incompatible norms at once, consensus and dissensus.[29]

And now, perhaps, we are convinced about the legitimacy of the formulation for nation-states with colonial histories—that civility is the stuff of modernity, and disagreement is the stuff of democracy. Given the hiatus and the apposite growth of these two entities historically noticeable in postcolonial societies like India, they are not compatible in a foundational sense. Therefore, for an Indian case, the argument for the difference between cultural modernity and political modernity or democracy is made at another remove. Here, both modernity and democracy are imputed unlike the West European cases. (Or is it possible to read so much against the grain that democracy can be shown to have been imputed even in the classical modular formations?) However, all along, the colonizing logic or ruse of colonial governance was to bring the native to some kind of deliberative and decisive competence for self-ownership. Here, therefore, the deliberative competence that is often asked for is seen with some justifiable and historically evolved suspicion. This is not unfounded. The communicative competence to insert civility into political questions (as we noticed in the Indian phase of invectives) would have to undergo, perhaps for always, a hermeneutics of suspicion. This historically correct caveat would precede any require-ment for an impersonal civility to be instituted through impersonation and be smuggled to the domain of democracy.

That is again enough to give debates, particularly among political executives in the Indian democracy on constitutional questions, a specific and undecidable turn that is eternally subject to the contingencies of local party politics and the decisive imagination of professional politicians; the

[29] Ibid., 175.

same applies to complaints against misbehavior. Incivility can then feature only as a political question and as a kind of original contamination felt by constitutional questions. *Byaktigat/byaktigoto* or personal inscribed within the norms of *bhodrotabidhi* or norms of civility is very differently political here. And this difference was historically recovered the moment we pushed the question of personal attacks to higher degrees: political pornography where the political and the erotic or the uncivil interrupt each other at the moment when power erupted and corrupted even the monarchical absolute.

## Argument Two: The Argument from Discursive Violence

But is "discursive logic" instead of personalized persuasion enough? The liberal argument will disagree. They would not be acceptable, even if discursive, when the circumstances in which they are expressed are such as to constitute their expression a positive instigation to some mischievous act or violence. This as we could see is totally in agreement with the classical liberal formulation of John Stuart Mill, who outlines a grave example. "An opinion that corn-dealers are starvers of the poor, or that private property is robbery, ought to be unmolested when simply circulated through the Press, but may justly incur punishment when delivered orally to an excited mob, assembled before the house of a corn-dealer."[30] Only sheer propositional, issue-based statements are, therefore, not enough; they should not be delivered before a corn dealer's house, that is, much will depend on the mediation that will render it objective, harmless, and without a bite. The aesthetics of reception will matter more than its production. There we have the abusive or assaultive paradigm in some other form (excitable speech:[31] to use the proper word). To answer the contemporary as well as the classical tenet of nonviolent speech advanced here as permissible, we could take recourse to another thinker commenting on the impossibility of deriving the right to kill the vanquished from the state of war; there, he concedes that

---

[30] John Stuart Mill, "On Liberty," in *Utilitarianism, Liberty and Representative Government* (1910; repr., New York, NY: JM Dent and Sons Ltd, 1936), 114.

[31] See Judith Butler, *Excitable Speech, A Politics of the Performative* (New York, NY: Routledge, 1997) for an interesting exposition.

> Men living in their primitive conditions of independence have no intercourse
> regular enough to constitute either a state of peace or a state of war; and men
> are not naturally enemies. It is conflicts over things, not quarrels between
> (men)[32] which constitute war, and the state of war cannot arise from mere
> personal relations, but from property relations.[33]

An extension of this Rousseauistic finding will lay to rest any theory
formulating violence as an aberration or disturbance as being an "injury
by design," since the state of peace can similarly be construed as imputed
from the outside, or having been imposed—resembling an aberration.[34]
From this, we could argue that, in the wake of "personal attacks" being
understood as a generic speech figure and articulated as disturber of
peace,[35] it urges us to look at the varieties of peace available in the political
market. What happens in times of peace?

  With violence, the stakes are clear; but with peace, we enter into
something more than violence-producing speech. How truce or peace
could be politically deployed or be subsumed under the political rubric
is offered in the next section for examination.

# Politics in the Times of Peace: "Personal Attacks"[36] as Itemized Within a Pure Political Imaginary

Politics in the times of peace! This is far from defining politics as "the
way to organize and optimize the technological seizure of beings at
the level of the nation."[37] It is rather the technological seizure of beings

---

[32] Wars over (wo)men—when pointed out—will be, according to such an argument, possible
when they are considered as things.

[33] Jean Jacques Rousseau, *The Social Contract,* trans. Maurice Cranston (Harmondsworth:
Penguin, 1984), 55–56.

[34] A state of curfew for instance. Curfew is an instance of violent peace.

[35] Rousseau has more things to say on peace: "What do people gain if their very conditions
of Civil tranquility is one of their hardships? There is peace in dungeons, but is that
enough to make dungeons desirable?" See Jean Jacques Rousseau, *The Social Contract*,
trans. Maurice Cranston (Harmondsworth: Penguin, 1984), 54.

[36] Throughout we've taken "personal attacks" as they have been projected (within quotation
marks) without distinguishing it from assaultive speech, libel, abuse, insinuation, invective,
and insult in terms of rhetoric and oratory. This specific legal-juridical exercise is beyond
the scope of this chapter.

[37] Miguel de Beistegui, *Heidegger & the Political* (London: Routledge, 1998), 71.

at the level of the person—the stuff of what some theorists[38] in the West have called it thinly, the "the politics of dirty hands,"[39] and that is perhaps because it debunks the neat distinction between the public and the private. We shall call "pure politics" made up of deception, betrayal, treachery, malice, lying, and such others. And an impossibility of refusal to accept these—say an affirmative denial, juridically or whatever—projects a recluse only in personal attacks that might end up even in a murder. Given a chance, such perpetrators(s) would confess in these words,

> I'll lie when I must, and I have contempt for no one. I wasn't the one who invented lying. ... We shall not abolish lying by refusing to tell lies, but by using every means at hand. ...;

> [or]

> For years you will have to cheat, trick and maneuver; we'll go from compromise to compromise.[40]

Lying is dirty mouth, though trying to deal with every means at hand. But what is the phenomenon of dirty hands itself? This designation of "dirty hands" might have been a product of a meditative listening to Sartre wherefrom this excerpt would be informative

> Hoederer: How afraid you are to soil your hands! All right stay pure! What good will it do? ... To do nothing, to remain motionless, arms at your sides, wearing kid gloves. Well, I have dirty hands. Right up to the elbows. I've plunged them in filth and blood. But what do you hope? Do you think you can govern innocently?

> Hugo: You'll see some day that I'm not afraid of blood.

> Hoederer: Really! Red gloves, that's elegant. It's the rest that scares you. ...[41]

---

[38] An early statement of this is Michael Walzer, "Political Action: The Problem of Dirty Hands," *Philosophy and Public Affairs* 2, no. 2 (1973): 160–80. Evidently though, the limitation of Walzer is in limiting the problem of dirty hands to governmental or public outcomes only.

[39] "The problem of dirty hands is thought to be situated somewhere in between public and private. In this view, it is understood as a kind of discontinuity between the two spheres." See J. Van Oosterhout, *The Quest for Legitimacy: On Authority and Responsibility in Governance* (Rotterdam: Erasmus Research Institute of Management [ERIM], Erasmus University, 2000), 73.

[40] Philip Green and Michael Walzer (eds.), *The Problem of Choice,* in *The Political Imagination in Literature,* eds. (New York, NY: The Free Press, 1969), 206–19.

[41] Jean Paul Sartre, *"Dirty Hands,"* in *The Political Imagination in Literature,* eds. Philip Green and Michael Walzer (New York, NY: The Free Press, 1969), 206–19.

Now, is it possible to make sense of the politics of dirty hands in a phenomenological manner? This is necessary because we've been listening to the politics of dirty hands as far as the manifestation of certain effects are concerned, but what form does it assume before an experiencing consciousness?

While the legal juridical discourse and the bureaucratic administrative apparatus do administer various applied notions of the person—public or private—the political deployments of such categories—that too with the cultural unconscious in action—would be fluid, strategic, and success-oriented is perhaps expected. The question of distant, objective, impersonal reflection on value-neutral questions and disagreement in both politics and culture are always already delivered to be governed by practical political imperatives—whether it entails instances of political deliberation or cultural expectancy. (And normative deliberation can be practiced only when it is freed from brute empirico-practical and practical-political considerations.)

Now, to subject everything to the practical and eternally immediate is to accept

> [t]he philosophical priority of the existent over being … it finally makes possible the description of the notion of the immediate. The immediate is the interpellation and, if we may speak thus, the imperative of language. The idea of contact does not represent the primordial mode of the immediate. Contact is already a thematization and a reference to a horizon. The immediate is the face to face.[42]

Then, with the immediate, deferred exigencies of "dirty" politics, we approach what we'll call the appearance of a pure political imaginary of the person whose comportment is toward other persons; (We use pure in the sense where an object's form and content cannot be distinguished[43] and imaginary in its now established usage as being "not a set of ideas; rather … what enables, through making sense of, the practices of a society."[44])

---

[42] Emmanuel Levinas, *Totality and Infinity: An Essay on Exteriority,* trans. Alphonso Lingis (Pittsburgh, PA: Duquesne University Press, 2000), 51–52.

[43] "Egoistic and professional forces may become conflated in reality and indistinguishable in practice. Machiavelli's advice illuminates this difficult problem." See Laurie Calhoun, "The Problem of 'Dirty Hands' and Corrupt Leadership," *The Independent Review* 8, no. 3 (2004), 363–85.

[44] Charles Taylor, "Modern Social Imaginaries," *Public Culture* 14, no. 1 (2002): 91–124.

Contextually, a political scientist commenting on violence and its relation to Sadat Hasan Manto notes,

> Manto's uniqueness lies in the fact that he refused to accept the parameters of either ethics or economy in talking about the violence of 1947. He had no recourse to a morality that was given to him either by god or by transcendental reason. Nor would he allow himself to be seduced by the economic calculations of governmental violence. For him, the violence of partition called for a response that was, if I may put it this way, an act of *pure politics*, where morality and economy had to be created all at once, all by oneself, de novo, from the bare elements of human interaction.[45]

This, we think, is a Machiavellian moment, and we've talked considerably about it.[46] The moment has approached all politics slowly but decisively, and now it only awaits a fair chance. And to address this question of the Machiavellian "pure"[47] moment, where the content of the experience and the experience cannot be distinguished, we need a political phenomenology—the way we experience the political and within horizons.[48] To exemplify such a phenomenology, to capture this moment and illustrate

---

[45] Partha Chatterjee, "Democracy and the Violence of the State: A Political Negotiation of Death," Paper Circulated for CSSSC Cultural Studies Workshop at Bharatpur Rajasthan, 1999. (Italics mine).

[46] And Machiavellism, with all its moral pessimism and secular empiricism, "can be applied with the same force not only to the work of Kautilya but to the entire range of Hindu economic, legal and political literature." See Benoy Kumar Sarkar, *The Positive Background of Hindu Sociology, Introduction to Hindu Positivism* (Delhi: Motilal Banarasidas, 1985), 640.

[47] "Pure violence 'shows' itself precisely in the fact that it never appears *as such.*" For instance, lying or deception in order to be successful resembles a truth structure. This is the figurative essence of politics as I understand it, and I agree that they have the force to foreground identities. But I do not use it in the sense that it is the condition of every performative act (like saying "all truths are fictions" or falsity is the phantasmatic base on which truth, indispensably, operates) entailing an unmediated immediacy or "pure mediacy" so much so that "that would mean, then, the death of the subject because the duality subject/object would have been entirely eliminated." See Ernesto Laclau and Lilian Zac, "Minding the Gap: The Subject of Politics," in *The Making of Political Identities,* ed. Ernesto Laclau (London: Verso, 1994), 26–27. In this sense, we retain the Kantian use of "malice" as something more than violence (and, therefore, different from violence as such) and we use the rubric "politics" to refer to all of these.

[48] "Whatever else a phenomenology of the political may offer, it should begin as a reflection on the first-person experience of the political [...] to begin with a reflection on political experience." See Steven Galt Crowell, "Who is the Political Actor? An Existential Phenomenological Approach," in *Phenomenology of the Political,* eds. Kevin Thompson and Lester Embree (Boston, MA: Kluwer Academic Publishers, 2000), 11.

what is pure politics, here is a slice of an example; better said, here is a narrative and a figuration. We quote parts of a news report which appeared in *The Statesman* on February 4, 2000.

<u>Bhubaneshwar, February 3</u>

Mr Navin Patnaik today expelled BJD political affairs committee chairman, Mr Bijoy Mohapatra from the party. He also snatched Mr Mohapatra's Assembly nomination and gave the ticket to a local journalist instead. Mr Mohapatra was left too stunned to react. All he could say was he had been back stabbed. BJD leaders and workers were outraged. Mr Patnaik's completely unexpected move was described state wide as "treacherous." ... The move that removed the ground from under Mr Mohapatra's feet was obviously planned meticulously and timed brilliantly by Mr Patnaik. The rebel leader with whom Mr Patnaik had ostensibly signed a truce, was sacked and debarred from the polls at the eleventh hour. ... too late for Mr Mohapatra to file papers as an Independent, and the outwitted rebel had no choice but to watch helplessly. ... No one could read the BJD chief's mind. Mr Mohapatra had been the party's key negotiator during the tortuous seat sharing talks with the BJP. He had had a major role in selecting candidates for various seats. Even Congress and BJP circles who consider Mr Mohapatra as the lone political leader of mettle and strategist in the BJD, were taken aback.

To the readers' surprise, and a challenge to surmise, what kind of political science or political sociology would explain this enchantment? All such disciplinary categories as civil society, political society, family, and the State just vanish into thin air before this. We all have had such moments in our lives but rarely have felt that those narratives would be included in political science textbooks. Those losses were ours and they will remain ours; those secrets will die with us—each separately. "Too stunned to react" is an adequate description because reaction could be a meditation on a prior act; here is an action without a reaction. In the disciplinary study of politics and criminal offence—stabbing being a metonymy of murder and violence—has often been mentioned or studied; where do we get to know what is "back stabbing"? Another important phrase is "timed brilliantly." What does it stand for? Punctuality is to go according to other's time: passive timing. Timing in politics is the dominative monitoring of others according to one's own time where he/she himself/herself is the frame of reference: active timing. I am waiting for the right moment to teach him/her a lesson, I know it, he/she doesn't, I am waiting for him/her to enter my duration. Here time as a trap and emerging as a "means of orientation"[49] is destructive of other's time—the space in which the victim thrived and swam along his/her moments. So I "ostensibly sign ... a truce," give him/her a show of importance to mislead him/her and then "remove the ground from under" his/her "feet." Notice the word truce, a signifier of peace, and how it has been deployed. When we were dealing with speech generating violence, this is the point we wanted to argue: let us look at the varieties of peace and how they are being used for what purposes. Truce used to back stab? Here is the moment.

This is a classic instance of the politics of dirty hands, but with our rider "pure" because this overwhelms and surpasses the implied notion of individuals of public, political, and representative significance indulging in unavoidable, moral wrongdoing for a greater, public good. This is sheer, deeply internal politicking where the solace of institutional differentiation and decisional segmentation undercutting the first personal action system of a lone politician does not even arise. Mr Mohapatra is not even allowed to contest and, therefore, the topic of democratic answerability cannot be mooted.[50] The standard discourse on dirty hands invokes guilt or shame felt by the perpetrator of dirty hands; some have proposed "tragic remorse,"[51] which is a more unified product than mere guilt, shame, or "personal aguish."[52] Is there any remorse here, or is there a shining, stubborn sense of competitive joy and success in having had one's way by crushing another rival? "The cases of dirty hands" (do good by doing evil) and "imperfect procedures" (to do evil by doing good), however,

---

[49] We borrow this phrase and use it to our purpose from Norbert Elias, "Time and Timing," in *On Civilization, Power and Knowledge: Selected Writings,* eds. Mennell J. Goudsblom (Chicago, Il: The University of Chicago Press, 1998), 253–59.

[50] Though this is in refutation of Sutherland's forceful thesis that the "The dirty hands leader, by definition, operates quite alone in a supra ethical realm of elitist thinking," which is at odds in a democratic milieu, his other modification is largely acceptable where he raises doubts about such lone actions: "The meaning of a particular politically intended action, rather, is not a pure philosophical concept, but can be puzzling even to the actors, who may have had confused motives, and is ultimately lost to the protagonist, being negotiated in society." See S. L. Sutherland, "The Problem of Dirty Hands in Politics: Peace in the Vegetable Trade," *Canadian Journal of Political Science* 28, no. 3 (1995): 506–507.

[51] "Tragic remorse is the sentiment we feel when we are moved by moral concerns to commit moral violations and in so doing suffer anguish ... and a sense of moral pollution in addition to the usual feelings of guilt and shame that ordinarily accompany moral violations." See Stephen De Wijze, "Tragic Remorse—The Anguish of Dirty Hands," *Ethical Theory and Moral Practice* 7, no. 5 (2005): 470.

[52] Michael Walzer, "Political Action: The Problem of Dirty Hands," *Philosophy and Public Affairs* 2, no. 2 (1973): 176.

are two areas in which not only the normal model but also the "relentless, pursuit of justice fails"[53] This is why we've termed this irresolvable and. in a sense, pure.

Where do we end then? What is the use of studying this phenomenon called personal attacks that name the persons with dirty hands? Peter Digester thinks we should be unforgiving toward the practice of dirty hands but forgiving toward imperfect procedural (in)justice. Then unforgiving as it is, we shall be stunned when we are cheated, betrayed, fired, suppressed, deprived, or discriminated against in an uncommon silence (and be "too stunned to react"). Those are the moments when we shall feel the hand of politics on our back, but nothing will save us, no category; they will be moments of pure experience. The politics of dirty hands will cleanse everything, remaining residually and strictly alive on the borderlines of our everyday being. We might feel exploited, but that will remain only as a moral feeling, because the apparatus required to structure the feeling has been slowly but evenly decontextualized. The state socialist project was criticized as being one of the most ruthless regimes of techno-scientific, objective, impersonal, and instrumental rationality where human beings without a personal touch were simply lost in a maze of bureaucratic cleaning. Now, if the death of all the grand narratives thereby have been conveniently announced, we need to engage with small and smaller events and listen to the narratives of pure, petty politics. Are we not doing this, in this chapter too? Also, to pure politics, the fragment or the micro-local is not a metaphor of place; for it, the fragment is that what we resist from allowing it to coincide with the norms of the public or the private and is limited to the overriding magic of the person.

> The rules and rituals of separation that function to maintain the purity of the categories of public and private also support the contemporary legal fiction that public servants act not as concrete individuals but as articulations of the abstract body of the polity and, accordingly, are neutral, objective, and free from the passions and interests that may plague their private existence. The pragmatic problem here is that everybody knows this to be a fiction. Everybody knows that Bush as public servant cannot be abstracted from Bush as private citizen, that his religious fundamentalism, corporate alliances, and personal affiliations directly impact his conduct as president. The logic operant here is one of cynicism; we know that the idea of a public

---

[53] Peter Digester, "Forgiveness and Politics: Dirty Hands and Imperfect Procedures," *Political Theory* 26, no. 5 (1998): 717; the bracketed elaborations are from page 708.

that is free of private interests and passions is fictional, nonetheless, we demand that all involved act as if this were not the case. We demand that the illusion of a real and substantive public be maintained even though we may not fully believe it.[54]

Then, bereft of illusions and abandoning grand investigations, we need to undertake studies of the micro politics of dirty hands: being dirty, the term political pornography, therefore, is improperly apt.

> Power thus relies on an obscene supplement—that is to say, the obscene nightly law (superego) necessarily accompanies, as its shadowy double, the "public law".… Obscene unwritten rules sustain Power as long as they remain in the shadows; the moment they are publicly recognized, the edifice of Power is thrown into disarray.[55]

Pure politics deals with this obscene underside of public and private law, and for this, regrettably, personal attacks are its primary raw materials. We need to have then narratives of manipulations, machinations, intrigues, and malice more sinister, more ghostly than violence causing speech or violence itself: Kant states: "He who openly declares himself an enemy can be relied upon, but the treachery of secret malice, if it became universal, would mean the end of all confidence. This type of wickedness is more detestable than violence."[56] Because we are to engage in the later part of the work with charity, optional benevolence, and finally, social work, it would not be misplaced to spend a few more words on malevolence—or malice—which is always orientated toward the others in a destructively negative co-relation. What is the response to Kant's malice, after all? Kant himself is at odds. That no theory can deliver us is clear from his account; what he endorses is right conduct as a kind of constant and consistent life-practice. The recent masterwork[57] on malice seems to discredit even Kant's conclusion. Beginning with Locke's formulation of childhood where the child is a little tyrant—a small despot with his/her love of dominion and fisticuffs, with his/her unbearable crying to attract everybody to come to his/her service, and his/her tearing everything including dolls, the first self-tuition

[54] Peter Bratsis, "The Construction of Corruption, or Rules of Separation and Illusions of Purity in Bourgeois Societies," *Social Text* 21, no. 4 (2003, Winter): intermittently.

[55] Slavoj Zizek, *The Plague of Fantasies* (London: Verso, 1997), 73.

[56] Kant, *Lectures on Ethics,* 215.

[57] Francois Flahault, *Malice,* transl. Liz Heron (London: Verso, 2003).

in infantile mutilation—we encounter the big other as we grow older and confront a bad infinity: "we cannot stand a particular person for this or that reason."[58] The more I want to extend myself, the more I encounter the limits posed by others, and this is in itself limitless. "[T]he set of relationships within which if the existence of one is to grow, the existence of the other must diminish. Here there is antagonism, malice and destruction."[59] Therefore, I confront it through another abstraction, but in a concrete form of existence: being malicious is one way of it. "Being decent, just and benevolent is a way of existing. Being malicious is equally a way of existing."[60] Kant's recommendation could be inferred in this light. Malice being an existential predicate is a subject of existence and not a subject of knowledge, thereby, external to all social and moral knowledge; the latter unable to cognize it as a concrete concept to be mastered, but is a witness to a show of images—palpable and passing, albeit missing. Therefore, accounts of malice and cunning could not be had in social bookkeeping—they are hardly archival records of history; they are present, as we shall expound later, in narratives. Flahault thinks fictional narratives are best because "[w]hat a narrative says about the subject of existence is something that the subject of knowledge is not in a position to hear."[61] To grasp and absorb malice fully, and transform it, is to acknowledge, while going against its grid, that it is an external entity and can be managed. To reject this view, Flahault projects an inner source of malice—that is—as if, it is within us and then, in the next step, he ontologizes it: "disparagement and hatred, destruction and the inflicting of suffering, primo, bring the us a more-being which benevolence would be unable to provide."[62] And here he nearly runs into Carl Scmitt, but without his politics, "This reversal of the friend into foe, confrontation and duels—all this extends a certain fascination."[63]

> As Burke wrote—and precisely before taking the Book of Job as his example: "the idea of pain, in its highest degree, is much stronger than the highest degree of pleasure." It has to be acknowledged that dark "negative," depressing ideas can exert an irresistible seductive power over us—an attraction with which "positive" pleasant and constructive (therefore

---

[58] Ibid., 165.
[59] Ibid., 168.
[60] Ibid., 167.
[61] Ibid., 10.
[62] Ibid., 171.
[63] Ibid., 169.

relative and limited) ideas cannot compete. [Mutual love and recognition, "being enriched by our differences," is wonderful. But that does not mean that there are not still times when—not to put too fine a point on it—other people piss us off[64]] Malice, dissatisfaction, and a liking for depressing ideas derive from the same source.[65]

The same inner source, that is, but Flahault hardly can explain why: "[S]oldiers in Vietnam who were unable to stop themselves from vomiting the first time they were ordered to machine gun civilians from their helicopters."[66] He seems to suggest that an element of neutralization, later, can work wonders, and when the first flurry of empathetic overflow subsides and we steel ourselves, we are ready to take up any menial job.

But is the moment when the steel is tempered enough on sufficient grounds? History cannot be halted simply by condemnation; it has to address events where an open declaration of enmity is absent and such wickedness—so to say—runs riot. Now, it appears as a lesson to be learnt and exists only as a secured item in the inventory. A simple guilty conscience hardly suffices and, therefore, what is required is such a counter-declaration,

> To sell oneself for thirty pieces of silver is an honest transaction; but to sell oneself to one's own conscience is to abandon mankind. History is a priori amoral; it has no conscience. To want to conduct history according to the maxims of the Sunday school means to leave everything as it is.[67]

We've returned to Machiavelli and the unspeakable confessions or suggestions of wickedness it entails. We are convinced about the personal nature of this politics, but it might be argued as an objection that, in the absence of a private language or a language that grasps the subject of existence, this genuinely personal would not be, and quite truly, communicated. But still this experience could be narrated as argued earlier. And that is the stuff of pure politics. After an elaboration, we've arrived at it, finally. But is it not a straight corollary that the personalized pure politics of dirty hands will be responded to, or answered back in personal terms too? If it is in the affirmative, then it is necessary to historicize it

---

[64] Ibid., 8.
[65] Ibid., 88.
[66] Ibid., 172.
[67] Arthur Koestler, "Darkness at Noon," in *The Political Imagination in Literature*, eds. Michael Walzer and Philip Green (New York, NY: The Free Press, 1969), 199.

since the politics of personal political attacks or the political appropriation of them could not be ruled out. And, therefore, the following detour, and then we shall able to see how they impact the impersonal public sphere and transform it radically.

# Resuming Responses to the Pure Politics of Dirty Hands: Personal Invectives in the West—From the Ancient Greek and the Middle Ages to Modernity

If we could discern three broad historical phases of "personal" invectives or uncivil rhetoric in the Western political history of humanity, then the footfalls could be three. First, the Greek sources with Cicero or Diogenes pioneering the first and Aristotle giving us the theory. Second, against the church in the 15th and 16th centuries, And the third during the 18th century, which interestingly turned against the state.

Invectives present in the corpus of assembly speeches delivered in classical Athens portray the master orator Cicero in his Philipic speeches asserting with fury the following words:

> Surely that is real moderation—to protest about Anthony and refrain from abuse! For what was left of Rome, Antony, owed its final annihilation to yourself. In your home everything had a price … Laws you passed, laws you caused to be put through your interests, had never ever been formally proposed. … You were an augur, yet you never took the auspices. You were a consul, yet you blocked the legal right of other officials to exercise the veto. Your armed escort was shocking. You were a drink-sodden, sex ridden wreck. Never a day passes in that ill-reputed house of yours without orgies of the most repulsive kind. In spite of all that, I restricted myself in my speech to solemn complaints concerning the state of our nation. I said nothing personal about the man.[68]

It is perhaps no wonder that Cicero would, thus, settle for a strategic catch phrase and would utter: "Men decide far more problems by hate, or

---

[68] Cicero, "Attack On an Enemy of Freedom (The Second Philippic Against Antony)," in *Selected Works,* transl. M. Grant (England: Penguin Books, 1981), 105.

love, or fear or illusion, or some other inward emotion, than by reality."[69] But an interesting point in this context is that the ruling templates of the time did sanction Cicero's venom, while—and this is what is historically interesting—what we call modernity devises in the wake of public opinion, also being tied to an impersonal rational public sphere, an ethics of deliberation for the first time.

Aristotle—if taken in entirety—would be difficultly poised to intervene in this debate since he both approves and disapproves the Ciceroian gesture in the same breath. First, let us consider the way he would censor Cicero: for children being susceptible to imitation or the art of acquiring "a taint of meanness from what they" [first] "hear and see," the "legislator," Aristotle urges, "should be more careful to drive away indecency of speech; for the light utterance of shameful words leads soon to shameful actions."[70] But not only this, he goes so far as to promulgate a sort of indecent representation act of ours: "And since we do not allow improper language, clearly we should also banish pictures or speeches from the stage which are indecent."[71] The second moment—the way Aristotle would endorse Cicero—is reflected in the way he reserves a category for "speeches of eulogy and attack."[72]

> All eulogy is based upon the noble deeds—real or imaginary—that stand to the credit of those eulogized. On the same principle, invectives are based on facts of the opposite kind: the orator looks to see what the base deeds—real or imaginary—stand to the discredit of those he is attacking, such as the treachery to the cause of Hellenic freedo[m].[73]

Further, in absolute concurrence with Cicero, Aristotle urges the skilled speaker's "power to stir the emotions of his hearers."[74] Cicero, thereby, was then a representative who pushed this thought to extremes.

[69] Cicero, "De Oratore" and "Orator," in *The Rhetorical Tradition: Readings from Classical Times to the Present*, pp. 283–343. 2nd Ed. edited by Patricia Bizzell and Bruce Herzberg. New York: Bedford St. Martin's, 2001, 328.
[70] Aristotle, "Politics," in *The Basic Works of Aristotle,* ed. Richard McKeon (New York, NY: The Modern Library, 2001), 1304.
[71] "[E]xcept in the temples of those gods at whose festivals the law permits even ribaldry … "; within the realm of his permission, Aristotle tends to include mature people also. See Aristotle, "Politics," in *The Basic Works of Aristotle,* ed. Richard McKeon (New York, NY: The Modern Library, 2001), 1304.
[72] Aristotle, "Rhetorica," in *The Basic Works of Aristotle,* ed. Richard McKeon (New York, NY: The Modern Library, 2001), 1409.
[73] Ibid., 1418.
[74] Ibid., 1318.

With this, we reach a certain benchmark of the first phase of invectives—and the way to understand them. But besides Cicero there was Diogenes. Hegel, while wanting to address the cynics and talking about Diogenes, remembered him for "his biting and often clever hits, and bitter and sarcastic retorts,"[75] and narrates to us an illustrative anecdote: "In Plato's house he once walked on the beautiful carpets with muddy feet, saying 'I tread on the pride of Plato'. 'Yes, but with another pride', replied Plato, as pointedly."[76] But could Diogenes's bitter retorts be taken as a precedent for invectives in political modernity? Hardly so, Diogenes's cynicism was, Hegel points out, "more a mode of living than a philosophy."[77] This "mode of living" (where philosophy itself was a way of life) in Diogenes bore peculiar results: he is said to have been gifted with the habit of masturbating in public. When asked, he is reported to have said that he was experimenting whether hunger could be appeased in a similar manner—just by rubbing the stomach.[78]

In this light, what is so distinctive about Aristotle—and which cannot be invoked in justifying today's deliberative democratic reasoning, or its exceptions—is that political deliberation in Aristotle is enframed within an art of rhetoric as a form of skill or technique giving directions to decisions and a particular way of life. While it was to persuade the hearers about a particular action (for instance whether Athens should go to war), today's political deliberation begins with the vow to settle disagreements. Aristotelian deliberation is not a means to pursue political legitimacy as in today's governance. It is, rather, oriented to a form of practical rationality. And perhaps for this reason he had a place for personal invectives and emotions because they invoke separate kinds of proofs and syllogisms. This supreme rhetorical necessity (not being a rational necessity) is unimaginable in impersonal modernity.[79]

---

[75] G. W. F. Hegel, *Hegel's Lectures on the History of Philosophy*, transl. E. S. Haldane (1892; repr., London: Routledge & Kegan Paul, 1955), I: 484.

[76] Ibid., 486.

[77] Ibid., 484.

[78] David Sacks, *Encyclopedia of the Ancient Greek World* (New York, NY: Facts on File, Inc, 1995), 83.

[79] And, therefore, contemporary attempts at trying to revive relevancy for Aristotle or similar commentaries in order to redefine a contemporary deliberative (Habermasian or Rawlsian) project, seems to me, absolutely misplaced. For attempts of such kind, see Bernard Yack, "Rhetoric and Public Reasoning: An Aristotelian Understanding of Political Deliberation," *Political Theory* 34, no. 4 (2006, August), 417–38; Amartya Sen, *The Argumentative Indian: Writings on Indian History, Culture and Identity* (London:

Amidst the medieval imagination of invectives, the most famous legacy has been borne by anti-clerical writers "in the generation immediately preceding the reformation"[80] who were energized by the writings of Luther. A historian studying this lineage mentions,

> Much of the resulting literature of invective and abuse had been produced by the most learned humanists of the age, but they had generally written in self-consciously demotic style, usually publishing in the vernacular and often presenting their arguments in the form of plays and satires in verse.[81]

The bulk of its abusive content is its attack on the church who is "depicted as Mother Fool" and who "spends her time plotting and machinating with all the fools of the age."[82] This results in the expected insistence "that all clerics are lecherous, and that all money given by the pious laity for the saying of masses is 'spent among wanton lasses'."[83]

While this time it is the church, the next turn is marked by invectives turning against the state itself. In the 18th century, we have to reckon with the hatching of a political pornography in a descriptive sense—the theorization of which is derivatively based on the so-called porno-theorists (sometimes called low life litterateurs of the French Revolution and excavated by low literature historians like Darnton[84]) and directed against the state. (Though enlightenment heroes like Diderot would, through *Memoirs of a Nun*, still explore the sexual corruptions of the church, but that critique had become, by then, clearly redundant). These researches reveal that intense personal-political attacks based on pornographic "scatological imagery" in pamphlets performed a historical and revolutionary role[85] against Marie Antoinette during the late 18th century;

---

Penguin Books, 2005). Also, in this context, we feel that if expressed in Aristotelian language, today's parliamentary deliberation—which has become a model of democratic deliberation in a sense—is simply "ceremonial"; emptied of all content—it has no precepts to offer to action.

[80] Quentin Skinner, *The Foundations of Modern Political Thought,* Vol. Two: The Age of Reformation (1978; repr., Cambridge: Cambridge University Press: Cambridge, 1992), 27.

[81] Ibid., 27.

[82] Ibid., 28.

[83] Ibid., 29.

[84] Specially Robert Darnton, *The Forbidden Best Sellers of Pre-revolutionary France* (New York, NY: Norton, 1995).

[85] But how such radicalism could degenerate into underground commercial pornography as well, see Iain McCalman, *Radical Underworld, Prophets, Revolutionaries, and Pornographers in London, 1795–1840* (Oxford: Clarendon Press, 1993).

while the Bourbon king Louis XV was dubbed as sexually promiscuous and libertine, pornographic pictures of Louis XVI were circulated among the population showing him as impotent. These, according to an author, went on to "discredit the monarchy as an institution and to desacralize the King's body ... the aristocracy, and clergy."[86] De-sacralizing the royal body finally engendered the birth of the republic. But the force of a personalized persuasion was not lost—at least not historically. It was picked up by the Fascists in the 20th century. But to shortchange the Fascist propaganda as sheer racial libel provoking the German public to undertake anti-Semitic violence, would be to miss the point. One who studied this project in some tenuous but reliable detail is Theodor Adorno who starts with a very helpful, thumbnail observation:

> It is personalized propaganda, essentially nonobjective. The agitators spend a large part of their time in speaking either about themselves or their audiences. ... they incessantly divulge real or fictitious intimacies about their lives and those of their families. Moreover, they appear to take a warm human interest in the small daily worries of their listeners. ... Another favorite scheme of personalization is to dwell upon petty financial needs and to beg for small amounts of money.[87]

Their identification with the audience being complete, they pretend to be mere means or "messengers" of the person or the Messiah to come (substitution of a collective ego for paternal imagery[88]) and, thus, limit themselves to elaborating on the means of the movement as the immediate task and avoid explicating its positive ends or a concrete future. With this "propaganda itself becomes the ultimate content ... a kind of wish fulfillment."[89]

This is one of its most important patterns. People are "let in," they are supposedly getting the inside dope, taken into confidence, treated as the elite who deserves to know the lurid mysteries hidden from the outsiders. Lust for snooping is both encouraged and satisfied. Scandal stories, mostly

---

[86] Mary L. BellHouse, "Erotic 'Remedy' Prints and the Fall of the Aristocracy in Eighteenth Century France," *Political Theory* 25, no. 5 (1997, October), 68.

[87] Theodor Adorno, "Anti-Semitism and Fascist Propaganda," in *The Stars Down to Earth and Other Essays on the Irrational in Culture*, ed. Stephen Crook (London: Routledge, 2002), 218–31.

[88] Ibid., 219.

[89] Ibid., 220.

fictitious, particularly of sexual excesses and atrocities are constantly told; the indignation of filth and cruelty is but a very thin, purposely transparent rationalization of the pleasure these stories convey to the listener.[90]

Supposedly for Adorno, the fascists, thus, aim the irrational and can successfully impart their "mental defects" to the listeners. This they do not by sheer abuse but by a crafted method of persuasion[91] (previously we had shown in the wake of Cicero how this has had its sources and justifications in Aristotle's Rhetoric.) It is irrational because, as Adorno tells us, it is nonargumentative, anti-theoretical, and not based on a discursive logic of reasoning footed to convince people. What is its substance then? According to Adorno, they are "oratorial exhibitions, what might be called an organized flight of ideas."[92]

If the Greek Ciceroian to the communist or the fascist orator are master politicians of personalistic dirty hands, we've shown and shall talk about more on how the nonviolent times of democracy could be more subversive—though in the standard literature, impersonal, formal legal regimes and the separation of powers in the public political arena have been argued to be stumbling obstacles to the "overman" blocking his authoritarian plot. And what if this has been shown to have been a fiction? In a classic article, C. A. J. Coady concludes, "It is one thing to hold that politics might require moral crimes, quite another to insist that it involves a life style which closes off certain morally attractive options. … If this is dirty hands, then it is merely the human condition."[93] Now,

---

[90] Ibid., 220.

[91]

> The relation between premises and inferences is replaced by a linking up of ideas resting on mere similarity, often through association by employing the same characteristic word in two propositions that are logically quite unrelated. This method not only evades the control mechanisms of rational examination, but also makes it psychologically easier for the listener to "follow." He has no exacting thinking to do, but can give himself up passively to a stream of words in which he swims.

See Theodor Adorno, "Anti-Semitism and Fascist Propaganda," in *The Stars Down to Earth and Other Essays on the Irrational in Culture*, ed. Stephen Crook (London: Routledge: London, 2002), 223.

[92] Ibid., 222–23.

[93] C. A. J. Coady, "Politics and the Problem of Dirty Hands," in *A Companion to Ethics*, ed. Peter Singer (UK: Blackwell, 1993), 373–83 Or, for that matter, as against such an exhortation, one would be at a loss to comprehend the fact as to how Coady could previously talk about the "circumstances" that require dirty hands (p. 379), or that dirty hands is more pervasive in political arena than private life, and the question could be posed,

this supra-generalization is the result of a liberal, helpless pessimism since, as we noticed, in order to compare and classify some acts or mechanics as dirty, one has to have a horizon of morality. If the lifeworld is itself dirty in the special sense, then nothing could be cast against its relief as clean and compared. The (life) world "like the earth … stands behind and forms the background to what we see … but the world is clearly not itself a perceived object."[94]

# How the Seduction of Pure Politics Disengaged the Person-al, or, Results for the Personal Transformation of the Public Sphere

We tended to stumble against the impersonal nature of the public sphere in the wake of political modernity after having examined the historical trajectory of the so-called personal attacks, where the personal—being subjected to the regime of personal attacks—appeared without a mask. The politics of liberal idealism, in this sense, seems to offer "a clean glove of legitimacy"[95] for dirty hands. At a particular site that is, politics, and at the level of rhetoric or speech we engaged with such a liberal-idealistic concrete counter discourse famous for its complaint that personal attacks push out the impersonal discourse of "principled governance" and pollute a democratic-political and a growing, albeit good modern, civic culture. This is in genuine consonance with the classical Weberian formulation. Now, in such a context where the personal-particular subverts and transcends the public-universal garb, it is often that personal attacks try, with or without success, to pierce this silencing, civil veil and address the illegitimate. And for the second objection—in this context, it was easily concluded (though it is not central to my argument) that the notion of

---

more forcefully, for "representatives" related to the state that must be legitimate, impartial, etc. His universal pessimism emerges, perhaps, from his failure to hold on to his liberal distinction—in the face of our onslaught—or anything similar to it—anticipated by him.

[94] David Carr, *Phenomenology and the Problem of History: A Study of Husserl's Transcendental Philosophy* (Evanston, IL: Northwestern University Press, 1974), 143.

[95] Richard Bellamy, "Dirty Hands and Clean Gloves: Liberal Ideals and Real Politics," *European Journal of Political Theory* 9, no. 4 (2010), 412–30.

civility, for instance in India today, is a matter of political sphere and not at all of civil society; therefore, an advice of civility has to be politically negotiated than be received as "unmediated" discourse on civic virtues. In short, civility and violent disagreement could never go together. How peace and civility could be seen as being complicit with an "un" fairly (we are remembering Rawls here) unjust system[96] was also examined in the wake of the phenomenon of agreement with approved ways of protest. While we do a lot of lip service against violence, let us not forget to examine peace too. Pure politics or the politics of dirty hands made up of betrayal, malice, fraud, deception, and treachery is politics in the times of peace: this was Machiavelli with a modern turn.

But this ought not to mean that we are engaged in that infantile tryst to justify the personal through personal attacks. It would be similar to arguing, like Mandeville, that private vices necessitate public benefits and exposure of such vices would reap public benefits. To those aggressive practitioners of this theory, this mutual castigation through personal attacks is perhaps not wrong. Followed continuously, this mutually focused political aggression turns itself into a ritual and finds itself involved in another unintended radical translation. Despite their private intentions, their public conduct becomes the same (in a Kantian sense), thus, giving Mandelville's formula "Private vices: Public benefits" more than an agreeable twist.[97] Such an argument would rarely look insurmountable today for various predictable reasons. A rational choice theory would surmise that if private interests are at stake equally, it may be so that both will avoid exposure beyond a threshold; further, they can be feigned, they can be staged, and they might just be deployed to override the propositional form of public reasoning, or they can be used as a convenient form of silencing or listening. Our argument is not this at all. We are satisfied having shown

---

[96] "The principle of cooperation ['with evil'] and double effect are accessible to private individuals, as well as public representatives, and thus there cannot be two moralities." See Leslie Griffin, "The Problem of Dirty Hands," *The Journal of Religious Ethics* 17, no. 1 (1989), 53.

[97] Luxury, expenditure, and corruption of convenience—according to Mandeville—result in industriousness. In nearly an anarcho-capitalist discourse, Mandeville argues how vice produces civilization and makes society necessary for the physically deficient; second, vice in the sense of moral defect (greed, lust, luxury, and envy) makes production and social co-operation desirable. See M. M. Goldsmith, *Private Vices, Public Benefits: Bernard Mandeville's Political Thought* (Cambridge: Cambridge University Press, 1985), 40–41. Goldsmith also argues that this view attacked the existing ideology of early 18th century Great Britain.

that personal attacks did reveal to us the overriding nature of the personal over the public and the private. It helped us arrive at the examination of the public nature of political modernity itself. And the moment we ventured into so-called "political pornography," dangerous vistas appeared. Similarly, our relational and other, even official affinities suddenly seem to have been tattooed, if we look in this light, by deception, betrayal, malice, backstabbing, envy, and other propaganda. And we find it everywhere, from our first orientation to the second person to our last orientation to the third person plural. Examples are rife and always happening. With this, we've departed from the established, surveyed usage of "dirty politics" in terms of politicians where "[t]he practitioner of politics—the politician—is assaulted with the same basic English. He is mauled and smeared with the student's favorite political adjective "dirty." "The politician will do anything, no matter how dirty, to get what he's after."[98] And as a countervailing explanation, the interviewer-author asserts: "Admittedly, the politician is an opportunist, a trimmer, a fixer. Perhaps he is, as Lincoln was described, 'scheming, contriving, manipulating'. He has to be. His tasks compel it."[99] Therefore, it is—as if—for public interest that his/her hands are dirty; we've done away with this long-lasting explanation and brought the phenomenon down to the floor of our everyday living, which also—in a way—corroborates our argument that it is not always that a just war is being waged, under compulsion, with unjust means, and it is with persons as private or public individuals who transcend the norms of privacy to engage in dirty hands. The context of an explicit, open violence is clearly redundant.

> If there were a clear line which marked the limit of manoeuvre, then there would finally be no Dirty Hands problem.[100] But we order or at least license our agents to pursue policies which cannot be translated into action, if honesty and openness are required too. The casualties of urban renewal, for instance, are greater if the plans are known in advance. The resulting blight then has to be remedied by wider destruction of property and community. Yet secrecy demands a firm lie in the face of questions. Thus, the family promised safety today will be Glencoed tomorrow. This too is violence, even if the weapon is not a musket but a clearance order.[101]

---

[98] Maurice Klain, "'Politics': Still a Dirty Word," *The Antioch Review* 15, no. 4 (1995), 458.
[99] Ibid., 464.
[100] Martin Hollis, "Dirty Hands," *British Journal of Political Science* 12, no. 4 (1982), 397.
[101] Ibid., 396.

I will disagree; I shall argue that this clearance order is in the times of peace.

It would not be perfect, or well-tailored, to call this violence since this is not war; this is politics in the times of peace, and why this is worse than violence will be told later. We've named them under one rubric: "pure politics." Now, perhaps we are aware of the problems that this pure in phenomenology has suffered in the hands of say deconstructive criticism. But we are not trying to deploy "pure" in the sense of absolute inwardness, solitary, free, etc.; we're using it in the Piercian sense of brute facts (and a few more words will be laid down further). This apart, it may be found in Derrida himself, if we are not wrong, a catalogue of lexemes named as un-deconstructible: hospitality, justice, etc. Now, will it be quite a sacrilege if undeconstructible is referred to as pure?

Let us grapple with an evident objection to this which could be the following: "The truth is that, relative to the 'pure' position of transcendent judgement, such political acts are always, one way or another, 'dirty', mixed, impure, compromises or approximations."[102] Therefore, if we are to say that the status of transcendental, political judgment is pure, the politics expressed or experienced is always already impure, dirty; what does it mean then to express pure politics? A neutral, more universal and harmless explanation is offered by the same author here: "Politics—even political philosophy at its most pure—is 'dirty'. Dirtiness is not a flaw or a degradation; rather it names the necessity that politics itself emerges insofar as power is presented in judgement."[103] In this view, immanent judgment—in this or that, everydayness—is already a fall and predestined to be dirty. The weight of this argument, turned on itself, surely must make space for a transcendentally impure politics; it denies, or it cannot think transcendence in immanence.[104]

---

[102] Douglas Burnham, "Heidegger, Kant and 'Dirty' Politics," *European Journal of Political Theory* 6, no. 1 (2007), 73.

[103] Ibid., 84.

[104] A much more promising and provoking line of objection to my way of arguing the politics of dirty hands expressed as immanent transcendence is this:

> Accordingly, politics is again a dirty game, in the additional sense that a critical analysis will always find its metaphysical grounds to be impurely taken up, riddled with contradictions or simply an expedient hotchpotch. To the extent that politics always involves ethical action, because of the primacy of the practical, then the 'dirtiness' of the metaphysical grounds of politics must raise ethical problems. As we have seen, ethical action cannot be grounded in or understood through the resources available to metaphysical thought.

However, we did not make it explicit—though we mentioned—that only a phenomenology of the political could make sense or go near as to what could be pure politics, and how one could begin talking about it is well said by Pierce (who remains unsung in this context with Husserl, Schutz, and Ricoeur hogging all the light),

> A court may issue injunctions and judgments against me and I not care a snap of my fingers for them. I may think them idle vapour. But when I feel the sheriff's hand on my shoulder, I shall begin to have a sense of actuality. Actuality is something brute. There is no reason in it.[105]

Second, what we mean by "experiencing the political" is not an ever-increasing stock of happenings and events catalogued in a particular cognition; it would rather entail—if we are correct—what we would call a feeling of the political or, a bit more inexactly, "political feeling." This feeling, again drawing from Pierce, is not subject to psychological laws and is not within the contours of a political psychology. An intimate touch may be likened to a good feeling of fondness or may be revolting or anything else: it is nearly impossible to generalize this at the level of the feeling. "It is a state ... a quality of immediate consciousness." To foster this sense, we wrote that the experience of the "pure" political could be narrated or described, but a narratology out of it is quite distant and, more often than not, an impossibility.

Politics in the times of peace is smeared with fierce politicking, and it has destroyed more people than all wars and pogroms added; so in order to dispel some aura around it, we also proposed a negative theory of peace. This theory does not entail debunking peace—the way Rousseau does it in the text quoted in the section—rather, it would lead, the moment we find its liaison with the politics of dirty hands, to a state of neither war nor peace. But this teleology apart, what could be such a formulation of peace? We think one of the primary theories of peace may be traced back to Aristotle, where peace is connected to leisure since "leisure which comes with peace," and also peace is the end of war and leisure is the end of toil. Peace is a kind of virtue that is derived from leisure.[106]

---

See Douglas Burnham, "Heidegger, Kant and 'Dirty' Politics," *European Journal of Political Theory* 6, no. 1 (2007), 85.

[105] Charles Sanders Pierce, "The Principles of Phenomenology," in *Philosophical Writings of Pierce*, ed. Justus Buchler (New York, NY: Dover Publications, 1955), 75–76.

[106] Aristotle, "Politics," 1299–1300. We shall reiterate this in the second chapter which thematizes Gandhi's nonviolent light.

Now, the state of political pornography, which we try to articulate as a collection of statements on the politics of dirty hands, can be had, derivatively, from the aforementioned. Peace with its alliance with leisure also gives truth its power of governance. Truth is tied to leisure and comfort, and such a liaison can take un-assumable forms—even that of lying. When its alliance is harangued or broken, it tends to become obscene and, thus, pornographic. In the main text, we talked about it but in a sweeping mode. Here let us do some tinkering. "[W]hat we need to see does not involve any interior secret or the discovery of a more nocturnal world."[107] Rather, it feeds, parasitically perhaps, on the factsheet spread before us like bones under nonviolent light. So long as this mission is maintained, in order not to sacrifice one's own nature, even lying is comfortable (in Bengali there is a saying, "It is better not to speak than utter *opriyo satyi katha* [uncomfortable truths]);" this endorses that what establishes truth as truth is its kinship with comfort rather than any substantive nuance. And as we tried to designate pornography by saying that it is "giving names to persons or things beyond a threshold," we meant just this. Related to the (un)speakable experience of the political—the scream after being backstabbed or betrayed—here we are dealing with its felicity conditions. "[N]othing that Machiavelli said ... was really novel to his readers. They knew—everyone had always known—that politics is a dirty business."[108] Given my argument—and reiterated time and again—this phenomenon has to be stretched to all departments of existence and not only limited to the affairs of the State as Machiavelli and Kristol or Walzer does; at least, that is the only way to reckon with Bengali novels where the middleclass *bhadralok* will inevitably scream at least for once, "sab jaigay politics" [damn it, everywhere there is politics].

Here, let us anticipate another possible question and try to answer it: If we are saying that lying, deception, betrayal, and backstabbing are techniques, one might wonder—for instance—whether they are at all political or not! Is lying or deception innately political? Or are there conditions when lying or deception become political? It will not be quite right to think that lying or deceiving are innately political categories; I think they are phenomenological, and in this sense they are pre-political (the sense in which Althusser connects Machiavelli with "primitive

---

[107] Michel Foucault, "A Preface to Transgression," in *Essential Works*, Vol. 2: Aesthetics, Method and Epistemology (London: Penguin: Books, 2000), 82.

[108] Irving Kristol, "Machiavelli and the Profanation of Politics," in *Reflections of a Neo Conservative: Looking Back, Looking Beyond* (New Delhi: Allied Publishers, 1986), 127.

political accumulation"): they provide the conditions by which the experience of the political becomes possible. And because they are a sort of a priori and are, in this sense, pure, they cannot themselves be subjected to the contingency of facts. A proof of this? We know what lying is, but we are still cheated every day. And with a vulgar but tempting variation of Levinas[109]—we might argue or designate—the way in which the liar presents himself, exceeding the idea of lie in me, is the face of the liar. And Machiavelli is obscene when—as one will have found in the chapter—he wants to regulate facts as value-ideals to be adopted to be successful; he is best when he says there are no fixed rules and he does say so.[110] And Kant is bang on the point when he discusses malice in this regard:

> Men prone to this vice will seek, for instance, to make mischief between husband and wife, or between friends, and then enjoy the misery they have produced. ... The defence against such mischief makers is upright conduct. Not by words but by our lives we should confute them.[111]

# Concluding Remarks

The undeconstructible, pure nature of this experience becomes explicit by now. With this, it would be possible to close up by following up once again how this whole discussion is relevant to our subject—personal as beyond private and public—and how this could be related to divergent but related discussion on the same subject. Firstly, politics in the times of peace! This is far from defining politics as "the way to organize and optimize the technological seizure of beings at the level of the nation."[112] It is, rather, the technological seizure of beings at the level of the person. We may begin or end with this vision. But as we had noticed, personal was required to have been expelled from the public sphere for its incalculable, irrational-emotional, and deceptive signification. There are several ways, which have been tested throughout, to normalize this consequence: Aristotle expounds virtues for the political speakers, and the moment we understand that these virtues can be feigned, we are into the scandal

---

[109] Emmanuel Levinas, *Totality and Infinity: An Essay on Exteriority*, trans. Alphonso Lingis (Pittsburgh, PA: Duquesne University Press, 2000), 50.

[110] Niccolo Machiavelli, *The Prince*, trans. and ed. Robert M. Adams (New York, NY: W. W. Norton & Company, 1992), 29.

[111] Kant, *Lectures on Ethics*, 219.

[112] Miguel de Beistegui, *Heidegger & the Political* (London: Routledge, 1998), 71.

proposed by Nietzsche and Machiavelli. This deception at the level of the person forms a cornerstone of this work. In fact, it could be documentarily shown, by recovering documents, that the arguments for organized charity or welfare from Hegel to those eager to institute the welfare state were panicked by the deceptive, incidental nature of personal charity. Even Rammohan, before he became a reformer, he used to meditate for some time on deception (this will be pursued in Chapter 5). Finally, where this discussion might lead to in more worthy hands could be well pointed out by the help of Althusser, who was, it seems to me, positively stumped by the presence of Machiavelli:

> We can say: there are not two ways of governing men—by laws" [I'll say—by consent] "and by force—but three—by laws, force and fraud. But as soon as this statement has been made, we realize that fraud is not a mode of government like the others; it is not on the same level. Laws exist—let us as say as human institutions, recognized rules and opinions; force exists—let us say as the army. In contrast, however, fraud possesses no objective existence: it does not exist. If fraud is a way of governing, given that it has no objective existence, it can be employed only when it is based on laws or force. Fraud, then, is not a third form of government; it is government to the second degree, a manner of governing the other two forms of government: force and laws. When it utilizes the army, fraud is stratagem; when it utilizes law, it is political guile. Fraud, thus, opens up a space, beyond force and laws, for diverting their existence—a space in which force and laws are substituted for, feigned, deformed, and circumvented. Mastery of fraud in the Prince [and all of us] is the distance that allows him [and us] to play at will on the existence of force and laws, to exploit and, in the strongest sense of the word, feign them.[113]

The personal then opens us up to a third invisible form of governance, and our beginner's argument as to how the personal overflows the public and the private and can play with them by fraud, deception, and treachery—or dirty hands—we believe, now comes full circle.

How do we conclude then? Does the personal to impersonal transit in modernity proposed by Weber undergo an abortion because of an illegitimate marriage between Nietzsche and Machiavelli? Or to put more sharply, is Weber destroyed by Nietzsche? Does Althusser comment on the theory of modernity, which harps again and again on the private/public division, or wants us to forget that the person and the personal are capable of playing with both? But Weber was not so naïve: in the wake of the

---

[113] Louis Althusser, *Machiavelli and Us,* trans. Gregory Eliott (London: Verso, 1999).

scienticization of the public sphere, he did see a withering away of the value-ideals, with rational scientific activity failing to fill the lack of what it has destroyed. What Nietzsche showed was that these values, considered genealogically, could be shown to have been inconsistent: altruism for weakness, honeyed words for wickedness, etc. Machiavelli's counter work was to re-state these facts as values. For instance, this was formulated by Machiavelli way back in 1513, "Everyone sees what you seem to be, few know what you really are and those few do not dare take a stand against the general opinion. The masses are always impressed by the superficial appearance of things. ..."[114] This was unnecessary, since we already live in the world of these facts. People misunderstand Machiavelli by alleging that he had documented anti-values wanting to regulate them as "virtues"; but this is mistaken; he was involved in an impossible project where facts and values suffer a reversal: he restated facts as values and scandalized everybody. But this is unnecessary and excessive, in brief—giving names to things and persons beyond the (empirical) threshold and, thus, an act which is pornographic. Irving Kristol sensed it quite well but touched the wrong chord when he called Machiavelli a political pornographer.[115] Kristol may have intended a discourse—which while stating facts in this way avoids a figurative language that could have hidden much of its sting. In this sense also, the description is apt: what is pornography if not the absence of figures or figuration. But this also, considered at a higher level, goes against the primary description of the political as pertaining to the problem of identity as a founding fiction masquerading as the essence of the political. In recent attempts to isolate the "poetic or figural (figurative, even) essence of politics,"[116] and therefore hit at the institutional root of Western political thought, it would not be too fanciful to find its beginning in these Machiavellian insights. The Machiavellian in his affirmation to open up, always, to the unstable play and ploy of figural identification in politics, denies to settle at a particular site of identification. And therefore the recent interrogation marked by questions like, "Is there something which would allow the political to be thought outside of the will to figure? Can the political be thought, finally, in a way which does not stem from

---

[114] Machiavelli, *The Prince*, 49.

[115] Kristol, "Machiavelli and the Profanation of Politics," 127.

[116] Philippe Lacoue-Labarthe and Nancy Jean-Luc, "Editor's Introduction," in *Political; Ficta'* in *Retreating the Political*, ed. Simon Parks (London: Routledge: London, 1997), xxi.

the will to realize its essence as figure?"[117] has to be acknowledged as having been originally, though differently, formulated by Machiavelli. (Machiavelli, not having access to our modernity, addressed himself to the person of the sovereign—this should be remembered well and all the time. The deeply debated distinction between facticity and validity or between facts and norms was not available to Machiavelli in the contemporary sense. Nevertheless, one finds even Althusser in his book on Machiavelli rightly celebrating him for reasons that we have already mentioned earlier.)

Finally, could Weber not sense this while he was charting the disenchantment of the personal world of informal communities in modernity? He did not offer any solution. Through the structure of "probity," the person in an act of self-legislation has to choose or abandon value-ideals within a particular life-sphere. Henceforth, virtue or sin, nothing comes with a warranty any more—which means that the person will speak to Aristotle to end preaching his catalogue of virtues; he/she will tell Machiavelli or De Sade not to display their table of brute "facts" to be adopted as value-ideals too. No general option can be regulated because, and this is what is interesting in Weber in as much as what he tried to show, modernity has entailed the differentiation of life-spheres into irreconcilable compartments: political, aesthetic, religious, economic, etc. It is irreconcilable because, as Weber and Habermas have reminded us, they have emerged with their own criteria of validity. But there is a twist here. Weber has an interesting item to add: the erotic. (Habermas has a list too: science, morality, and art, but the erotic is missing.) Now this is interesting. The erotic is then not reconcilable with the political. (Hannah Arendt and Habermas would insist much against a feminist social worker's fury that "take the private to the public" for redressal is finally problematic in the face of their own distinctive validity claims.) What happens then to political pornography, pure politics, etc. of which we have talked considerably?

Let us just dramatize this energy of irreconcilability by recalling how in modern times, or even contemporaneously, a singer, a writer, or an academician embedded in the worlds of music, social science, or literature, respectively, would complain of politics again and again happening to

---

[117] Max Weber, "Science as a Vocation," in *Max Weber's Complete Writings on Academics and Political Vocations*. trans. Gordon C. Wells (New York, NY: Algora Publishing, 2008), 30.

them? Consider this from Weber himself while he was considering people
who choose science as their vocation:

> But we also have to ask all the others to examine their conscience and
> answer the question: "Do you believe you could bear to see mediocrities
> getting ahead of you year after year without feeling inwardly embittered
> and crushed?"

Or consider this from Geoffrey Boycott, the legendary batsman cricketer,
talking about Fred Trueman, another great:

> Of course it is me. It's my character. But it's their character, too. Take
> Fred Trueman. He started it … when the club decided to dispense with my
> services he slagged me off. He could not even bring himself to say I were
> a good player. He said, "If I get back on the committee I still won't give
> Boycott a contract." Well that was tantamount to saying, "F*** you, then."
> … He had to belittle me. I was hurt. … It was dirty tactics, that. … If he
> walked through the door now I'd say, "what have I ever done to you?"[118]

How is politics within the academia and "dirty tactics" related to cricket?
How is this possible? But while such complaints could be made and
even entertained, they definitely cannot be resolved within these life
spheres—and that is the reason why such complainants could feel aghast
and helpless; helpless being challenged by the internal norms of valida-
tion of these departments of existence. What are we to do? Shall we call
for an integrity of the public and the private? Or shall we invoke a strict
separation? For this we shall be offering a case study in the next chapter
where such an irresolution reaches an interesting impasse from where we
can take off and enter well into our main text.

[118] Nigel Farndale, "Geoffrey Boycott," in *Flirtation Seduction Betrayal: Interviews with
Heroes and Villains* (London: Constable & Robnson Ltd, 2002), 35, 39.

# 2

# Gandhi and the Ethics of the Personal: Is Personal the Terroristic Unity of Private and Public?

*I think the political life must be an echo of private life and that there cannot be any divorce between the two.*

—Mahatma Gandhi (Gandhi 1996: 109)

*I write the truth as I personally see it.*

—Mahatma Gandhi (Gandhi 1996: 236)

The genesis of the postcolonial critiques of Gandhi could be paradigmatically rendered in two or three constructions where the Gandhian discourse could be seen to have been—if we are to abide by their conclusions—either a self-contradictory discourse of manoeuver[1] or an originary critique of enlightened modernity. The first position articulated Gandhian discourse as a site where the practical-political implications of an inclusive, nationalist politics where peasants were mobilized against the coercive structures of the state through the moral-universal impulse of nonviolence, and then subjected to a sort of private morality that extended its grasp to all and everyone by inviting the large majority to suffer hardships in the hands of a domineering minority. The second group, to my mind, seems more baffling in its claims. Such claims have rested, quite securely, on two major premises, of which the first can be understood with help from

---

[1] Partha Chatterjee, "The Moment of Manoeuvre: Gandhi and the Critique of Civil Society," in *Nationalist Thought and the Colonial World: A Derivative Discourse?* (Delhi: Oxford University Press, 1986), 54–130.

Dipesh Chakraborty: "In one stroke, as it were, Gandhi collapsed the distinction between the private and the public on which the theoretical side of the political arrangements of Western modernity rest."[2] Thereby, while "destruction" is the matrix of the first group of postcolonial theorists, Gandhian "integration" or the annihilation of separation between the private and the public has been the keen, categorical watchword of the second group (from the traditional Gandhi admirers to the critical neo-Gandians), and for them, predictably, the syntax "I think the political life must be an echo of private life and that there cannot be any divorce between the two" with which the chapter had begun, could become forcefully titular.

But also, this is the statement that has led hordes of critics astray (from the traditional Gandhi admirers to the critical neo-Gandians) since it has been assumed—through this—that integrating the private and the public is not only the secret of the Gandhian ethic but that it rehearses in its womb a thousand years of ethico-theological (in Gandhi's case "spiritual") desire as a counterpoint to liberal modernity—the latter being strictly founded on a distinction between the private and the public. A philosophical century ago it was the question of integrating the outside and the inside,[3] or the mind and the body;[4] in Gandhi's schema of an alternative modernity, this

---

[2] Dipesh Chakraborty, *Habitations of Moderntiy: Essays in the Wake of Subaltern Studies* (New Delhi: Permanent Black, 2004), 62.

[3] The outside and the inside founded by a myth were perpetuated by a dialectic "of division" later to be translated in their corresponding, taxonomic correlation: public outside, private inside. The most profound theorist of the founding myth, to my mind, has been Jean Hyppolite, who is said to have spoken of "a first myth of outside and inside" [where] "you feel the full significance of this myth of outside and inside in alienation, which is founded on these two terms." If that has been the mythical appropriation, the dialectics of inside/outside is foregrounded in a dark intimacy; they are themselves not distant, "outside and inside are both intimate." The dialectical dissolution of this myth is driven by a blasting of this marginal, territorial space of intimacy demarcating nearly a threshold of being/nonbeing, "And then onto what, toward what, do doors open? Do they open for the world of men, or for the world of solitude? Ramon Gomez de la Serna wrote: "Doors that open on the countryside seem to confer freedom behind the world's back?"' See Gaston Bachelard, "The Dialectics of Outside and Inside," in *The Continental Aesthetics Reader*, ed. Clive Cazeaux (London: Routledge, 2000), 151–63. One might justly conjecture that the outside and inside are united in the door pre-empting the dialectic of private/public to be dissolved in the person.

[4] Quoting Rousseau, "I've said a hundred times, if ever I were confined in the Bastille, it's there that I would draw the picture of Liberty," Marshall Berman concludes that this was an attempt to free "'the head' from subjection to 'things as they are'—but only by detaching it from the body, which remained confined in the Bastille. It split men in two, and so diverted their discontent from its source in their lives." See Marshall Berman, *The Politics of Authenticity: Radical Individualism and the Emergence of Modern Society*

assumed the form of integrating the private and the public.[5] And now, in an age of heightened hypocrisy and terrible double standards, his words carry a strong, vigorous and relevant ring.

In this chapter, I shall argue against this established array of arguments, why such an integration is not possible, if it were possible then at what cost, and how Gandhi wanted to pay for such a will—if there was one. But first, a story to begin at the beginning.

## Integrating Wine and Bifurcation of the Simple

In the years of 1920–21, Motilal Nehru is reported to have played a leading role in anti-liquor picketing.[6] Three years after this, it was 1924. Read the tract of a dilemma via the voice of Gandhi—who having received a dubious paper cutting from a journalist, writes to Motilal Nehru,

> The writer has sent me the enclosed cutting (from The Leader). I had not read it before. He says that at another dinner you are reported to have said: water has been called pure. But wine is made after being thrice distilled. It is, therefore, purer than water … if the report is to be relied upon, I cannot but be grieved that you, who lead the antiliquor campaign, should publicly drink it and, what is worse, chaff at teetotalism. … [ PS.] I know that if a man drinks privately, he may drink publicly too. A *public man,*[7] *however,*

(London: George Allen & Unwin Ltd, 1970), 109. Thus, integrating the mind and body meant not only exercising the freedom of the mind but also freeing the physico-material circumstance in which the physics or the body finds itself confined.

[5] Though the origins of this integration could be meekly traced to Plato's *Apology* where Socrates, being indicted for corrupting the youth, speaks in his defense, "Throughout my life, in any public activity I may have engaged in, I am the same man as I am in private life"; it must also be acknowledged that the Greek understanding of the private and the public only remotely resembles our modern understanding. See Plato, "Apology," in *The Trial and Death of Socrates,* trans. G. M. A. Grube (Cambridge, MA: Hackett Publishing Company, Inc., 1975), 21–42.

[6] For Motilal Nehru's own version of the success of those events, see Motilal Nehru, *Selected Works of Motilal Nehru,* eds. Ravinder Kumar and D. N. Panigrahi (New Delhi: Vikas Publishing House Pvt. Limited, 1984), 3: 45.

[7] The cultural-cognitive self-understanding of the word "public" or "private" in the colonial or the postcolonial predicament, let us also note, did deviate from the standard Western notions. While *public* started to mean *janta, aam aadmi,* etc., private meant *byaktigat, niji, apni* and quite mistakenly coalesced the personal and the private. My hunch here, of course, is that Gandhi is deploying the word "public man" in a very specific sense (stripped of its aam [mundane] uses imminent in its Indian translation), which must be gotten from the Western inventory. But this is no limitation: such maneuvers are strangely creative

**46** Is the Personal Beyond Private and Public?

*may not drink publicly, if he is likely to offend. I distinguish between private drinking* and secret drinking.[8]

Motilal Nehru, in a lengthy reply, avoided answering the main question: whether it is apt to lead an anti-liquor campaign as well as drink at the same time. He instead wrote,

The charge divides itself into two counts: (1) that I have drunk wine *publicly*, and (2) that I said in the course of an after dinner speech that "Water has been called pure but wine is made after being thrice distilled. It is therefore, purer than water." My answer to the first count is an unequivocal "yes." As to the second, I am sure I did not institute any comparison between the respective merits of wine and water. The statement, as reported, is too silly (Jayakar 1958: 333–34). In fact, during the forty years preceding 1921, I had seldom missed my evening drink for 11 months in the year. I abstained for one month in every year simply to avoid getting enslaved to the habit ... I must also respectfully differ from the distinction you draw between "Private drinking and secret drinking." In my humble opinion, it is a distinction without a difference. ... pray do not misunderstand me. I do not mean that I am going to take to regular boozing at this time of my life because of the stupid attacks made on me. I may or may not drink at all. This is my own concern. But if I do, nothing in the world will make me seek privacy for doing so. I would have the world judge as I am and not as others would wish me to appear ... The tongue of slander will not deter me from what is right and proper. ... It is for you to judge which is the graver offence—the levity in which I indulged in the course of a *private talk* with a friend or the publication of the talk by that friend.[9]

Two synoptic inferences should be made here: Gandhi is proposing an integration between the public agenda that a public man puts forward and whether he believes and practices the same in his private life—as far as

---

with Gandhi—recall the way he deployed Carpenter, Ruskin, Thoreau, and Tolstoy, all in the service of an indigenous "defamiliarization." See Partha Chatterjee, "The Moment of Manoeuvre: Gandhi and the Critique of Civil Society," in *Nationalist Thought and the Colonial World: A Derivative Discourse?* (Delhi: Oxford University Press, 1986), 98–100.

[8] Mahatma Gandhi, *Collected Works of Mahatma Gandhi* (India: The Publications Division, Ministry of Information and Broadcasting, Government of India, 1967), 25: 350–51 (italics mine). And in this sense only—I assume—Gandhi could be called religious: "religion exists once the secret of the sacred, orgiastic, or demonic mystery has been, if not destroyed, at least *integrated*, and finally subjected to the sphere of responsibility." See Jacques Derrida, *The Gift of Death,* trans. David Wills (Chicago, IL: The University of Chicago Press, 1995), 2 (italics mine).

[9] M. R. Jayakar, *The Story of My Life* (Bombay: Asia Publishing House, 1958), II: 334–35 (italics mine).

that is practicable—unless he is ready to take recourse to the secret; at the same time, he is also proposing a model of the "public man": a private person may drink publicly, he does not offend anyone; a public person cannot do so, he offends because he has preached to the contrary. (And let us remind ourselves here that to the picketer Motilal boozing was an evil—not a temporary one but an "evil incarnate," evil in itself.)[10] This has been referred to in ethical debates as the problem of integration,[11] which I assume should be pegged at the level of the person-al,[12] and Gandhi

[10] Nehru, *Selected Works of Motilal Nehru*, 3: 45.

[11] For an initial philosophical account of the discourse of integrity, see Alan Montefiore, "Identity and Integrity," in *Multiculturalism, Liberalism and Democracy*, eds. Rajeev Bhargava, Amiya Bagchi, and R. Sudarshan (New Delhi: Oxford University Press, 1999), 58–79, where he describes integrity as being inscribed within a larger discourse of "essential identity" and how such integration is always deferred and incomplete. A classical example of this is perhaps available in Nietzsche "when it really happens that the just man remains just even toward those who have harmed him." See Friedrich Nietzsche, *On the Genealogy of Morals and Ecce Homo*, trans. Walter Kaufman and R. J. Hollingdale (New York, NY: Vintage Books, 1989), 74. The Gandhian sentence in the text "we may not return anger but gentleness even against anger" quoted from Mahatma Gandhi, *The Essential Writings of Mahatma Gandhi*, ed. Raghavan Iyer, (Delhi: Oxford University Press, 1991), 113, is reflexive of integrity as essential identity in Gandhi. The result, as a comment on both the above, I speculate would be this: there will always be some people (and Gandhi was often reproached for this) who will still feel let down even by an integrated person, who going by the indices of an essential, integrated identity is not supposed to let others down. Gandhi uses the word "compromise" to designate this change of prior position. A person of Gandhian integrity—a la Gandhi—would "admit of no compromise" in the face of eternal principles; and "must be prepared to displease the dearest ones for the sake of principles" (Gandhi, *The Essential Writings of Mahatma Gandhi*, 191). And when, compellingly, compromises are made, Gandhi considers this as a moment of exception not to be recommended to others (Gandhi, *The Essential Writings of Mahatma Gandhi*, 191).
While Gandhi's uncompromising position on "universal principles" resolves the issue emphatically and for once, it does agree with the Kantian categorical imperative. The philosophical discussion on this, however, has only recently started to recognize Gandhi in a serious philosophical light (Akeel Bilgrami's work has been justly instrumental here). Being unaware of Gandhi, however, Alan—as a theorist of integrity as identity—thinks, taking full responsibility of an acknowledged change of position would do the job here; but rememorating the Hegelian objection to Kantian U norm, we might recall that the same strategy could be easily deployed by an immoral person too (That this was my position then; now what I think is, this; Gandhi seems to have been perceptively aware of this in rejecting this resolution). Some think this paradox could be avoided when an "I" is integrated into "we" accounts. An examination of this proposal is beyond the scope of this paper; yet, I'm sure Gandhi would disapprove of this position too.

[12] While I have previously pointed out the Greek availability of private/public integration, how the problem of integration at the level of the individual person became a modern

does exactly the same by making a distinction between persons. Unless there is a third, the question that shall haunt this binary while forging a unity is which is being sacrificed to what: either the public will melt in the private or the private will lose itself in the public. Therefore, Gandhi rightly needs a third where these two could be brought together to have a dialogue: that is the person. This is, however, very different from making the private and public one as upheld in dominant Gandhian secondary discourse. The private and the public become indistinguishable only in the person in the instance of personal integrity: Gandhi's unforgettable exhortation that "we may not return anger but gentleness even against anger"[13] is axiomatic of such integrity. Methodologically, Gandhi has the instance of the person and his character, where the impersonal private/public registers would be united in a principled, living moment. This is what he has to say in a context which is provoking and yet pertinent:

> Shastra is not anything written in a book. It should be a living thing. Hence the words of a wise man of good character whose actions are *in accord* with this speech are our shastra.[14]

Not only is action in accord with speech, Gandhi goes so far as to bring speech in accord with thoughts, "Let us not tell the world that there is one thing on our lips and another in our thoughts."[15] This bringing "in accord" (using Gandhi's own words) is what we designate—borrowing the language of moral philosophy—as integration.

Further, he is firmly and rightly of the view that the person and his/her phenomenology is capable of transcending the public–private divide along which the separation of sovereignty was cast. The person imbibes the living principle:

> [I]f a person has violated a moral principle in any one sphere of his life, his action will certainly have an effect in other spheres. In other words, the belief generally held that an immoral man may do no harm in the political

---

problematic is an interesting and intriguing case to note. In a perceptive history of the Western public man, Richard Sennett informs how the molecule public/private broke the moment individual character was used to form a social principle. "From this idea of individual personality as a social principle came ultimately the modern impulse to find political measures worthwhile only to the extent that their champions are 'credible', 'believable', 'decent' persons." See Richard Sennett, *The Fall of Public Man* (Cambridge: Cambridge University Press, 1976), 105.

[13] Gandhi, *The Essential Writings of Mahatma Gandhi*, 113.
[14] Ibid., 189 (italics mine).
[15] Ibid., 132.

sphere is quite wrong. And so is the other belief that a person who violates moral principles in his business may be moral in his private life or in his conduct in family affairs.[16]

Through the axis of the person, then, Gandhi overrides the private/public disjunction. Gandhi invokes the question of integrating (or in his own words, bringing "in accord") the public and the private at the level of the person (the person is the third here in the sense that if the public and the private form the first and the second is an isotopy [in the semiotic sense], then the person is the third isotopy[17]); but there is a catch here. Quite strangely, Gandhi does not regulate the question of such integration for all persons; he makes a distinction between public persons and private persons. Gandhi ends with his will to integrate the public and the private for public persons. For private persons, he would not make this compulsory since—it seems—they could not be held to have a message at the public level, thereby, any question of violating them does not arise.

Therefore, what we have here is the axiom that public/private can be brought together at the level of the person-al third according to Gandhi's hierarchy (though not the third person) by this maneuver of him; maneuver because the binary is—otherwise—locked in its own insurmountable and instrumental opposition. And this overcoming, as it is evident, Gandhi would hold active only for public persons and not for private persons. But this will not work.

We enter into a discussion of this by asking a preliminary question: What kind of consequential understanding does it entail for the concepts of public and private? We enter this domain (but) by acknowledging first that Gandhi—at least for this moment—is well within the liberal distinction; the only transcendence that he can achieve is when he wants to forge a unity and discover a third. Second, unity is, of course, but allegedly or evidently for public persons only; but who are public persons anyway? From which inventory and by what taxonomy can they be defined? As discussed before—and which will frustrate his anti-enlightenment admirers further—there is no Indian cultural stock here to which Gandhi could refer. While this is true for the moment,[18] the fact that

---

[16] Ibid., 182.
[17] But as our historical investigation will show, the personal is the originary first and the public and private following it. But Gandhi's argument is not dependent upon the recognition of such historically correct seriality.
[18] This is also a welcome reminder when we subject Gandhi to many Western social science paradigms. While it is true that the Western colonial predicament and the consequent

Gandhi had been associated with anti-Western indigenous impulses and
a vibrant vernacularist outbreak—even in matters of taxonomy—is true
for Gandhi's overall position. But while it was otherwise and quite rare,
Gandhi intuitively knew what was at stake: "The word 'vow' is also an
unsuitable equivalent for the original *vrata*. But the best thing for me is
to explain what I mean and then leave you to find the exact word if you
endorse my position."[19] This hermeneutic wholeness (elsewhere: "we
mean the same thing but express it differently—you in Spanish and I in
Italian"[20]), where explanation and meaning precedes iteration, is a pointer
to the Gandhian philosophy of language (along with the radically political
conscience that the master's language can never be mastered, "We never
master the English language."[21] Thereby, where I speak about the lack
of Indian cultural stock for the moment, and while "public person" and
"private person" are immediately Western taxonomic predications and
we have a Western jurisprudence classic to speak for that, the question of
"personal integrity" at the level of the person—as we shall discover—is
also "spiritual" in the Gandhian original sense).

If we are convinced by now of the Gandhian apparent adoption of
Western taxonomy and then transcendence, here is Holland:

> By a "Public person" we mean either the State, or the sovereign part of it,
> or a body or individual holding delegated authority under it. By a "Private
> person" we mean an individual or collection of individuals, however large,
> who, or each one of whom is, of course, a unit of the State, but in no sense
> represents it, even for a special purpose.[22]

displacements it ushered in India could not be explained fully by indigenous theory, let
us rehearse that the same could not be accomplished by Western social theory either;
often, the indigenous and the vernacular acted as a site of resistance to the Western
invasion of apparatus and ideology. So the choice in this sense is "political" and not
simply heuristic. Today, to re-describe this juncture, we must recall the intense hybrid
nature of that encounter and its resultant. So while we subject Gandhi to Western social
science paradigms, we must always be sensitive to the transformation they have had to
undergo in his hands. It would be safer then to articulate Gandhi in between *ahimsa* and
nonviolence, *vrata* and vow, *satya* and truth, etc. But I must confess that I've not been able
to live up to this complicated deconstructive maneuver in this chapter always—though
I've put up cautionary notices here and there.

[19] Gandhi, *Essential Writings*, 201.
[20] Ibid., 202.
[21] Ibid., 290.
[22] Sir Thomas Erskine Holland, *Elements of Jurisprudence* (Calcutta: Progressive Publishers, 1924), 127.

Now, having known the statist ground of a "public person," it would be worthwhile to remember that while Gandhi calls for the integration for public persons (associated with the state), the agenda (drinking) he chooses belongs somewhere else. Drinking, like sexuality and allied choices, is a social life practice belonging to the realm of the society and not the state. This is the larger liberal binary within which the private and the public are subsumed: society and state.[23] Society is the realm of freedom from the interference of the state—the area of good life and irreconcilable conceptions of the good. Likewise, drinking as an entertaining social life practice is related to the ideal of a good life that I have—not to be regulated by a liberal state (unless I harm others). This puts Gandhi unto an irresolvable paradox: he has to integrate then state and society before he can pose the question of public/private integration even if it is only for a public person. Gandhi then—if, allegedly, integration is his agenda—has to integrate two sets of categories: society and state, and public and private. To integrate them requires a magic: what is that? We shall discover, and quite dangerously, that unless Gandhi takes recourse to an algorithm (we shall name the genre later) where society and state are undivided in one person, he cannot pose the question of such an integrity at all. This is the dilemma.

## "Adult Education" for Very Unreasonable, Involuntary Incest

Let us then start by asking a simple question: How is Gandhi to be situated in relation to the problem of drinking? In other words, how does he

---

[23] While state and society could be transposed to stand for public (state) and private (society), and a gamut of interrelated thinking could be predictably charted, their intertextual co-originality should not be undermined. Here is an excerpt from a monumental, classis work:

> When men tried to interpret the State as a "society," they were borrowing the term *societas* from Roman Private Law. When they tried to interpret government as the exercise of an authority which had been delegated by the "society," they were borrowing the conception of *mandatum* from the same source. These were matters of the borrowing of private-law terms and conceptions and their application to the sphere of public law. In other words, what was involved was the use of the rules of law relating to private groups and private activities in the state to explain the character and the activity of the State itself. Difficulties naturally arose. ... from this transference of the ideas of one sphere to explain the life of another.

Ernest Barker, "Introduction" in Natural Law and the Theory of Society 1500–1800 by Otto Gierke, ed. and trans. Ernest Barker (Cambridge: Cambridge University Press, 1950), xxi.

discover and translate it as a problem? It should be obvious to anybody having preliminary acquaintance with Gandhi and *Gandhiana* that there is a broader narrative always with him to absorb every fragment of experimentation or protest he proposes. Drinking, therefore, predictably as "evil" is a "national evil" to Gandhi—and that he can allow secret drinking for a public person or private or public drinking for a private person is a testimony to the fact that, and as he confessed once, apart from the categorical commission, he did not want to make a "fetish of consistency." Thus, being inconsistent allowed differences and encouraged a positive, nearly unpredictable plurality. However, this difference is abolished the moment we hear his call for absolute prohibition on the sale of drinking. Why drinking after all and why subsequently a call for prohibition?

First, "prohibition is to mean a great moral awakening in India" and the campaign for prohibition led by women would be an immense civic education of the masses (Gandhi uses a peculiar ascriptor here: "adult education"—we'll soon come to that). But this evil, as it is evident, Gandhi knows, is shared both by the ruler and the ruled, the colonizer and the colonized, and the rich and the poor without distinction. So here it is necessary to wrench oneself away, not supposedly from an evil infused by a colonizer but from the evil or the habit itself. But what is so evil or morally degenerate about drinking?

Here we come to the most interesting part and that which will anticipate more surprises when it finally takes the interpretive turn.

Gandhi clearly and repetitively dubs drinking as a "robber of reason," so much so that he asserts that the alcoholic tends to forget "the distinction between wife and mother, lawful and unlawful."[24] Gandhi shivers imagining this dark night of incest and this time; he wants to protect reason—eluding his anti-enlightenment admirers—but at the same time it must be acknowledged, to the latter's relief, that this is communicative reason and not a substantive reason of the enlightenment. And when it comes to incest, he is into a more serious, severe sexual economy. "The drunkard forgets the distinction between wife, mother and sister and indulges in crimes of which in his sober moments he will be ashamed;"[25] but this evil levels all, "I have seen respectable Englishmen rolling in the

---

[24] M. K. Gandhi, *Prohibition at Any Cost*, comp. R. K. Prabhu (Ahmedabad: Navajivan Publishing House, 1960), 5.
[25] Ibid., 3.

gutter under the effect of alcohol."[26] What needs to be done to invoke this moral reasoning where sexual reasoning and prohibitions are not done away with?

Primarily "adult education" (in earlier matters stamped with the symbol A, perhaps!)

> Women ... will visit those who are addicted to drink and try to win them from the habit. Employers of labour will be expected by law to provide cheap, healthy refreshment, reading and entertainment rooms where the working men can go and find shelter, knowledge, health giving food and drink, and innocent fun.[27]

Fine, but will this—ultimately—in terms of effectiveness and finality, work? "[I]t would be a wrong thing for you to say that education has to precede legislation. Education will never be able to cope with the evil."[28] Gandhi is aware of the obstacles in his path to eradicate the earlier stated (or any) evil of unreasonableness exemplified in involuntary incest, and for which he justifiably thinks his "adult education" insufficient. He is well aware that either private or public rights would be invoked to hurt this agenda. To Gandhi, a woman becomes a "public woman" by selling sex which is an intimately private "virtue" not to be sold or sacrificed; further, evident in the statement "Those who speak in the name of individual freedom do not know their India"[29] is the anxiety that if the language of liberal freedom as a right is projected or allowed to interpellate, then, "There is as much right of a person to demand drinking facilities from the state as there is to demand facilities for the supply of public women for the satisfaction of his animal passion."[30] And, therefore, Gandhi would neither invoke the mixing of public and private—keeping the example of "public woman" and demand for liquor—nor would he surrender to the liberal language of rights that would act as hindrances to the abolition of the "evil." Here then, we've been served with certain answers to questions we've been posing throughout. However, the public/private impasse seems to be overbearing; what would Gandhi do then? Gandhi requires a transcendental magic: what is that?

---

[26] Ibid., 6.
[27] Ibid., 18.
[28] Ibid., 8.
[29] Ibid., 11.
[30] Ibid., 11.

To protect the prohibition on incest, then, what does Gandhi suggest? Prohibition of liquor of course, but an iota more than that and here is the long awaited answer:

> If I was appointed dictator for one hour for all India, the first thing I would do would be to close without compensation all the liquor shops, destroy all the toddy palms such as I know them in Gujarat, compel factory owners to produce humane conditions for their workmen and open refreshment and recreation rooms where these workmen would get innocent drinks and equally innocent amusements. I would close down the factories if the owners pleaded want of funds. Being a teetotaler I would retain my sobriety in spite of the possession of one hour's dictatorship and therefore arrange for the examination of my European friends and diseased persons who may be in medical need of brandy and the like at State expense by medical experts and where necessary, they would receive certificates which would entitle them to obtain the prescribed quantity of fiery waters from certified chemists. The rule will apply mutates mutandis to intoxicating drugs.

> For the loss of revenue from drinks, I would straightway cut down the military expenditure and expect the Commander-in-Chief to accommodate himself to the new conditions in the best way he can. The workmen left idle by the closing of factories, I would remove to model farms to be immediately opened as far as possible in the neighbourhood of the factories unless I was advised during that brief hour that the State could profitably run the factories under the required conditions and could therefore take over from the owners.[31]

This is not to inscribe within the Gandhian discourse an elemental hour of contradiction and prove discursive incoherence; our engagement is not with the psycho biography[32] or truth of Gandhian discourse in general

---

[31] Ibid., 9.

[32] This is not to undermine the possible world of a psycho-biographical, personality-psychological, or psychoanalytical study of Gandhi. David Hardiman in executing an exercise of historical biography of Gandhi and, connecting comparative time, does notice (elsewhere in the book) how the shadow of the Fuehrer was lodged always above and inside the heads of Gandhi and his disciples. And yet, he arrives at this instance but fails to give it a context and the evidence from which we could infer the truth of his inference. However, the instance is interesting:

> A year later, Harilal and Gulab were married. Gandhi told him to return to south Africa alone, but instead Harilal came with his new wife. Gandhi resented the obvious love the couple had for each other, and tried to take her in hand in an authoritarian way, causing her great emotional suffering. He was very annoyed when she became pregnant

so that it can be countered by a contrasting utterance made by Gandhi elsewhere. Truly, in dealing with the irreconcilable differentiation of life-spheres in modernity and, subsequently, public and private, we have been examining the origin and future of a discourse trying (not) to make them compatible. What I shall try to argue here is that this dictatorial apparatus is not a matter of intellectual or infinite, manifest desire belonging to an agency (peculiar to Gandhi) but an immanent necessity (and could be deployed by anybody) that rises in response to the need to transcend public/private and unite them in one. But this is not the originary moment. It is elsewhere.

## Defenceless Enclosed Arena of Tumult

The incestuous excess induced by drinking has to be countered by a power that is excessive: Why?[33] In other words, it could not be confronted by the "politics of pure means." Because such a practice not only is inextricably, and elementally tied to nonviolent peace or the discourse of pure means; it is its habitus. "Unproductive expenses: luxury, mourning, ceremonies, wars, cults, the erection of splendid buildings, games, theater, the arts, perverse sexuality (that is, detached from genitality) represent activities that atleast originally have their end in themselves".[34] Without a single

and later gave birth to a daughter, as this revealed that the couple were having sexual intercourse despite his injunction. He punished them by demanding that Harilal be the first to court arrest and go to jail during the satyagraha of 1908. Gandhi acted as his lawyer during his trial, insisting before the judge that the punishment should be as severe as possible. In a public statement made a week later, he said that his twenty-year-old son was "only a child" and that it was "a part of Harilal's education to go to gaol for the sake of the country." Harilal spent nearly a year in prison in all, constantly anxious about Gulab. He had good reason to be, for Gulab developed an alarming cough, excruciating earache and sores all over her body.

See David Hardiman, *Gandhi in His Time and Ours* (Delhi: Permanent Black, 2003), 98–99.

[33] "[S]trictly speaking, only excess power is truly powerful, because in order for something to set limits to something else it must be equal to it. The weaker is no limit for the stronger, both must thus compel and be compelled reciprocally with equal power." See G. W. F. Hegel, *Natural Law,* trans. T. M. Knox (University Park: University of Pennsylvania Press, 1975), 86.

[34] Jurgen Habermas, *The Philosophical Discourse of Modernity: Twelve Lectures*, trans. Frederick Lawrence (Cambridge, MA: MIT Press, 1993), 223.

strike of doubt we may incorporate drinking and sytagmatically relate it to the perverse sexuality of incest in the list of unproductive expenses. Thereby Gandhi's proposal to institute "cheap, healthy refreshment, reading and entertainment rooms where the working men can go and find shelter, knowledge, health giving food and drink and innocent fun," or drinking as allowed to fulfill a "medical necessity" (all within a rubric we might name as "productive expense and consumption") is not to be had in the temporality of pure means where activities are ends in themselves.

Invoking such a context of "peace," it is possible to relate it to leisure; by arguing that one of the primary theories of peace may be traced back to Aristotle where peace is connected to leisure since "leisure which comes with peace" and also peace is the end of war and leisure is the end of toil. Peace is also a kind of virtue that is derived from leisure.[35] Here interestingly it finds a support in Habermas arguing this for Bataille, "The self sufficient activity performed for its own sake (Aristotle), as displayed in the luxury of the leisure classes, still reveals something of primordial sovereignty."[36] This excess that gives content to the discourse of pure means: nonviolent peace or primordial sovereignty, could not be overcome from within that discourse but only violently from without: forcible prohibition "without compensation." In other words, the excess of drinking leading to a loss of reason and sexual economy, could be overcome yet by another power that is excessive: the dictatorial negation. Gandhi is true to this structure, therefore, by immanent necessity; there is veritably no other alternative. (And let us note, this "structural" inference is in a sense impersonal and not a qualitative comment on the Gandhian discourse in general.)

Let us put this schematically in the form of an elaboration. If we look at the list of unproductive expenses above, we shall find a curious heterogeneity of items: from "war" to "orgies" and "perverse sexuality." In other words, that what we shall classify today under private and/or public are rooted in a disastrous unity there. But this is not an artificial, synthetically superimposed unity of differences; it instances the medieval, monarchical sovereignty which is the origin of this unity. There is no state/society distinction by which these objects could be allocated. The person or the body of the monarch holds them all without distinction;

---

[35] Aristotle, "Politics" in *The Basic Works of Aristotle,* ed. Richard McKeon (New York, NY: The Modern Library, 2001), 1114–1316.

[36] Habermas, *The Philosophical Discourse of Modernity*, 223.

since any discrimination would divide his person/body and his powers. Hobbes stated this classically when he said somewhere in the monarchical context that the representer—his unity is the sovereign, not the represented. This argument, what to say of the middle ages, would flow correctly and absorb even history during the ancient regime.

> The society of the ancient regime represented its unity and its identity to itself as that of a body—a body which found its figuration in the body of the king, or rather which identified itself with the king's body, while at the same time it attached itself to it as its head.[37]

With the onset of the democratic revolution this unity "burst out when the body of the king was destroyed, when the body politic was decapitated and when, at the same time, the corporeality of the social was dissolved."[38] The historical opposition to universal suffrage, where the represented is the (so-called) sovereign, was, thus, well placed because "Number breaks down unity, destroys identity."[39] With the state/society and public/private division now inaugurated, there was no looking back. Divisions in the "ungraspable" society now looked clear and could not be demythized by a formal equality before law. A violent reaction was inevitable. With Marx came the first blow and with the fascists the second. Both retained dictatorship in some theoretical form to transcend the disintegrating fractures proposed by the liberal divide charted according to the registers of the state/society and public/private division. Marcuse in his memorable explanation of the fascists documented this attempt in meticulous theoretical detail. But this unity could not be forged artificially for that second time; divorced from the person of the king it could never be de-differentiated again. The private and the public could never come again in the person-al figure of the king. The language used to deplore dictatorship is charted in these terms and history perhaps proves the anachronism of such experiments.

To repeat, the public private once upon a time were united and that in the body of the sovereign monarch. Post anti-absolutist movements and the rise of liberal capitalism bifurcated this simple and once divided they were never to meet again. Any attempt in this direction and that too in the

[37] Claude Lefort, "The Image of the Body and Totalitarianism," in *The Political Forms of Modern Society,* ed. John B. Thompson (Delhi: Disha Publications, 1989), 292–306.
[38] Ibid.
[39] Ibid.

times after its sovereign times are over has to meet with the reprobation that assumes the form of a strong and outright, severe rejection—even without a dialogue, of the dictatorial imago.

But this narrative has its ruptures: Somewhere in the middle of this nowhere, some one like Gandhi would invoke "an hour" of dictatorship to transcend "evils" that are genealogically aligned with peaceful leisure, by prohibiting them forcibly without compensation. But alas only an hour! Not wrongly because this springs from Gandhi's own idea of "not more than what is strictly needed"[40] an idea which is behind the strong notion of voluntary poverty resurrected with lovely force by some critical neo-Gandhians. Even the great utterance inscribed on the head of De Sade—which Giorgio Agamben is so fond of quoting everywhere, "There is no man ... who does not want to be a despot when he has an erection"[41] may be demystified similarly by pointing out that going by this economy, one wants to become a dictator only when he has had an erection; in other times he is purportedly a democrat. But this is—given its phallic logos—precariously a masculine interpretive imagery. Bypassing it we may now brace ourselves to understand (narrated in the first chapter) why pornography in 18th century Europe wanted to de-sacralize the king's [holy] body and break its unity (a graphic cartoon which captures a king in the act of sodomy, bore the caption "This is what Louis XIV did to the people").[42]

Therefore Gandhi's "healthy refreshment" and "innocent fun" try to avoid the excesses of alcohol induced incest and other pornographic

---

[40] M. K. Gandhi, *Voluntary Poverty*. comp. R. K. Prabhu (Ahmedabad: Navajivan Publishing House, 1960), 7.

[41] Sade cited in Giorgio Agamben, *Homo Sacer: Sovereign Power and Bare Life,* trans. D. H. Roazen, (Stanford, CA: Stanford University Press, 1998), 135. But Agamben's hunch in deploying Sade is to show how Sade stitches together the being of biologically bare, sexual *homo sacer* with that of the sovereign: "in a dimension in which the public and the private, political existence and bare life change places." (Giorgio Agamben, *Homo Sacer: Sovereign Power and Bare Life,* trans. D. H. Roazen, [Stanford, CA: Stanford University Press, 1998] 134).

[42] Now, though this was achieved through the genre of political pornography (and, thus, pornography was clearly aligned with and abetted the evolution of democracy), the liberal critiques would condemn pornography as authoritarian in essence: that is, they sexually excite the readers to the extent of committing (sexual) violence or, in other words, making them rapist-ly authoritarian by forgetting the value of consent. If not in this, then they force the readers to indulge in an autoerotic practice like masturbation, which is "unproductive" and "wasteful"; Gandhi was a great critique of masturbation. Sade's statement *vis-à-vis* Agamben should be understood in this spirit.

"despotic" predicaments. But to restore the moment of "national and moral awakening" and weed out the evils of alcohol induced incest, Gandhi brings in, compellingly the dictatorial hour—which in turn blossoms in a (nondemocratic) state of un-divided (public and private combined) unity of the monarchs' body, sexual extremity, peaceful leisure and war combined in one (primordial sovereignty). An irresolvable contradiction but also involves an economy. What kind of economy is this? Let us examine by way of conclusion.

## Concluding Remarks

The well-established view that Gandhi wanted the public and the private to be the echoes of each other, if I'm correct, stands demolished. But this is to endorse the point of their irreconcilability only, and Gandhi was at times within this paradigm—always. In fact, Gandhi is rather suspicious of the radical translation the two categorical sets (public/private and society/state) might entail: "public woman" or "private rights" (and his distrust of the liberal language of rights is all the more evident here). He finds them as obstacles not to be diluted by means of the politics of pure means—his brand of what he calls "adult education." Not because it is amidst nonviolent peace tied to leisure itself that all unproductive excessive practices such as "drinking," "perverse sexuality" blossom. Nonviolence cannot annihilate, therefore, the "evils" that originate on its own land. Gandhi's own means of nonviolence, therefore, rendered paralyzed, he would very rightly transcend them by means of dictatorship (again, this is a structural comment and not reflexive of the Gandhian discourse in general). Dictatorship because "the Fuhrer is no longer an office in the sense of traditional public law, but rather something ['a whole body that is neither private nor public'] that springs forth without mediation from his person."[43] If we want to connect it to its past, dictatorship is the modernist transformation of the monarch: transforming a Hegelian discursive fragment, he is "'a person, but the solitary person who stands over against all the rest' [constituting] 'the real authoritative universality of that person'" which is "'but a natural result of the personal hunt for content and determinateness' ... 'their impotent' 'self-consciousness is

[43] Agamben, *Homo Sacer*, 184.

the defenceless enclosed arena of their tumult' ... whose 'activities and self enjoyment are equally monstrous excesses'."[44]

But there is a rider: Gandhi requires this monstrous excess to counter the excess induced by drinking, not as an instance of his own emotional pathology but as the reenactment of an indispensable, unconscious structural genealogy. The modern dictator tries to absorb, override, or forcibly transcend the public/private and society/state divisions but fails; He/she fails because once the divisions have been made and they have emerged with their own irreconcilable validity claims, they survive on their differences. They cannot be mutated as one in the post bifurcation times. They were one in the person of the monarch who did not have to unite them synthetically like the modern dictator. He was the original habitus of the division where they peacefully and [practically] slept as one; he was origin of all values—his voice was conscience, his speech, law. Today, this monstrous excess of the person would be too strongly condemned and denounced by the help of the divisions that originated in him (say the protection of society or the protection of privacy). Gandhi understands this and, inspired by his economy, calls for an "hour" of dictatorship.

An hour, but only an hour. But this hour must be a very lonely hour, and loneliness, put in brief, is a terrible temporality. And now, if we are convinced of the causes and consequences of this terrible temporality—so to say—we must think twice while invoking transparency in public and private life by calling for an integration through investigation with the help of technologies of the self (conscience) or a tele-visual technology of the sting operation (the proverbial spy cam), or whatever. This pursuit and trap could be elided only when we take Gandhi's exhortation and attempt it in an overgrasping spiritual sense without distinctions: admitting this partly, we might conclude that Gandhi both sets up and eludes this trap—by which Gandhi attracts us even now—more than anybody else.

But this problematic, and the corresponding reading of it, urges us to delve deeper into the histories of the personal. Chapter 3 will enrich us with this opportunity.

---

[44] G. W. F. Hegel, *Phenomenology of Spirit*, trans. A. V. Miller (Delhi: Motilal Banarasidass Publishers, 1998), 292–93.

# 3

# Universal and Cultural Histories of the Personal

## I

Today, the lexical presence of public/private has become a part of our everyday, implicit vocabulary, so much so that their meaning seems self-present (self-evidence that shows itself without a corresponding sign chain) and equipmentally ready at hand. *Public* means all the citizens of a state and also "unconcealed, not private" (S. 8, expln. 2, Indian Evidence Act [1 of 1872]). The operative principle here is, "everything that appears in public can be seen and heard by everybody and has the widest possible publicity."[1] Etymologically meaning "of the people," the public is strongly built into the optic of the "public sphere"—where public opinion evolves among people who are political equals (no distinction of class or rank is made) through the mediation of publicity forms (media), and it is connected to certain forms of representation (elections and referendum), deliberation (for example, debates in the Parliament), and political authority (that government, whose authority rests on a changing public opinion, is most legitimate). In Hindi, *janta* is the closest equivalent of the word "public," meaning crowd or a collection of people, and *aam janta*—another word—specifies the average, ordinary character of the word *public* in India. *Private* classically means that which is not open to or belonging to all; it does not rest on the principle of publicity or equality of persons (an example of which is the family). In post-medieval English and Latin usage, private stood for an existence withdrawn from public life or for

---

[1] H. Arendt, "The Public and the Private Realm." in *The Human Condition*, ed. H. Arendt and M.Conovan (Chicago: The University of Chicago Press, 1958), 22–78.

anyone not working in an official capacity. Again, private stood for that which belongs to the individual and not to the state. In India, following our colonial induction, private has been defined as not public, or opposed to public, not open to public, apart from the state; belonging or concerning one or more individuals (S. 75, Indian Evidence Act [1 of 1872]). The individual as a private person (when not acting in official capacity) and family (often organized around private property), sex, and such matters assign a content to the private and privacy. Privacy, though (till lately) not a constitutional right as in the USA, is defined in the Indian Penal Code (IPC) as freedom from unauthorized oversight or observation; seclusion (S. 509, IPC [45 of 1860]).

The public/private binary—whose historical roots have been traced to classical Greece—acquired its modern meaning through the mediations of medieval Roman Law and 18th century Europe. Aristotle made a distinction between household (*oikos*) and the space of the city-state (*polis*) where, through deliberation (lexis) and common action (praxis), a shared, common, and in a loose sense "public" life beyond bare essentials or necessities was sustained. The private realm of necessities (subsistence and reproduction) was the household. Therefore property, "and the art of acquiring property" was considered a part of "managing the household"[2] and participation in the polis was restricted by one's status or rank as a master of oikos.

In the medieval age, in Roman Law, one encounters terms such as *publicus* and *privatus* but without the standard usage[3] because everything public/private ultimately resided in the person of the monarch (more on this latter.) However, in Roman Law—the first systematic legal document—the privacy of the home (*domus*) was sanctioned[4] and Roman Law itself was "private law," in that it would have application only for individuals or relations of coordination. Public law would administer affairs of the state or relations of domination. But similar to the Greek city state, it was the status of the individuals that determined their participation in the medieval public sphere. We enter modernity when men entered

---

[2] Aristotle, *The Politics*, trans. Benjamin Jowett (Cambridge: Cambridge University Press, 1988), 5.

[3] Jurgen Habermas, *The Structural Transformation of the Public Sphere: An Inquiry into a category of Bourgeois Society*, trans. T. Berger (Great Britain: Blackwell Publishers & Polity Press, 1996), 5.

[4] A. Black, "The Individual and Society," in *The Cambridge History of Medieval Political Thought*, ed. J. H. Burns (Cambridge: Cambridge University Press, 1988), 593.

the realm of contract from that of status, from duties to that of rights (18th century Enlightenment and the French Revolution remain the canonical examples). Formal equality of persons was a prerequisite of such a contract. Particularly, at the break of the medieval age, in the wake of civil or commercial law in 18th century Europe, a democratic climate was created where apparent equality of all before the law and the market was preempted. And the public sphere was, thus—in a sense—opened to all. This meant the formation of public opinion through the media (enabled at that time by the advent of print capitalism) and institutionalization of state sovereignty that would rest, henceforth, with the people or the public. A new category of legitimacy was created. This also engendered the rise of civil society where the subjects would fulfill two roles at the same time: as a property owner or bourgeois, he/she would pursue his/her private interests, and as a citizen in the public sphere, he/she would bear equal rights granted by the state. This also—as a part of the public sphere— ensured the separation of society (family) from the state, and that the state would not intervene in societal matters and, expectedly, privacy would be located in the societal realm henceforth. (Separated from the state, classi-cally, the church was the first private to have imparted the secular color so characteristic of modernity.) The state would ensure privacy, but would not intervene; its closest analogy was the market: the state would ensure a free market by itself not intervening in it, and the free market was not only of commodities but a great market place of ideas and exchange of opinion in which anybody could participate, irrespective of birthmarks and the stink of status. The modern public sphere had arrived. It was just a step further when Marx would denounce universal suffrage and invoke the proletariat as the class with "universal suffering,"[5] and would mock this artificial equality of publics before the law and the market (alleging that they masked real inequalities) and thought of smashing the private/ public divide by abolishing private property—which he thought was at the core of this suffering. The rest is history and its repetition. No wonder that the public/private divide has been considered as the core of our modern existence.

An interesting part of recent academic discussions is that while there is a growing interest in the public and the private, critical discourse on

---

[5] Karl Marx, "A Contribution to the Critique of Hegel's 'Philosophy of Right' (1843)," in *The Young Hegelians: An Anthology*, ed. L. S. Stepelevich (Cambridge: Cambridge University Press, 1983), 310–22.

the personal nearly draws a blank. (The state of the personal is somewhat dubious and absent in all classic European discussions—even in Jurgen Habermas and Hannah Arendt).

Although Habermas does cursorily refer to the process through which the "modern state apparatus became independent from the monarch's personal sphere," he rarely engages with it.[6] For instance, here goes this recognition in the form of a footnote to one of his famous articles: "The important thing to understand is that the medieval public sphere, if it even deserves this recognition, is tied to the personal. The feudal lord and estates create the public sphere by means of their very presence."[7] But the personal sphere of the monarch[8]—and what it means in the Western tradition—is somewhat available, not in Habermas but in G. H. Mead, from the standpoint of a social behaviorist. Mead meticulously charts the components of this personal sphere where the people within the same state "can identify themselves with each other only through being

---

[6] Habermas, *The Structural Transformation of the Public Sphere*, 29.

[7] Jurgen Habermas, "The Public Sphere: An Encyclopedia Article," *New German Critique* 3, no. 51 (1974), 49–55.

[8] Marx's caricature of Hegel describing "the will's final decision is the monarch" and not the "will of the monarch is the final decision" rings ironical in the face of facts. Did Marx ever think that Hegel's progressive graph of tyranny or feudal monarchy to constitutional, "well organized" monarchies was able to resolve the antinomy between the monarch—"the will of the empirical singularity," and its real opposition—the civil society or "the will of the empirical generality"—as Marx puts it? Therefore, if there is a view that constitutional monarchy is a cut remove from, and modifies the monarchical person (who mutates to becoming just a dotted i) to the extent of revising the graph proposed above, because it grants "free subjectivity" to the people, one needs to revisit Hegel again to see that the person element of the monarch tied to final, ultimate decisions ("I will") is retained, contradictorily, in more ways than one. Also reread Marx's brutal, and detailed indictment of such a revision (if it is one) where the personality of the monarch, to begin with, appears to have been mediated (the basic, abstract personality becoming the "personality of the state" or "personality of the whole"), but according to Marx, such mediations fail (like the attempt to make civil society legislative through estates reflecting public affairs though actually limited to private interests only); what remains perhaps, is the abstract self-mediation of the monarch, for the "self-originating principle" of the monarch to which Hegel refers to is never resolved (for the monarch cannot derive himself from the constitution, too). Marx uncovers nearly a logical, and insurmountable muddle. "Real extremes cannot be mediated precisely because they are real extremes. Nor do they require mediation, for they are opposed in essence. They have nothing in common, they do not need each other, they do not supplement each other." I have therefore stuck to the unmediated, and noncontradictory version of the monarchy in its classical topoi.

subjects of a common monarch."[9] Mead traces the phenomenon to the ancient empires of Mesopotamia and observes that "[i]t is possible through personal relationships between a sovereign and subject to constitute a community which could not otherwise be so constituted." In the Roman Empire, through the mediation of Roman Law, Mead notes that while the emperor–subject relationship was "defined in legal terms"[10] through sacrificial offerings made to the emperor,

> [The subject was] "putting himself into personal relationship with him, and because of that he could feel his connection with all the members in the community". .... "It was the setting up of a personal relationship which in a certain sense went beyond the purely legal relations involved in the development of Roman law".[11]

In India, considering the King's person as sacred, it was assumed that he had influence over crops, cattle, rain, and general prosperity. So again, in order for the subjects to relate to cattle, the mediation of the King was involved in a metonymic gesture through whose presence people could relate and be present to themselves.[12] Personal is that which predates both the public and the private, and what is historically interesting is to discover when and why the collapsing of the personal and the private began.

---

[9] George H. Mead, *Mind, Self, and Society, From the Standpoint of a Social Behaviorist,* ed. Charles W. Morris (Chicago, IL: The University of Chicago Press, Chicago, [1934] 1972), 311.

[10] What Mead is trying to argue here is a modification of the argument where formal Roman property laws relating to persons are transcended through personal relationships directed to the monarchical center. The Roman distinction between persons will later be debated by Kant and Hegel, which we shall discus further. For Hegel, in Greece, the medieval *subject* could not be posited because a subject (exterior to an object) implies a disjunction between the universal and the particular, accomplished by a division between custom and law or state and religion—while Athena is both God and *Polis*. It was in the Roman law of private property that the change was first offered:

> The Roman form of private property was enshrined in a legal system which separated law, in the form of private property law, from custom, from the other relations of social life. Those other relations, such as the family, were defined in terms of the same property law, by its distinctions between persons; with the right to bear property, and "things" who have no such right, such as women and children.

See Gillian Rose, *Hegel Contra Sociology* (London: Athlone, 1981), 114.

[11] Mead, *Mind, Self, and Society*, 312.

[12] A. M. Hocart, *Kingship* (London: Oxford University Press, 1927), 9.

For this last instance we can borrow from Max Weber the diffused origins of the public law-private law distinction, which as Weber shows was

> once not made at all. Such was the case when all law, all jurisdictions, and particularly all powers of exercising authority were personal privileges, such as especially, the "prerogatives" of the head of the state. ... [Who was] not different from the head of the household.[13]

This world of the personal, or as Weber calls it, "patrimonial monarchy," forms the prehistory of the private/public distinction, and again I repeat that what is historically interesting is to discover when and why the collapsing of the personal and the private began. Habermas, therefore, does away with a vast repertoire.

So far as Arendt is concerned, commentators have tried to make a case out of the energy generated by the latter's "personal," having previously been at pains to argue that the "political" and the "personal" in the wake of Arendt's celebration of these moments later had become the "public" and the "private." "With the emergence of women's liberation a decade or so after *The Human Condition* appeared, the relation between the 'political' and the 'personal' moved to the forefront of politics, and this eventually took the form of the public and the private"[14] with their corresponding emphasis on "personal life" becoming a "third challenge to the liberal dichotomy:"[15] a really queer mix-up in history. The reason perhaps is that we tend to have a mix-up between the private and the personal,[16] and

---

[13] Max Weber, *Economy and Society: An Outline of Interpretive Sociology*, eds. Guenther Roth and Claus Wittich (Berkley, CA: University of California Press, 1978), II: 643.

[14] Eli Zaretsky, "Hannah Arendt and the Meaning of the Public/Private Distinction" in *Hannah Arendt and the Meaning of Politics*, eds. Calhoun and Mc Growan (Minneapolis, MN & London: University of Minnesota Press, 1997), 207–31.

[15] Zaretsky, "Hannah Arendt and the Meaning of the Public/Private Distinction." 214. For consideration of the failure of this appraisal in its true light, judge the following comments of Craig Calhoun,

> Arendt would never endorse social engineering and, against such threats, certainly would protect privacy. Even more, she would protect the personal and the distinctive from absorption into the impersonal. But she would not assimilate the notion of the personal to that of the private as Zaretsky does.

See Craig Calhoun, "Plurality, Promises, and Public Spaces," in *Hannah Arendt and the Meaning of Politics,* eds. Craig Calhoun and John McGrowan (Minneapolis, MN & London: University of Minnesota Press, 1997), 232–59.

[16] For feminism, I pursue how the personal is mixed up with the private in their slogan "personal is political" in a different paper, See Arnab Chatterjee, "Beyond Private and

this is its contemporary moment. But, this easy and historic conflation of personal as private is perhaps not the end of the story.

In the Western history itself, there is also a suppressed narrative (suppressed because it does not suit the liberal project) where the two are not the same; in fact, the two cannot be the same. But first I'll take the opportunity to narrate how the personal/private coalescence occurs and then I shall try to recover the personal from the sediments.

## The Moment When the Personal Loses Itself in the Private

Is it possible to appreciate the fact that the appearance of the personal through the sieve of the private is basically a historical maneuver?

This major point then needs mention: the qualitative leap realized when personal came to be identified with the private. Now, private property is as old as Greek antiquity: Aristotle had argued in favor of and Plato had wanted to abolish private property. That is not the point; the first signs were available in the natural law (or natural rights) tradition, and despite a lot of caveats, one of its representative voice still remains John Locke. In this tradition, property, for the first time, is placed in the person:

> Though the earth, and all inferior creatures be common to all men, yet every man has a "property" in his own "person." This no body has any right to but himself. The "labour" of his body, and the "work" of his hands, we may say are properly his. Whatsoever ... he hath mixed his "labour" with, and joined it to something that is his own, and thereby makes it his "property" ... that excludes the common right of other men.[17]

When "his property" or private property derives from personal capacities of labor, the first motivated mix up between the personal and the private occurs. And then having had its 18th century initiation, it became a cornerstone of liberal theory where property becomes an attribute of

Public: New Perspectives On Personal and Personalist Social Work," *The Indian Journal of Social Work* 67, no. 3 (2006). A revised version of it is in Arnab Chatterjee, *Categorical Blue: Personalytic Ethics in Social Work and Other Structures of Helping* (Shimla: Indian Institute of Advanced Study (IIAS), 2017).

[17] John Locke, *Two Treatises of Government* (London J. M. Dent & Son's Ltd. (Everyman's Library), (1690), [1924, 1982] [Sec. 27.]), 130.

personality. If you take away property from me, I become a nonperson because (private) property is in my person. Here, there is natural ownership before there is a legal ownership. Here is a classical example in Hegel: "Not until he has property does the person exist as reason."[18] Hegel goes at length to show how property is required to supersede "the mere subjectivity of personality."[19] In fact, this is the personal in Hegel invested with some kind of immediacy but lacking in content, that is, Hegel's "abstract personality" in order to become concrete and objective awaits a trick: "Since my will, as personal and hence as the will of an individual [des Einzelnen], becomes objective in property, the latter takes on the character of private property ... "[20]

This would be picked up by liberal capitalism, and now onward—property being in person and that which makes objective, tangible personality possible—private becomes the realm of liberty, reprieve, and freedom. Marx would fall heavily on all of this and, in fact, this discourse finds its final resolution in Marx only. His argument was just the reverse: in a society without private property, the personal selves of men freely blossom to enter the true realm of freedom. Therefore, this hyphenation between the private and the personal is more an ideological investment necessary for liberal history than a structurally indispensable relation.

## Recuperating the Personal

Now, having presented the anatomical, bare rudiments of how the personal loses itself in the private, here I'll explore as to how it could be recovered and allowed to have a safe passage. I shall present four exemplary, paradigmatic instances; now, even though they are examples, and therefore comparatively brief, it is possible to push up this reading to map more thinkers and more thinking. Given the force of history, it would be wise to start with Hobbes.

---

[18]   G. W. F. Hegel, *Elements of the Philosophy of Right*, trans. H. B. Nisbet (UK: Cambridge University Press, [1820] 1991), 73.

[19]   Ibid.

[20]   Ibid., 77.

# Hobbes

The problem of author, authority, and representation—the quintessential nuances of the linguistic turn in the human sciences and political theory—were all pre-predicated by Hobbes some three centuries back. His description and division of natural and artificial persons have remained most significant and have ushered a new age where a natural person is his/her own author and presenter, but a sovereign is an artificial person authorized by his/her subjects and representing them (this rememorates, though not in its entirety, the social contract). An artificial person is also an actor with a script authorized by the authors or natural persons, but can also represent inanimate things "an inanimate thing can be a person ... and can act in law."[21] Hobbes is nearly predicting the legal personality of idols that would spring up later in history, but with so much of person and personality cropping up in and around Hobbes, recovering the pure personal in Hobbes is fairly straight.

This union of a collective multitude in one person and representing the multitude in a singular collectivity is the Hobbesian personal—where the realm of the common is not separately delineated.

> This union so made, is that which men call now-a-days a Body Politic or civil society; and the Greeks call it ... a city; which may be defined to be a multitude of men, united as one person by a common power, for their common peace, defence, and benefit.[22]

Let us mark this with an underlined emphasis: "multitude of men, united as one person by a common power." Having had a taste of this in Chapter 2, we are no more surprised at the introduction of this. Can we say that as common power, the person of the sovereign or the state is a "common man"? The state is the common man or the pubic person as Rousseau has had it. He/she is common because he/she represents all and himself/herself by essence that runs through him/her, not by the sheer force of numbers, or by the mere tact of representation. "(Commonwealth) is one person, of whose acts a great multitude, by mutual covenants one with another, have made themselves everyone the author." The authority granted to the authors (previously note the actor/author distinction) is by a mediating

---

[21] Cited in A. P. Martinich, *A Hobbes Dictionary* (Cambridge: Blackwell, 1995), 229.
[22] Thomas Hobbes, *The Elements of Law: Natural and Politic*, ed. Ferdinand Tonnies (New York: Routledge, [1969] 2013), 104.

moment of self-representation, not always sovereign, yet all in one and one in all—in width and latitude.[23]

A public person is not a private one. The point is, can they (the multitude) be misrepresented? Can the sovereign actor having had authority from the multitude-author deny or misrepresent the authors? But this is posed in somewhat a tedious way: people's representatives tend to abandon the people, and the promises (key to social contract theories) atrophy. Here, we use our contemporary bereavement as projective devices. But it could be posed by reversing the hierarchy too. Slaves in Roman law—despite being bereft of rights—were able to bear the burden of representing their masters—the way we send off our domestic helps to sign for us and submit the electric bill, or other errands with authorization. "The slave had no rights. The personality of the slave was recognized to some extent in the law of contracts and torts, but he was considered merely as the representative of his master."[24] So, here is an interesting reversal, representing the superior but just as a vehicle of the superior where the question of misrepresentation is shunned. But Hobbes is categorical on this that it cannot be posed in the way it is being done with a sovereign superior:

> In a body politic, if the representative be one man, whatsoever he does in the person of the body which is not warranted in his letters, nor by the laws, is his own act, and not the act of the body, nor of any other member thereof besides himself: because further than his letters or the laws limit, he representeth no man's person, but his own. But what he does according to these is the act of every one: For of the act of the sovereign every one is author, because he is their representative unlimited; and the act of him that recedes not from the letters of the sovereign is the act of the sovereign, and therefore every member of the body is author of it.[25]

---

[23] Like natural person and artificial person, Hobbes' distinction between natural (patrimonial monarchical) state and artificial (democratic) state—the latter being artificial by the feat of representation of others conferred upon it, and Hobbes' eluding, and somewhat varying preferences before *Leviathan* for artificial (democratic) state over natural personal monarchy, or vice versa (noted by Leo Strauss)—is a matter of Hobbes's psychobiography and not intrinsic to our argument. See Leo Strauss, *The Political Philosophy of Hobbes: Its Basis and its Genesis*, trans. Elsa M. Sinclair (Chicago, IL: The University of Chicago Press, 1963), 62.

[24] Joseph R. Long, "Notes on Roman Law; Law of Persons, Law of Contracts," (1912), https://archive.org/stream/cu31924021206804/cu31924021206804_djvu.txt, accessed August 11, 2017.

[25] Thomas Hobbes, *Leviathan*, ed. J. C. A. Gaskin (Oxford, New York: Oxford University Press, 1998), 150.

If the authors are actors, then can the role really be feigned? To whom are the dialogues and the utterances faithfully delivered? Is the audience not itself represented? Isn't the persona bound to a discourse? "The concept of the political covenant is not a means of limiting the powers of the crown; properly understood, it shows that the powers of the crown have no limits at all."[26] The state of nature and invasion are prominent thought exercises in Hobbes. But what do they invade for? "The first maketh men invade for gain; the second, for safety; and the third, for reputation."[27] And how is this third positioned? Men also invade "for trifles, as a word, a smile, a different opinion, and any other sign of undervalue, either direct in their persons or by reflection in their kindred, their friends, their nation, their profession, or their name."[28] So the highest kind of aggression in Hobbes (invasion) is also for their (the aggressors' persons) will to be reflected in their friends in the form of reputation. And why not? When people come together, they engage in idle talk, disseminating what Hobbes called "vain glory."[29] This is how they step out of the realm of necessity where the invasions of possessions, power, and security are remarkably positioned and proliferate; and this reflexivity, of course, signifies presence.

> That which men desire they are said to love, and to hate those things for which they have aversion. So that desire and love are the same thing; save that by desire, we signify the absence of the object; by love, most commonly the presence of the same. So also by aversion, we signify the absence; and by hate, the presence of the object.[30]

And what is absent but power. "The passions that most of all cause the differences of wit are principally the more or less desire of power, of riches, of knowledge, and of honour. All which may be reduced to the first, that is, desire of power."[31] When power is desire, it is absent, it is lacking, it is a slot which is empty. But presence forms an interesting event in Hobbes, and with it, the personal "feelings" of love and hate constitute in Hobbes a crude but essential axiomatics. And the way we have pitted the private

26 Quentin Skinner, "Hobbes and the Purely Artificial Person of the State," *The Journal of Political Philosophy* 7, no. 1 (1999, March): 1–29.
27 Hobbes, *Leviathan*, 1998, 83.
28 Hobbes, *Leviathan*, 1998, 83–84.
29 Hobbes, *Leviathan*, 1998, 101.
30 Hobbes, *Leviathan*, 1998, 34.
31 Hobbes, *Leviathan*, 1998, 48.

against the personal comes forth in Hobbes splendidly in relation to love only—where he tends to speak on the private exclusion of others:

> That which taketh away the reputation of love is being detected of *private ends*: ... the acquiring of dominion, riches, dignity, or secure pleasure to themselves only or specially. For that which men reap benefit by to themselves they are thought to do for their own sakes, and not for love of others.[32]

Again, "signs of private interest [are] enough to mortify the most lively faith;"[33] the private as a form of mortification then must be secured against its false substitution, which according to Hobbes is passing of "private opinion" as "opinion."[34] Concerning "irrational" animals also, he distinguishes between common good and private benefit. The way this charts itself relationally is when Hobbes seems to be talking about the origins of civil or criminal law:

> And so also in Commonwealths private men may remit to one another their debts, but not robberies or other violences, whereby they are endamaged; because the detaining of debt is an injury to themselves, but robbery and violence are injuries to the person of the Commonwealth.[35]

The private person versus the public person of the Commonwealth now comes out in the open in Hobbes. Hobbes also, while distinguishing political systems—public and private—confers common sources for the former and private sources for the latter. Richard Tuck is sincerely wrong when he says that in the Hobbesian state of nature private property is acknowledged. Martinich gives the answer: "There is no personal or real property ... in the state of nature. Property comes to exist with the commonwealth. ... In fact all property ultimately belongs to the sovereign."[36]

Finally then, what is the Hobbesian resolution?

> If the public interest chance to cross the private, he prefers the private: for the passions of men are commonly more potent than their reason. From whence it follows that where the public and private interest are most closely

---

[32] Hobbes, *Leviathan*, 1998, 48.
[33] Hobbes, *Leviathan*, 1998, 81.
[34] Hobbes, *Leviathan*, 1998, 69.
[35] Hobbes, *Leviathan*, 1998, 99.
[36] Martinich, *A Hobbes Dictionary*, 236.

united, there is the public most advanced. Now in monarchy the private interest is the same with the public.[37]

The monarchical sovereign where the private and the public are united in one person is the conclusion in Hobbes. It trumps both but alienates and unites in one.

## Locke

We have already noticed how Locke's argument became instrumental in foregrounding private in the personal.[38] But even in Locke, it is possible to find another discourse of the personal besides property and the private dominion. While discussing property as an extension of the person, and particularly Adam's property as "private dominion," which is supposed to have arisen from God's "grant" or "donation" and that of fatherhood from the act of begetting, Locke meditates on how this divine donation was made "personally" to Adam to which his heir could have no right.[39] Locke argues that even if it belongs to the parents "personally," after their death, their property does not go to the common stock of mankind but is inherited by their children as heirs because humans have a natural propensity to continue their creed.[40] This power of begetting in another form—and that what roots continuity—founds inheritance. The point relevant to our case is that this "personal" belongingness is a middle-term that appears with some autonomy and mediates person and property—seen as an extension of each other in Locke. And because the mutual-extension argument, I guess, in itself cannot explain inheritance, Locke is taking recourse to a different premise; the "personal" appears to give a language to this premise.

## Hegel

As established earlier, the reading that entails Hegel as a canonical case where the personal-private mix-up receives the force of an argument is not

---

[37] Hobbes, *Leviathan*, 1998, 124.
[38] For Lockes' allergy toward communal or collective ownership, see C. B. Macpherson, "The Theory of Property Right," in *The Political Theory of Possessive Individualism, Hobbes to Locke* (London: Oxford University Press, 1972), 197–221.
[39] Locke, *Two Treatises of Government*, 60–61.
[40] Ibid., 62.

wrong, and as rendered by Marx, it carries an immense sway with it. But it is as well possible to discover in Hegel a curious personal impatience not to be suppressed by the interested world of the private. Take for instance the distinction between real property and personal property that could be traced to the Roman law from which Kant borrowed his interesting theory of rights and where we find personal appearing with a rider: "personal rights of a real kind." Hegel made a critique of Kant's formulation; drawing on that critique, let me here try to illuminate the distinction that I think was unconsciously made by Hegel himself.

Deriving from the Justinian Roman legal division of right into rights of persons, things, and actions, Kant in 1797 had proposed, taking into account the "form" of the rights, a threefold division: "a right to a thing; a right against a person; a right to a person akin to a right to a thing."[41] The first is a property right, the second is a contract right, and the third is a "personal right of a real kind;"[42] in other words, it is a right about "what is mine or yours domestically, and the relation of persons in the domestic condition ... [including] ... possession of a person,"[43] such as the rights of spouses over one another, the rights of parents over their children, etc. The third is the most interesting because it resembles what today we call personal laws supposed to distribute "private" affairs within a household. And this is what Hegel attacks. Hegel thinks that the division is a confusing one; second, while family relationships form the content of "personal rights of a real kind," in actuality, family relationships are based on the "surrender of personality."[44] Hegel further notes that

> For Kant personal rights are those rights which arise out of a contract whereby I give something or perform a service ... Admittedly, only a person is obliged to implement the provisions of a contract, just as it is only a person who acquires the right to have them implemented. But such a right cannot therefore be called a personal right; rights of every kind can belong only to a person.[45]

What is interesting in Hegel's engagement—relevant to our project—is the way he extricates the personal from being stamped with the badge of

---

[41] Immanuel Kant, *Practical Philosophy* (UK: Cambridge University Press, 1999), 412.
[42] Hegel, *Philosophy of Right*, 71.
[43] Kant, *Practical Philosophy*, 426.
[44] Hegel, *Philosophy of Right*, 72.
[45] Ibid., 73.

household rights or the power to accomplish a civil contract;[46] in other words, a personal right not masquerading as a private right. (Later while engaging with the theory of the personal, I shall make the point how in the person itself the public or the private becomes real or are diffused; in the above Hegelian quote there is a distinct anticipation.) In brief, what Hegel may have argued here could be that there are no "personal rights of a real kind."

But let us underline this binary: personal versus/and real, which is significant and requires of us to reiterate that a distinction between real property and personal property was a strong feature of English law. Real property had "some degree of geographical fixity."[47] In order to examine this distinction in the form that it is found in a 1827 tract, I think the notions of the personal could still be recovered in a very different sense. In personal property "the general rule is, that possession constitutes the criterion of title; ... hence the vendor of personal chattels is never expected to show the origin of his right ... [but] real property like land is held not by possession but by title requiring 'the production of documents'."[48] Please note the somewhat loose coverage that personal property requires compared to real property. Now if it is pointed out that personal property does have property as a signified, even if in a loose sense, it may be rebutted by saying that, in the same text, Mathews goes on to mention "peculiarities personal" or as to how "personal disability" may be enough to "repel the presumption of a grant."[49] Does this personal call for documents or is a means to establishing a title? No. In fact, these are blatant uses appropriate to our cause existing in a legal tract meant to discuss property personal or real.

---

[46] Carole Pateman does not agree that Hegel is successful in his attempt, and according to her, he is rather limited to transcending just one part of the Kantian argument that saw personal right, among others, in the manifest act of pointing out "this is my wife" where a "thing" is, accidentally, a person. See Carole Pateman, "Hegel, Marriage, and the Standpoint of Contract," in *Feminist Interpretations of G. W. F. Hegel*, ed. Patricia Jagentowicz Mills (University Park: Pennsylvania State University Press, 1996), 209–23. But I disagree with Pateman and reiterate that there is a moment of personal in Hegel that precedes the contamination of property.

[47] Andrew Reeve, *Property* (London: Macmillan, 1986), 80–81.

[48] John H. Mathews, *Treatise On The Doctrine of Presumption and Presumptive Evidence as Affecting the Title to Real and Personal Property* (London: Joseph Butterworth and Son, Law Booksellers, 1827), 27.

[49] Ibid., 14.

## Marx

The well-placed common knowledge that the key to understanding modernity is the public/private divide and a corresponding failure to find a way beyond the binary, with which I had begun writing the book, would find—if considered carefully—an approval with dignity in Marx because Marx curiously is a symptom of both: he said for the first—which I have already cited—that "the state is founded upon the contradiction between public and private life,"[50] and for the second:

> [I]f the modern State wished to end the impotence of its administration it would be obliged to abolish the present conditions of private life. And if the State wished to abolish these conditions of private life it would have also to put an end to its own existence, for it exists only in relation to them.[51]

Now, throwing in the fact that private property is just a singular and isolated moment in the discourse of private life, Marx's agenda—I guess—looks readily defamiliarized here.

Marx would fall heavily on all of this and, in fact, this discourse finds its final resolution in Marx only. It is not a fact that in a system without private property and a sanction against "unlimited appropriation," all are nonpersons and there would be nothing personal. Therefore, this hyphenation between the private and the personal is more an ideological investment necessary for liberal history than a structurally indispensable relation. Let us document a few discursive fragments where this collapsing has been done away with. Now, notwithstanding the will to go beyond private/public divide, it may rightly be asked, could Marx be used to endorse the personal that I am proposing? Yes! And choosing only one instance, love, we may document this flower unfolding in Marx.

> Assume man to be man and his relationship to the world to be a human one: then you can exchange love only for love, trust for trust, etc ... if you want to exercise influence over other people, you must be a person with a stimulating and encouraging effect on other people. ... If you love without evoking love in return that is, if your loving does not produce reciprocal

---

[50] Karl Marx, *Selected Writings in Sociology and Social Philosophy*, eds. T. B. Bottomore and M. Rubel (Harmondsworth: Penguin Books, 1961), 222.
[51] Ibid., 223.

love; if through a living expression of yourself as a living person you do not make yourself a beloved one then your love is impotent—a misfortune.[52]

Is this not the personal in Marx, which—I'm sure—he would willingly exclude from the domain of private life he wanted to abolish for history? I think the reader agrees.

## A Contemporary Example

Marx apart, curiously, the human rights discourse does have, it may be pointed out, a phrase like "personal property." What does it qualify? In fact, it endorses the distinction that we are making between the personal and the private. A theorist of such rights comments,

> By personal property I mean individual ownership and control of possessions such as clothing, furniture, food, writing materials, books, and artistic and religious objects. Considerations of personal freedom provide strong reasons for instituting and protecting personal property. These reasons are related not to production but to the requirements of developing and expressing one's own personality. Ownership of personal property is a matter of personal liberty, not a production-related right.[53]

Therefore, it is possible to attempt a historical reconstruction of the personal where the personal could be said to have filtered through the monarchical metonymy right down to human rights discourses via Roman Law, Kant, Hegel, and the English Common Law. While the prehistorical personal comes to be contaminated by the private, the human rights discourse is significant in its attempt to do away with this conflation. While it tries to do away with the infiltration, genealogically, it perhaps proves the point that there was this contamination or over determination.

Now, while we have unraveled the philosophical, and in a sense the canonical-global history of the personal vis-à-vis the private and the

---

[52] Cited in Norman Geras, "Seven Types of Obloquy: Travesties of Marxism," in *Socialist Register*, eds. Ralph Miliband, Leo Panitch, and John Saville (London: The Merlin Press, 1990), 1–34.

[53] The ownership of means of production is called "private productive property" in this discourse. See James W. Nickel, *Making Sense of Human Rights: Philosophical Reflections on the Universal Declaration of Human Rights* (Berkley, CA: University of California Press, 1987), 152.

public, it is time to explore its cultural roots. Having reviewed the state of received history in Western social theory—past and present—and while we ask for the extrication of the personal, an impasse occurs immediately: while it is possible to launch an immanent critique and recuperate the personal from the lineaments of the private/public dilemma, it is equally impossible to normalize that text of recovery according to codes that are peculiarly available only in a cultural setting. To put it more picturesquely, we need to explore and test the distinction in various cultural practices. It is curious to note that when we come to understand what is "our personal" in terms of a cultural, cognitive self-understanding instead of the universalized "personal," we shall soon find out how the same problem arises—that of the contamination of the personal by the private and the corresponding emergence of the public sphere, and in India and other postcolonial societies with a history of having been through colonization— how the personal soon came to be identified more and more with that institutional introduction of private property and all its corollaries. It is no wonder that today we too tend to confuse the private and the personal, irrespective of the cultural system that envelops us. But how about the contamination being originarily infected? Therefore, perhaps its best to examine, after a historico-theoretical attempt, the state of the contaminated and the emancipated personal in terms of a self-regarding cultural history. And then only the emancipation of this personal as a signifier, from the lineaments of historical contamination—if any—could be more meaningfully grounded.

# II

# The Personal/*Byaktigoto:* Toward a Cultural History of the Collective Person

## *Introduction: Culture, Cognition, Self-understanding*

While we talked about the monarch and monarchical sovereignty in the sovereign person in the middle ages in the last chapter, it is a no mean coincidence that Georges Duby—one of the great cultural historians of our times—while commenting on the "culture of the high middle ages," comments that it "culminates in the person of the sovereign as the image of God."[54] Duby's larger project is, of course, different: he seeks to show "the movement of cultural popularization" in "feudal aristocracy;"[55] What is interesting however, in our context is, Duby's earlier acknowledgement that the whole "medieval culture" discloses itself or dissolves in the sovereign person. But this we have already narrated, and in a sense scripted; in this chapter, we shall hold on to the other register "culture."

The problem could be stated in these words of Jacques Derrida, where we make a contextual but legitimate replacement of a particular lexeme to give it the force of an event:

> [A]t the very moment when pronouncing ["personal,"][56] we sense the impossibility of deciding whether this name belongs, properly and simply, to one tongue. And it matters that this undecidability is at work in a struggle for the proper name within a scene of genealogical indebtedness. In seeking to "make a name for themselves," to found at the same time a universal tongue and a unique genealogy, the ["English"[57]] want to make the world see reason, and this reason can see simultaneously colonial violence (since they would thus universalize their idiom) and peaceful transparency of the human community.[58]

By subjecting this to translation, if we are to stay with Derrida, we "limit its universality: forbidden transparency, impossible univocity. 'Translation becomes the law, duty, and debt, but the debt one can no longer discharge'."[59] But after having indulged in it, we realize the untranslatable-translatability. To put it more picturesquely, we need to explore and test the distinction in various linguistic or cultural practices— even try modestly to locate person/al in cultures of translation. It is the time when we come to understand what is an "our personal" in terms of a cultural cognitive self-understanding of communities.

[54] Georges Duby, "The Diffusion of Cultural Patterns in Feudal Society," in *French Studies in History*, eds. Maurice Aymard and Harbans Mukhia (Hyderabad: Orient Longman, 1990), V.II: 214–22.

[55] Ibid., 217.

[56] Derrida's favored word here is "Babel."

[57] The Derridean original here is *Semites*.

[58] Jacques Derrida, "Des tours de Babel" in *Psyche, Inventions of the Other, Vol. 1,* eds. Peggy Kamuf and Elizabeth Rottenberg (Stanford, CA: Stanford University Press, 2007), 191–225.

[59] Ibid., 199.

Before we begin, it would be best to clarify the meaning of this "cultural-cognitive self-understanding" metaphor. To name it, we precisely designate by that term the kind of understanding available in the symbolic order of the life world of a specific community.[60] While "our personal" is apparently well defined in terms of a negative translation, a too-quick granting of a stable positivity to it would be misleading. As Sibaji Bandyopadhyay rightly reminds us, "culture is not the site where contending practices so arrange themselves as to produce a happy blending or synthesis, a stable symbolic order, but instead it is a site of contestation, inextricably linked to the material conditions and contradictions of life."[61] Here, one investigates, therefore, the cultural contestations or even the dialectic involved in the "personal" as a cultural signifier after reckoning with the fact that the colonial system is also a cultural sign system and a postcolonial nation like India cannot but involve itself in the rigors of it: this is the political secret of the cultural-cognitive self-understanding of the signifier "personal" that we've been referring to. The word cognition is significant here because "cognitive comforts are just the kind of thing which cultures, and cultures alone, can produce."[62] The comfort is this: "cultures bestow on their members/

---

[60] This attempt at reconstructing a cultural self-understanding may not be limited to non-Western identities giving them undue authenticity. Homi Bhabha invokes Adrienne Rich in situating the negroes in the USA as "quasi colonial" and, thus, eliciting a kind of vernacular minoritarianism that could be shared by a kind of affective doubling by both the classically colonial and the quasi colonial. See Homi Bhabha, *The Location of Culture* (London: Routledge, [1994] 2009), xviii, xvi. Elsewhere, Paul Manning in a perceptive piece ("Owning and Belonging: A Semiotic Investigation of the Affective Categories of a Bourgeois Society," *Comparative Studies in Society and History* 46 no. 2, [2004], 300–25) notes that while authors have deployed "the soundness of English common sense displayed in the polysemy of terms like 'belonging' to argue that political economic relations of ownership can be directly assimilated to broader vernacular understandings of 'belonging'" … [which] "too quickly assimilates the affective regime of political economy (property) to that of kinship, like morality (propriety)" (p. 301), lacks historicity—which might just sanctify, as Manning tries to accomplish, "the displaced polysemy of the English vernacular notion of belonging, "which moves from kinship to property just as surely as the Welsh one does" with some historical antecedents (p. 301). Therefore—as it is evident—while we go for "our" cultural cognitive self-understanding, the same privilege must be granted to the originary Western notions too; and secondly, this cultural discourse must ostensibly be historicized at the same time.

[61] Sibaji Bandyopadhyay, *"East" Meeting "West": A Note on Colonial Chronotopicity* (Calcutta: Jadavpur University, 1994), 17.

[62] Ernest Gellner, *Reason and Culture: The Historic Role of Rationality and Rationalism* (UK: Blackwell, 1992), 19.

participants ... the warm gratification of possessing both a self and a world. ... The world is there to be known and appreciated by the self, the self has its best aspirations supported and endorsed by the world."[63] And the moment we go for a culture-free cognition, we repeat—as Gellner has so effectively shown us—the Descartian mistake, encased within a kind of performative contradiction. The result of going for a culture-free rationality that itself needs a cultural system to sustain is sinister: "perhaps there can be no culture free cognition, any more than there can be a genuine vindication of any world. We cannot escape a contingent, history" [custom and example] "bound culture; and we cannot vindicate it either."[64] To transform this to the context of our case example would stand to mean that it is impossible to rely on a culture-free (meaning, stain-free) rationality of the public sphere. At the same time, it seems impossible again to vindicate, in turn, this irreducible failure. The way this is relevant for us is, while the instrumental and deliberative reason and norms of justice associated with the public sphere have been taken as a model to settle so-called oppressive private matters, what has been bypassed is that "it is virtually impossible to specify clear and exclusive criteria for satisfactory personal relationships[65] ... any more than there can be a genuine vindication of any world." Because, "[i]n culture, unreason is an important gatekeeper."[66]

This cultural cognitive self-understanding is sometimes referred to—in other words—as a "vernacular"[67] understanding instead of the

---

[63] Ibid., 18.

[64] Ibid., 19.

[65] Ibid., 149. With no collective comfort and criteria—this personalist reduction involving a "personal agony" invites a queer but interesting 'personal' solution from Slavoj Zizek—"The role of fantasy hinges on the fact that ... no universal formula or matrix guaranteeing a harmonious sexual relationship with one's partner" [exists]; "because of the lack of this universal formula, every subject has to invent a fantasy of his or her own, a 'private'" [I'll say "personal"] "formula for the sexual relationship—for a man, the relationship with a woman is possible only in as much as she fits his formula." See Slavoj Zizek, *The Plague of Fantasies* (London: Verso, 1997), 7, or vice versa.

[66] Gellner, *Reason and Culture*, 19, 149.

[67] The *vernacular*—as Ann Berger reminds us—in its taxonomic origin "designates the slave born in the house." And this vernacularism because also moots derivatively a language which is domestic, natural, private and not popular or public enough to found a nation, belongs, ostensibly to the age of families before the age of nations. See Ann Berger, "The Popularity of Language: Rousseau and the Mother Tongue," *The Politics of Deconstruction: Jacques Derrida and the Other of Philosophy,* ed. Martin McQuillan (London: Pluto Press, 2007), 98–115. This was Rousseau. Now, the *Oikos* as we had noted

universalized "personal" in which we shall soon find out how the same problem arises—that of the contamination of the personal by the private and the corresponding[68] emergence of the public sphere, but through special forms of historical mediation, and in India and other postcolonial societies with a history of having been through colonization—how the personal soon came to be identified more and more with that institutional introduction of private property and all its corollaries. It is no wonder that today we too tend to confuse the private and the personal (in byaktigoto), irrespective of the cultural system that envelops us. But how about the contamination being originarily infected? Therefore, perhaps its best to examine, after a (universal) Western historical attempt, the state of the contaminated and the emancipated personal in terms of a self-regarding cultural history. And then only the emancipation of this personal as a signifier, from the lineaments of historical contamination, if any, could be more meaningfully grounded.

in the last chapter was also a unit of withholding slaves. The affinity between servitude and the vernacular existence has been interestingly reinforced (post Rousseau) by Hegel and then illuminatingly transformed by Nietzsche. Klossowski (though much in debt to the Kojevian reading of this; Pierre Klossowski, *Nietzsche and the vicious Circle*, trans. Daniel W. Smith (London: Continuum [1997] 2005) puts it thus: if culture is the disavowal of external constraints, then the servile consciousness creates culture to free him from the master: this is autonomy. "Slavery belongs to the essence of culture" (p. 6). "Culture is the product of the slave; and having produced culture, he is now its conscious master (p. 8) … [This is] "The entire cultural, historical and human world that the servile consciousness had begun to construct under the constraint of the *autonomous consciousness,* and through which the *servile consciousness* in turn becomes *autonomous* and triumphs over the consciousness of the master. (p. 9)." But as the external constraints of the "serviles" are disavowed in culture, they do not vanish and remain still "externalizable" (p. 7). The antinomies are not abolished and the reconciliation in favour of social integration does not take place in art—the evidence of autonomous consciousness. "Who is the *adversary*? Who is the *enemy* to be destroyed? … In determining the enemy, thought is able to create its own space, to extend it, to breathe freely" (p. 6). Therefore the cultural (vernacular) self-understanding—particularly in the colonial (masterful) context becomes not only crucial but meaningful. And how the friend/enemy distinction foregrounds the personal will be commented on later.

[68] The specific forms of historical mediation have also undergone interpretations where the vernacular has been pitted against both the "classical" and the "colonial." For the most nuanced statement on this, see Partha Chatterjee, "Introduction: History in the Vernacular," in *History in the Vernacular*, eds. Raziuddin Aquil and Partha Chatterjee (New Delhi: Permanent Black, 2008), 1–24.

## *"Personal" in a Non-Western Definite Discourse: Law*

The general tendency of addressing the personal in the colonies has been in concurrence with the strategies of rational modernity charted in Chapter 1: "Personal in the Public Sphere: The Politics of Modernity." While examining "Orientalist Structures and Restructures" in his classic *Orientalism*, Edward Said makes such an endorsing observation: there he says, consolidation of the general discourse of Orientalism involves, through codification, a "metamorphosis" or conversion of "personal" ("autobiographical," "indulgent") narrative documents of "experience and 'testimony' of Oriental residence to impersonal official documents of 'Orientalist science' 'on which Orientalism in general and later Orientalists in particular can draw, build, and base further scientific observation and description'."[69]

But (not disputing the content of the personal—for the moment—as entailed by Said), while this is true for legal-political administration of the impersonal aesthetic, this might just be different in the domain of culture. In other words, while personal-impersonal translation may be entailed true for definite discourses, amidst indefinite (literary or cultural) discourses, it might be brought to a singular crisis.[70]

This is albeit to start with a disillusionment about which we've been rightfully cautioned. As far the legal-juridical discourse is concerned, there—even in postcolonial societies—we shall find that the public, the private, or the notions of the personal in their universal Western-modern usages are specifically present. These notions have become administered in the West.[71] The opinion that the Indian private sphere lives through "personal laws" is simply incorrect.[72]

---

[69] Edward Said, *Orientalism* (New Delhi: Penguin Books, 2001), 157.

[70] Critics like Ashis Nandy harp on this anticipated disjuncture between the autonomous culture of peoples (evident in wide religiosity and concomitant belief systems) and the statist system, which tends to practice and/or preach rules of administrative inheritance (e.g., secularism), as being germane to the ongoing crisis in non-Western societies. An examination of the merit of such an argument is beyond the scope of this chapter.

[71] "Public" in this "designative" discourse in India broadly means the people of a nation or all (and is inclusive of any class) of the citizens of a state or the community at large. Public also means "open to all the people;" unconcealed, not private. See P. Ramanath Aiyar, *P. Ramanatha Aiyar's Concise Law Dictionary* (New Delhi: Wadhwa Company, 2004), 689; Are we not listening to an audible western rumble?

[72] Let us not be misled by what goes on by the name of *personal laws*; they are but remnants of private or customary law.

Speaking in this legal sense, a person in India is a legal entity that is recognized by the law as the subject of rights and duties and who is capable of suing and be sued. Personal, as in Indian Penal code, is anything that pertains to a person, be it his/her character, conduct, motives, or private affairs. (Note here that private affairs belong to the person/al, and the person/al is not limited to that of the private.) Now, what about the "interactive" state of the private and the personal with us? In this wake, we've learnt and quite correctly that the public/private distinction in West Europe did not correspond with the *ghar/bahir* (i.e., home or inside vs. outside) distinction that had emerged in the nationalist imaginary in India. As a backdrop, it must be remembered all the while that the result of this, according to one dominant narrative, has been simply this: the "colonial rule created a public sphere but left the private sphere for the native elites;"[73] these elites were understandably male, and the so-called private sphere or ghar and the *paribar* continues to be governed by personal laws.[74] Marc Galanter needs special mention for having shown us that this proposition that argues that the personal in India lives through personal laws for the private sphere is no more valid. With the complete obliteration of the *Dharmashastras*—the source of Hindu personal laws—the latter are "administered in the common-law style."[75] And with the growing dispute on common civil code in postcolonial India, it is, however, evident that with the demand in the face of complaints of communal exceptionalism, personal laws will more and more comply with the paradigms of modern law and gender revision; add to this—as Galanter points out—how local laws are being increasingly brought to conform to national laws. Therefore, the proposed paradigm of personal laws for the private sphere, thus, proving their coalition collapses and it is safe to mark here at the most the mimetic similarity of Western paradigms of law as we had held earlier.

---

[73] Amir Ali, "Evolution of Public Sphere in India," *Economic and Political Weekly* 36 no. 26 (2001, June 30), 2419–25.

[74] To explore interesting reproductive similarity and differences in relation to this typology in colonial histories, see Aziz Al-Azmeh, ed., *Islamic Law: Social and Historical Contexts* (London: Routledge, 1988).

[75] Marc Galanter, *Law and Society in Modern India* (Bombay: Oxford University Press, 1992), 31; For a dependable account of how personal laws were demarcated and separated as a "special area of law" in 1860–61, see Samita Sen, "Offences Against Marriage: Negotiating Custom in Colonial Bengal," in *A Question of Silence: The Sexual Economics of Modern India*, eds. Mary E. John and Janaki Nair (New Delhi: Kali for Women, 1998), 77–110.

## *Personal vis-à-vis Private/Public in Non-Western Indefinite Discourses: A Cultural History*

To bypass this legal discourse where the Western inscription is directly visible, we have to inquire into the cultural-cognitive self-understanding of ours and take a linguistic turn.

A remote instance is given here. In 19th century Bengal, "personal hygiene" (*byaktigoto sasthyobidhi*) was the parallel classificatory scheme besides the emergence of "public health" and "national health" regimes.[76] To plot an easy binary from this, it would be personal versus public/ national without exercising the notion of the private, but such separate excerpts of numerous usage will not help us go very far. It would rather be instructive not to negatively define the personal anymore (as to what it is not or not private) but try and locate the personal in its (for the moment representable) positivity (as to what it is).

## *The Emergence of Byaktigoto (Our Personal) vis-à-vis the Private*

Now, how do we name and historicize the personal vis-à-vis the private for us and show the way the personal appears in a particular cultural lexicon? A very interesting anthropological study could be used to foreground the discussion before we historicize it. In a study on the construction of the person in Bengal and Tamil Nadu—two states in India—it has been contended that "[p]ersons are culturally constructed as relatives (*attaiya kutum*) in groups, and groups in alliance"[77] that reconstruct the personal as against "units of equivalence created by blood ties in a line and marriage ties among sets of lines."[78] One of these lines is neighbourhood, which generates personal relationship (*para attaiya*) through shared locality apart from blood and marriage alliances.[79] This notion of "shared locality" contributing to the formation of personal relationships besides the usual

---

[76] Pradip Basu, ed. *Samayiki, Puruno Samoyik Patrer Prabandha Samkalan*, Vol I: 1856 1901 [Bengali] (Calcuta: Ananda Publishers, 1998), 305.

[77] Lina Fruzzeti. Akos Ostor, and Steve Burnett, "The Cultural Construction of the Person in Bengal and Tamil Nadu," in *Concepts of Person: Kinship, Caste and Marriage in India*, eds. Akos Ostor, Lina Fruzzeti, and Steve Burnett (New Delhi: Oxford University Press, 1983), 8–30.

[78] Ibid., 15.

[79] Ibid.

contours of blood kinship or marriage contracts (in established discourse), please notice, is somewhere in between the private space and the public sphere where public opinion is formed and actually belongs to neither of them. This subjectivity rendered through para is peculiarly Indian. However, the most interesting part in this project, if we want to extend it, is that so far as our cultural-cognitive self-understanding is concerned, the lexeme byaktigoto in Bengali and *byaktigat* in Hindi are held to stand for both private and personal at the same time and byaktigoto originally meant the personal dimension without the privative rider (byaktigoto— that which goes to the person—a site of expression as if).[80] There are no separate words[81] to designate them differently; and because a word brings in a corresponding world, we think this is a crucial moment where the traditional binary that has been always pitted, that is, public/private, is demonstrably found absent in us,[82] but the moment one utters "byaktigat" or byaktigoto, personal and private are easily and wrongly coalesced (while we shall find that the personal is not necessarily opposed to the public). In fact, they must reflect separate moments: byaktigoto, in the first internal sense, entails the expressed notion of the individual in expression or matters that belong "to" the person (personal-personal); the second will entail the notion of byaktigoto *sampatti* or private property: this was the later development (i.e., the sense of private ownership) that came to be associated with byaktigoto. Hence, this limits and modifies our cultural self-understanding to an unlimited extent; but then because byaktigoto stands for both personal and private, one must be cautious about the contamination of property in byaktigoto and should not try to impose this view that the moment we use byaktigoto, it cannot but mean private and invoke notions of privacy where all others have to be ritually excluded. In the following section, we shall emerge with a case study where the collective nature of the personal enters severely and the vernacularisms attached to that of the public/private and the personal are brought to a significant moment of crisis and not sublated in a moment of resolution.

---

[80] Other social dialects will reveal other features; I apologize for knowing only these two Indian languages.

[81] The word private in English today is found apart from Indian law in such floating utterances in Kolkata when "bus drivers roundly curse cars that block their passage with the epithet 'Private!'." See Janaki Nair, "Beauty by Banning," *The Telegraph*, October 23, 2003, Kolkata edition.

[82] Though in some discourses, as will be argued, this is retained.

# A Case Study: "Our Personal" as Life-communal: Rabindranath and the Felt Community of "Public" Emotions

On the issue of a public condolence meeting after the passing away of Bankimchandra Chattopadhyay (the great Bengali litterateur and arguably the first theorist of modernity in India), there was a debate[83] between Nabin Chandra Sen and Rabindranath Tagore. Sen's contention was that grief is a personal emotion (in the privative sense) and, therefore, a public condolence meeting is quite meaningless and simply a bad European inheritance; the show is totally artificial with the public not at all aggrieved and rather going for an evening's amusement. Tagore retorted by saying that to consider personal grief as only a privative emotion would be a mistake. Or otherwise why is there ceremonial mourning at the death of our close ones? "At the death of one's father whether one is really aggrieved or not is unimportant; *samaj* [our community][84] says you are bound to express grief before me and that according to my customs."[85] Tagore argues, "The way in our country 'ceremonial mourning of father's death is staged in the open and as it is incumbent upon every bereaved one that he mourns the loss of his father also in the open,"[86] there is nothing wrong in holding a public condolence meeting. Tagore also emphasizes how through social mourning, the excessive nature of personal loss becomes somewhat tolerable. Therefore, from Tagore's argument we can infer three things:

1. Personal grief in our samaj is bound by customs and, therefore, is not private; it can be collectively shared through symbolic behavior;

[83] We are indebted to Partha Chatterjee for attracting our attention to this debate. See Partha Chatterjee, "On Civil and Political Society in Post Colonial Democracies," in *Civil Society: History and Possibilities*, eds. Sudipta Kaviraj and Sunil Khilnani (New Delhi: Foundation Books, Cambridge University Press, 2002), 165–78.

[84] Tagore's use of *samaj* (as a community/collection of communities) could be deployed to mark its difference from the Western *society*. See Partha Chatterjee, "Review of *Tika Tippani* by Pradyumna Bhattacharya", *Baromas* 20, no. 1 (2000), 175–77, (in Bengali). I've detailed elsewhere how the personal being *samajik* or customary and pre-historical has a collective-communitarian nature as against the *private* which blossoms forth in historical, Western 'society' established by contract (A. Chattopadhyaya, "Private/Public Dwander Baire: Personal/*Byaktigoto* Niye Notun Kichoo." *Ababhas* 5, no. 3 (2005), 91–108, (Bengali).

[85] Rabindranath Thakur, "Shoksawbha," in *Prabandha Samagra* (Kolkata: Bikas Grantha Bhavan, 2003), II: 505–10; insertion mine.

[86] Ibid., 507.

2. Personal grief being indeterminate, nobody knows whether one is really aggrieved or not; this helps grief retain its personal nature;
3. Extending further in such discourses, personal and private may be shown to have been different.

Let us expand on the above inferences:

*Personal Grief in our Samaj: Samaj as Life-community*
"Personal" or byaktigoto in India as will be seen and which we've been referring to, after this exercise, was and has never been an unencumbered one; rather, it was the existence of the algorithm personal-personal as life-communal (*jaiba-samajik*) that was endorsed by Rabindranath Thakur, thus, once more endorsing our thesis: personal is not private. Furthering this, we might want to argue that the "impersonalization of the public realm," activated by the colonial-imperial intervention as has often been alleged, now particularly in the critical neo-Gandhian discourse,[87] is not correct.

Let us follow Rabindranath as his argument unfolds. To justify a public condolence meeting after Bankim's death as against Nabin Chandra Sen who had argued that grief is a personal[88] emotion (in the privative sense), Rabindranath argues (as we've noted before) that while acknowledging that grief at a relative's death is a personal emotion, what do we do as part of the public, when someone dies who is not a relative but a well wisher of the public? Tagore will answer this later. Before that he argues that grief is essentially personal, but only till the time we find "what is mine and what belongs to society-municipality resists demarcation."[89]

Though samaj now has come to stand for the English society and *samajik* for social, the correspondence is again more of historical convenience than a necessary relation. Samaj or samajik as theorized in the indigenous discourse (most significantly by Bhudev Mukhopadhyaya) first resembles a mythical discourse more than a historical one, something

---

[87] Ashis Nandy, "The Illegitimacy of Nationalism: Rabindranath Tagore and the Politics of Self," in *Return from Exile* (New Delhi: Oxford University Press, 2001).

[88] And I think we should take more caution in translating *byaktigoto*, which when translated as "intimate" would have been more happily rendered if it were "personal;" intimacy in Bengali—even by plain lexiological standards—is *ghonisthota*, meaning *closeness*. And may we insert that intimacy in Western predicament and even in postcolonial spheres is absolutely a different paradigm.

[89] Rabindranath Thakur, "Shoksabha," in *Prabandha Samagra* (Kolkata: Bikas Grantha Bhavan, 2003), II: 505–10 (italics mine).

that is without a beginning, a middle, and an end—an organic indestructible body than an entity with linear growth; the hunch is that, because it has no origin, it cannot be destroyed either, though it may come under cloud during alien rule.[90] A weak but formative rendering of samaj would be—borrowing from Max Scheler,[91] who borrowed from Ferdinand Tonnies—life-community. "First, the society as opposed to the natural unit of life-community, is to be defined as an artificial unit of individuals having no original 'living with one another;'"[92] second, society's essential unit is based on conventions, usage, or contracts: the essential private Law. Mores, customs, and solidarity belong to the life-community. Fiction, force (the majority principle) contributes to the construction of the "common will" in society marked by a shared distrust of "of all in all,"[93] life-community is marked by true solidarity ("one for all" and "all for one") unlike "the elements of society [which] are ... of equal value because they enter the picture as such elements solely by virtue of their formal character as single persons, not by virtue of their nonformal [materialen] contents of individuality."[94] While in society "the principle of exclusive self-responsibility of each for his actions is realized,"[95] in life-community "the community itself is responsible, while everyone of its members remains coresponsible to the degree of his importance within the community."[96] "The basic nexus is this: there can be no society without a life community (though there can be life community without society)." Thus, there is no contract to keep contracts, but the keeping of contracts is placed within the symbolic network of mutual "moral faithfulness" (not a broader contract as Carole Pateman construes it.[97] My conclusion

---

[90] Bhudeb Mukhopadhyaya, "Samajik Probondho," in *Bhuudeb Rachanasambhar*, ed. Pramathanath Bishi (Kolkata: Mitra O Ghosh, 1968), 1–263.

[91] Max Scheler, *Formalism in Ethics and Non-formal Ethics of Values*, trans. Manfred S. Frings and Roger L. Funk (Evanston, IL: Northwestern University Press, 1973).

[92] Ibid., 528.

[93] Ibid., 529.

[94] Ibid., 530.

[95] Ibid., 531.

[96] Ibid.

[97] Carole Pateman does not agree that Hegel is successful in his attempt and is rather limited to transcending just one part of the Kantian argument that saw personal right, among others, in the manifest act of pointing out "this is my wife" where a "thing" is, accidentally, a person. See Carole Pateman, "Hegel, Marriage, and the Standpoint of Contract," in *Feminist Interpretations of G. W. F. Hegel,* ed. Patricia Jagentowicz Mills (PA: The Pennsylvania State University Press, 1996), 209–23. But I disagree with Pateman and reiterate that there *is* a moment of personal in Hegel (as will be evident in the later chapter) which precedes the contamination of property.

from this is simple: the personal (as within a life community) can exist without the private, but the private cannot do so without the support of the personal; in order to be actual it has to reiterate this forged kinship again and again and at the same time cloak it.

## Personal Grief Being Indeterminate: Indeterminate Grief

The question of indeterminacy emerges in stark relief when Tagore invokes the authenticity of grief at one's parents' death. "At the death of one's father whether one is really aggrieved or not is unimportant; samaj says you are bound to express grief before me and that according to my customs ('niyam')."[98] Why? "Because reverence for one's father is indispensable for the good of society." And, therefore, irrespective of great, unbearable grief, one still has to go through minute details of rituals that have been disciplinarily/conventionally/customarily (*anusashaner dara*) laid down through practice.[99] It seems, therefore, that Rabindranath is preparing the grounds to make his case for the public condolence meeting also by arguing that even before Europe had set such an example, we already had ourselves rule-bound and differentiated through discipline by and in our "samaj."[100] The elaboration upon this function by Rabindranath follows a specific route: he says, "our society is a familial society." Reverence for parental authorities is the bonding that sustains this society, therefore an expression of grief "is not merely private but within social customs."[101]

This much to endorse that byaktigoto in a Bengali-Indian culture has never been private-personal.

Truly, it is nearly impossible to predict, understand, and anticipate real pain, but that rarely makes pain "private." This unknowingness only makes pain determinately personal. But even personal and byaktigoto (or our personal)—are they the same? Where grief is not privately personal but within customary norms of the life-community, it may be hazarded that the

---

98 Tagore, "Shoksabha," 506.
99 Note this exhortation in one of his great novels *Gora*, "That marriage in our country is not private, but familial: Binay pursuing this topic has written extensively in newspapers with a lot of pride, and himself has not entertained any such wish in this regard too." See Rabindranath Thakur, "Gora," in *Uponyas Sangraha* (Kolkata: Juthika Book Stall, 2002), 1–320. Here Rabindranath is clearly pursuing the *byatktigoto* (rendered as personal) as within the deplorable *private-personal* register.
100 Rabindranath's usage of "*samaj*," as referred to before, stands for *a collection of communities* that may be used to endorse our notion of *life-communities*; also note that he often contrasts *samaj* with the nation-state.
101 Rabindranath, "Shoksabha," 507.

indeterminateness built into grief is, thus, undermined being imbricated within customs. Let us hear Rabindranath closely as to what he has to say on this: "[S]amaj approaches us and says, whether your grief is yours or not does not call for questions or answers," so whether your grief is yours or not invokes the indeterminacy innate in the substantive reality of grief and only formally identifies it without destroying its content—whatever it is.

## Our Public as Jonosadharon and Public Sphere as Janamatakhetra: The Emergence of the Nonpublic and Nonprivate

While personal is life-communal and not opposed to the public, as it is with the private, it is not merely political in the sense in which the private could be politicized. How personal could be political in a very different sense would be picked up later; in this section, we shall deal with the fact as to why, in the standard sense, this "publicalization" (if we may) fails at our cultural site. Arguably, it directly derives from the nature of the cultural entity that our "public" becomes. For this, we can extract from Rabindranath, albeit with or without his permission, the concept of an "our public" (which is, in fact, a nonpublic[102]) marking the impossibility of the discursive translation of the "private is public" (to preface *personal is political* in some genre of feminism), if not in infrastructural but in cognitive terms.

## The Emergence of "Our" Nonpublic

Recently, a historian has traced the colonial attempts to institute the Indian public to 1793 when the regulations of Lord Cornwallis were "printed

---

[102] The use of such a nonpublic should be distinguished from its standard formulations in Western political theory. Jurgen Habermas points out, that drawing from Hobbes, it was John Rawls who proposed that "the sought-for public agreement must be supported by private, non-public reasons." See Jurgen Habermas, *The Inclusion of the Other: Studies in Political Theory* (Cambridge, MA: The MIT Press, 1998), 85. This is the agreement or rational consensus based on public reasoning and public reasons. "But these reasons cannot be inspected by everyone in common, given that the public use of reason depends on a platform that can only be constructed on the basis of nonpublic reasons." (p. 86). My use of the term *nonpublic* is absolutely in terms of public pedagogical competence rather than the *moral-substantial* viewpoints of different persons (waiting to be transcended) as argued by Habermas.

and promulgated" for the Indian public and a special press was set up for the purpose.[103] But the most emphatic attempt at constituting the public and public opinion was through nationalist mobilization. Inevitable in it was the resisting tendency to use the emerging media forms and harp on a difference.[104] But as will have been evident, to try to institute the public is not necessarily to arrive at it; second, this arrival or departure will, therefore, be always incomplete, confused, and divisive. And that is what keeps our personal—if any—intact along with the raving inequalities that mock such formal equality even though a "proletarian public sphere" could not be found. Later, we shall see how Tagore repents this phenomenon. To understand that we have to inquire into the cultural-cognitive self-understanding of ours. Not only with public and private, but same with the personal. Simply put, the public in India was invested in symbolicity.[105] It emerged as a distant signified in the process of colonial accumulation of administrative meaning. (Certain sites especially symbolized publicness— ghats for bathing, bazaars or markets. Here market then is both a metaphor and metonymy of the public space.) A phenomenology of colonial everyday life, however, reveals a distinction between "office" and "home" that stood for such typologies but only remotely. And the distinctive displacement of the corresponding sign systems revealed for instance when Swami Vivekananda was advising his disciple Saratchandra Chakraborty to wear European dress at the office[106] and general Bengali

---

[103] Rajat Kanta Ray, *The Felt Community, Commonality and Mentality Before the Emergence of Indian Nationalism* (New Delhi: Oxford University Press, 2003), 548–49.

[104] The result, as has been pointed out in the subalternist discourse, was dominance without hegemony. Similarly, the nationalist narrative could not but exclude the autonomous domains of politics.

[105] Only later did it take the stringent and mostly administratively rigorous form of the distinction between the public sphere of the economy and the sphere that would belong to private interest and investment. The nuanced details of the evolution of this sphere in the realm of the economy, public administration, and planning included would reveal interesting and different details than the usual one where the public sphere emerges as always already within the category of the European bourgeois society and could be studied as a pale inflection of it. I owe this point to Dwaipayan Bhattacharya.

[106] Though Beteille correctly disputes this by arguing that anthropological examples show in our case, "household" and "office" were never fully separated; in the rural areas, when an anthropologist is taken around inside the house and all spaces are exposed to his field' vision, Beteille thinks, the notion of hospitality overrides the notion of privacy. See Andre Beteille, *Equality and Universality: Essays in Social and Political Theory* (Delhi: Oxford University Press, 2003), 103. There are also feminist accounts who discover the kitchen or the bedroom as constructing a house within a house with their own architectonic codes and subnorms of privacy; the household is therefore a split metaphor.

dress at home.[107] "Public" stood for terms like "*sarba sadharan*" in Bengali;[108] sarba sadharan was transmuted to mean *janasadharan* or *janagan* later.[109] In Hindi janta started to stand for this audience formed by anonymous individuals. It is clear that unlike the sphere of public opinion connected to political authority in the West, we refer to the public as a group of anonymous collectivities (close to the word "crowd" in the West). Second, public also invokes the notions of *sarkari* or governmental in us but not the hard notion of the Western public.[110]

Through the negotiation of certain disputes among these two then, we could use this opportunity to explore the status of "our personal" or byaktigoto in relation to the janata or *sadharon* and the political in India. Inscribed within the rigours of a nonpublic or janta, we may want to delineate the history of our nonpublic/nonprivate, janta, sadhahron, *byaktikhetra*, etc. (the vernacular forms of public and quasi public) in conversation with a number of useful standing notions drawn from the Indian discussion of the public sphere (here we shall limit ourselves

[107] It has been pointed out in one such commentary on this that such an advice coincided with the material/spiritual distinction of the native by which the women's question was defeated but at the same time helped imagine an "our" modernity at the cost of excluding the women from the public sphere. For our purpose it might suffice that this could also be construed to have been complicit with the Kantian paradigm of the enlightenment: obey when you are employed with a designated duty (in a particular civil post or office entrusted to him); you are free to criticize when you are left to yourself and "your public." See Immanuel Kant, "What is Enlightenment?" in *Critique of Practical Reason, and Other Writings in Moral Philosophy,* trans. L. W. Beck (New York, NY: Garland Publishing, 1976), 288–89.

[108] In this sense, in a perceptive essay on the notion of the public in India, Andre Beteille has correctly noted, "The way people use public, in that the substantive sense of 'all the members of the community taken together'" is sometimes present. See Andre Beteille, *Equality and Universality: Essays in Social and Political* Theory (Delhi: Oxford University Press, 2003), 99.

[109] Gautam Bhadra traces the word *sadharon* in Bengali to the second phase of 19th century Bengal. The word in its self-description carried the notions of the average and the ordinary—they being the opposites of extraordinary, "special" or *bishesh*. The task of converting this *sadharon* to the *public* was the task of modernity's pedagogic mission. Public meetings were seen in this sense as exercises in public instruction and advocacy. See Gautam Bhadra, *Jal Rajar Katha: Bardhamaner Pratapchand* (Kolkata: Ananda Publishers, 2002), 206. I shall return to this point again.

[110] But apart from legal discourse the word "public" is popularly transmitted in India via such idioms of contemporary popular culture instanced in the film song "*Yeh public jo hai, sub jaanti hai*;" the "it knows everything ... " of the song, suggests that the public knows more things than are generally up for grabs in ... the "marketplace of the knowable." See Shuddha @sarai.net, 'Discussing the Public Domain' in *Sarai Reader 01* (New Delhi: Sarai-CSDS, 2001), 1.

to making liminal but understandable references). Briefly, our idea of a nonpublic (not in the Rawlsian sense but in the vernacular sense of sadaharon [ordinary or mundane) or aam janta [average] or nonprivate, etc.) is derived largely from the idea of nobodies. Persons in India who are generally held to be publicly consequential, and a majority of the others who are condemned to move as private individuals only—without security cover, publicity, or mass importance—are not public persons. The beggars who copulate on the footpath are not, in terms of essence, even private individuals. The somebodies are those whose individuality— by virtue of property, office or "manipulative coping"—are never lost in the average vagueness or the forced inferiority of the "aam janta." But a nobody is he/she who as a member of the anonymous ordinary collective (janta) and even as an individual is "the 'one' who in fact lives the life of the individual," [and] "who in the end is no one."[111]

Now if this is the state of the pubic of Western discourse getting nearly displaced in a postcolonial society as nonpublic in terms of both competence and consequence for the rights bearing agents, it seems obvious Gandhi (explained in Chapter 2) was not hinting at the public of the Western rubric. To reiterate, the term public is rather retained for the elite property owning pseudo sovereign person attached to state offices and power. For them—according to Gandhi—privacy is more important or meaningful in the sense of significant, but instead of instructing on retaining the domain, Gandhi seems to suggest—going by our reading— that the private of the public persons should be asked to come to a collection and integrated at the level of the personal that is also the level of the message. This is in response to the original contamination suffered by the personal in the hands of property. The distinction then could be authenticated in the second part which is haunted by the question, what is this "public/social duty"? Rabindranath answers,

> The way in our country "ceremonial mourning of father's death" ("pitrishraddha") is staged in the open ("prokashye") and as it is incumbent upon every bereaved one that he mourns the loss of his father also in the open, similarly, in the case of a great person—who has had been the well wisher of the public—his death should occasion the expression of condolence in an open meeting.[112]

---

[111] To mark this existential drift of the nonpublic, I draw upon Theodore Kisiel, *The Genesis of Heidegger's Being and Time* (Berkley, CA: University of California Press, 1993), 257–60.
[112] Rabindranath, "Shoksabha," 507.

But what is the "public" in relation to the Bengali? Rabindranath holds, though public has entered/ infected or contaminated the familial—which is of course well understood, at the same time it is impossible to render it in Bengali, but irrespective of the impossibility of this linguistic translation, the ordinary/common people have comprehended the term "public" (*sadharener bodhgamya hoteche*), and "with the appearance of the public besides the family, the appearance of public duties seem inevitable."[113] What is the utility of this public mourning or shoksabha? Rabindranath elaborates: public appearance of emotions puts a brake on the overwhelming expression of private grief possible behind a closed door; which, however, does not make public mourning insignificant![114] Hence, the necessity of public condolence meetings! But Rabindranath at the same time senses a problem: our public (sadharon) at the present point of time rarely can identify its benevolent icons, it is still in its childhood—unaware of its duties—that is, public duties and that is why such meetings are significant twice over. Such meetings will educate the public in its social duties and bring them to adulthood.[115] Is this, to stay with Rabindranath for a while, the modern pedagogic mission of modernization through public education?

Two conclusions emerge from the previous account: Firstly, it could be—again—no more true that the personal existed in India in a deeply individualistic selfish mode that could give credence to the contemporary liberal appropriations and grievances trying to invoke an originary personal against a public which was—historically speaking—never there. Secondly, "public" resists direct cultural translation but is only governable through a hermeneutic self-understanding. Again, the Bengali word sadharan/sadharon meaning common, ordinary or average is noticed to have had been in circulation as "our metaphor" for the word public. The state of sadharon becoming public was considered to have been a matter of continuous public education by way of acquiring civic virtues. To say that our janta or sadharon have become public is to assume that this pedagogy is complete. But the public being incompetent, taking the private to the public is ineffective. And therefore, the standard, particular discursive publicalization (if I may) of the private will just flop having sensed this unbecoming.

When byaktigoto (subsuming both the private and the personal) is then reductively used to imitate the graph private/public, what is made

---

[113] Ibid., 508.
[114] Ibid., 507–08.
[115] Ibid., 508.

out is that—the familial or life-communitarian confronts the average-the ordinary and the incompetent.[116] Then it remains to be discovered what actually could work for us: how could our personal negotiate the political—atleast culturally?

## The Person and Politics! A Cultural-vernacular Answer

Therefore, having become convinced of the separation of the personal and the private in terms of culture, history: cultural history, it is incumbent upon us to undertake the examination of the longer moment when a simple-analytical or a specific-cultural notion like personal could assume the body of the political without a minimal or no recourse to the private becoming the public. That is—in fact—our challenge! The political nature of the person overflowing the private-public distinction was noticed in Chapter I. Here we arrive at it culturally.

### The Founding Moment: A (Colonial, Cultural) Political Epistemology of the Personal

One of the doyens of the "new age" in (modern!) Bengal, that is, the 19th century and the first years of the 20th century—Ramendra Sundar Trivedi—remembered for his interventionist writings trying to domesticate science in Bengal, in the article "Mukti"[117] turns his torch on the identity that is personal. In fact, he is one of the few authors who uses the word personal in original, untranslated English and tries to address it from a noncognitivist, albeit a cultural epistemic viewpoint. Having created a backdrop by arguing that, in India—particularly in nondualist philosophy—a rigorous distinction between the subject and the object is

---

[116] I have already noticed how Gautam Bhadra traces the word *sadharan* in Bengali to the second phase of 19th century Bengal. Note again that the word in its self-description carried the notions of average and ordinary—they being the opposites of "extraordinary," "special," or *bishesh*. For more on an incompatible public and private (though trapped within the binary), see T. N. Madan, "Of the Social Categories 'Private' and 'Public': Considerations of Cultural Context," in Mahajan 2003; Andre Beteille, *Equality and Universality: Essays in Social and Political Theory* (Delhi: Oxford University Press, 2003).

[117] Ramendra Sundar Trivedi, "Mukti" in *Jiggasa* (Kolkata: Granthamala, 1982), 171–209.

not maintained, Trivedi argues that it is, thus, possible for me to see myself "subject I" and the "object I" both in the same person. However, after this quick chip, Trivedi takes on the Western category on a comparativist scale,

> In English there is a word (*"katha"*) called personal identity;[118] it means yesterday's I (*"kalker ami"*) and today's I (*"ajker ami"*) are both the same persons; but this unity belongs to the realm of the object self (*gneyo amar*), not the subject-self (*gnata*) that is knowing. The way I saw myself yesterday, I do not see myself that way today, though the fact that the 'I' remains intact is understood by the significance of the statement. Difference in vision does not suffice to provoke anybody to suspect the unity of both the selves. My childhood self, my young self and today's aged self are the same: they all are me.[119]

But this unity, Trivedi cautions us invoking Western experts, is incomplete, unsaturated, and never full. Yesterday's me does not resemble in full today's me but still it is me.

Given the background assumptions operative here that foreground Trivedi's text curiously, it will be interesting to try and historicize it or recover a moment of prior politicization. Simply put, it is this: is he not trying to chart a difference for his colonized self by deploying the categories of personal identity (fraught with discontinuity)? (Yesterday's me is not today's me—as I know them, see or read them. In other words how can the pre-colonized or noncolonized self resemble the colonial self?) Because well, finally, one negotiates with the world with one's own self and the self is re-encumbered time and again. To give meaning to the re-encumbrance (if I may use the term) that will situate the colonial self in difference with the past times and will aid the knowing "I" to come to terms with the governed and the known "me" (an object of colonial knowledge?). Trivedi's project is only apparently epistemological in plain cognitive terms; in fact, one might argue, this is the native elite's colonial or cultural-political epistemology of vengeance. Our point, however, is to note the allegorical re-inscription of the personal to serve the political in those times and in these terms. More so, because the question of (personal) identity did not involve questions of privacy. Therefore, it is very possible to politicize the personal (the personal-personal algorithm) without taking any recourse to the standard private paradigm—taken as indispensable

---

[118] Originally in English (italics mine).
[119] Ibid., 198.

in various social identity movements. Trivedi, if I'm correct, would be remembered as one of the grand precursors of this departure.

Now, if this is Trivedi's moment of arrival and departure—the knowledge of the person considered from within a collective—it is best that we anticipate its results from within the canons of the theory of the personal.

## Concluding Remarks: The Emergence of Cultural Collective Persons and the Personal as Essence

The cultural narrative trajectory of "our personal" and byaktigoto then charts a discourse antithetical to a normalized, laboured recuperation of the personal as given in the previous section dealing with the mere history of the personal. In byaktigoto, the privative interpellation remains dispelled as if in an always already existing form; the contamination comes in an original form whose origin is, subsequently, lost. We shall meditate more on this, inquiring whether "culture" at all sanctions or abolishes this search for origins; for the moment, let us rehearse the findings of this chapter so that we can have the rightful transition to the next one.

In the cultural taxonomic predication, while byaktigoto in the first sense could be construed as our personal, there is an independent autonomous discourse of byaktigoto that could well serve as the prehistory of such an "our personal."

Tagore's ritual mourner is the cultural collective person; what he invokes is the emergent status of public rituals and the emergence of a new civic culture in the wake of justifying public condolence meetings. This is more possible because, as we might want to argue, personal is not opposed to the public. But the reverse contamination suffered by the public sphere in the hands of our vernacular culture makes it sure that it lacks the competence required to make it a vibrant one. Therefore, the translation of private issues to a public one would not elicit successful answers as one would expect in a Western one. The private emerges distinctly separate from such a personal (with a life-communitarian bent) in this discourse.

The cultural collective person as available in Scheler is a complex concept. Distinguishing the scholar ("who knows and discerns 'much'" of the fortuitous circumstances of things [polymathia—knowledge of many facts]) and the explorer ("the person with the greatest ability to predict and control development around him"[120]) from the cultured man, Scheler goes on to present his summary:

> The cultured person is one who has acquired in the world a personal structure, an inclusive concept of ideally mobile patterns superimposed on each other, in order to arrive at one single way to view the world, to think, comprehend, judge, and deal with the world and any of its fortuitous manifestations-patterns anterior to fortuitous experience, capable of utilizing and integrating the experience into the entity of their personal "world." This is knowledge of culture.[121]

The Schelerian concept of cultural collective person is a step ahead than this. But before we finally arrive at it, let us rehearse the prominent elements of his articulation:

> Culture is a category of being, not of knowledge and experience and that which mould the entire being of man ... shaping a living entity within the order of time ... this cultural being of the person corresponds in each case to one specific world, to a "microcosm," an entity in itself ... a world entity in which all essential ideas and values find themselves reproduced and organized into structural order. ... One such "universe," summed up and encompassed in one particular human being, is the world of culture. In this context, Plato, Dante, Goethe, Kant each have their world.[122]

The meaning, therefore, of having a world of one's own while being in the same world is a world that is self-encompassing, extending outward to an infinite externality and then folding back unto itself, as if harboring a narrative nature within.

On Trivedi's tirade with the political epistemology of the personal, let us conclude, it is a knowledge that is no knowledge at all. "[K]nowledge of culture is fully digested and assimilated knowledge which has become life and function ... in which origin and derivation can no longer be traced.[123] 'A knowledge about which one neither need nor can reflect'."[124] Scheler, therefore, denies the laboured politicization of the personal:

> It is a knowledge fully prepared for every concrete situation, ready to act, which has become "second nature" and fully adapted to the concrete

---

[120] Max Scheler, *Philosophical Perspectives*, trans. Oscar A. Haac (Boston, MA: Beacon Press, 1958), 47.

[121] Ibid.

[122] Ibid., 19.

[123] Ibid., 36.

[124] William James; cited in Scheler, *Philosophical Perspectives*, 36.

> task ... like a natural skin. [...] It is not an application of concepts, rules, and
> principles to facts, but a possession, an immediate perception of thing[s].[125]

This possession, as evident, is distinctly personal. And indeterminate.

The cultural politics can, therefore, only be unconscious. It is not "a desire to make egocentric self-planning ... the growth of culture happens and takes place behind the back of mere intent and mere will."[126] But that which has become second nature is also essential; it cannot be disparate, consciously arbitrary, and transitory. Then previously we've had the personal as contingent and circumstantially fortuitous (such as in Hegel); now the personal emerges as essential. A few more comments are in order.

A disparate anarchy of "fortuitous," distributed facts cannot be grasped or understood "except through an infinite series of experiences and observations" that reveal the "essential structure of the entire world."[127] According to Scheler, this is culture. "For culture, necessarily, includes a perspective, anterior to experience, of realms of essence of stages and levels of being, which we know exist but which we also know are devoid of content for us."[128] This knowledge and experience of essence is the source of the knowledge of culture that develops as its function and becomes, so to speak, its blood and life.[129] The love for the world becomes philosophia—the love for essence.[130] To "strive for culture means to try, with loving fervor, to participate ontologically and take all aspects of nature and history that are essential to the world, and not just fortuitous essence and circumstance."[131]

This essence could be sensed more easily if we rehearse that the personal has always been confused with that of the individual person, where the private emerges as the justification of the individualism of the individual person—the liberal and the communitarian conundrum—once again. But this is, as it comes out of the earlier stated—and more so from the Schelerian analysis—misleading and wrongly achieved. Truly so! The liberal and the communitarian debate is meaningless if we concur with Scheler: the individual person is co-original with other persons,

---

[125] Ibid., 24.
[126] Ibid., 31.
[127] Ibid., 19.
[128] Ibid., 37.
[129] Ibid., 38.
[130] Ibid., 20.
[131] Ibid., 20.

and in every act-content the community is co-given, "the person is equal in origin to the whole."[132] The "social person" is "either [an] individual person" or a "collective person." With this, we establish a link with the point with which we had started the concluding summary.

It is here that we can directly relate our discussion of "group personality"[133] to what Scheler articulates as group persons.

> The collective person is not a kind of "sum" or a kind of artificial or real collection of individual persons. ... The collective or group person is not composed of individual persons in the sense that it derives its existence from such a composition ... it is an experienced reality and not a construction, although it is a starting point for constructions of all types.[134]

Haldar's question could be asked here too; in fact, Scheler anticipates that, "If one asks whether the collective person has a 'consciousness-of' that is different from and independent of the consciousness-of of the individual person, the answer depends on the meaning of the question. No doubt the collective person does possess a 'consciousness-of' that is different and independent of the consciousness-of of the individual person."[135]

> [Further] the collective person with its world is not fully experienced in any of its member-persons in terms of duration, content, and range of effectiveness. Indeed, it belongs to the essence of all collective persons to have member persons who are also individual persons; but the collective person's existence, with its strict continuity as a collective person, is not connected to the same individual persons. In relation to the collective person the latter are freely variable and in principle, replaceable. Through death and in other ways they lose their membership in the collective person. And the same individual persons can also belong to different collective persons, for example, to a nation and to a church.[136]

This nearly coincides with the juridical description of legal group personality—one of our central points in the book, and more specifically pursued in the part on Hiralal Haldar (Chapter 5). Anticipating the

---

[132] Max. Scheler, *Formalism in Ethics and Non-formal Ethics of Values.* trans. Manfred S. Frings and Roger L. Funk. (Evanston, IL: Northwestern University Press, 1973), 524.

[133] Will be pursued extensively in Chapter 5.

[134] Scheler, *Formalism in Ethics and Non-formal Ethics of Values*, 522.

[135] Ibid., 522–23.

[136] Ibid., 523–24.

conclusion, let us rehearse here that the transit in modernity, is not—as Weber had it—from personality to impersonality but, as we shall show with demonstrative fervor, from one kind of personality (natural) to another (institutional, legal, or fictional).

# 4

# Toward a Theory of the (New) Personal

## I

## The First Philosophy of the Personal: Nietzsche

This collective person of culture that we were meditating on in the last chapter has had its stark and classical parentage, one would be surprised to note, in Nietzsche. The exercise begins with his deeply nourished disillusionment and disjunction with Aristotle. Aristotle is accused by Nietzsche of having destroyed the force of the personal by taking recourse to concepts and not metaphors. "For Aristotle, metaphorical writing is the sign not of an affirmative and flourishing type of life but of a lack of maturity, a state of incompletion."[1] Nietzsche precisely reverses this order. He invokes the pre-Socratics (or pre-Platonists) as a refutation of Aristotle and shows how the concept effaces the metaphor and drowns personality—"metaphor foregrounds the 'personality' which is effaced by and in the concept."[2] It can, given the opportunity, express a "proper," but one which is "provisional and multiple,"[3] enabling us and all to occupy the position of the other. Therefore, with our literary style, more so with our metaphorical manner—style and manner juxtaposed—we project, in the Nietzschean description, "a slice of personality," which is "the task of

---

[1] Sarah Kofman, *Nietzsche and Metaphor*, trans. Duncan Large (Standford, CA: Stanford University Press, 1993), 21.
[2] Ibid., 102.
[3] Ibid.

history to preserve."[4] The poor person is lost under the concept-weight of poverty. Therefore, to revert to style is to be with the personal—primally to be able to deny abstraction and invent virtues. And to be with the personal for the first time is to be with the pre-Socratics who posed the question of being and the presence, and the here and the now for the first time, later to be drenched, and forgotten. But it is Nietzsche who first denounced, in a fit of modest outrage, the Aristotelian and post-Aristotelian inheritance as the dialectical valence of loss and impersonal boredom where—to use Nietzsche's own words—"enchantment" has been "petrified" (now we understand the Weberian "disenchantment" of the modern world better—in the light of an early Nietzsche, that is). This loss pertains to the earlier mentioned "slice of personality."[5] Metaphorical writing shows off and preserves personality, unlike the dialectical tactics and skilled rhetorics' foul play entailing "the absolute silencing of the personal element. It is through this that those records become so tedious; for in systems which have been refuted it is only this personal element that can still interest us, for this alone is eternally irrefutable."[6] Only the personal element made up of metaphors are not arguments and, thereby, cannot be refuted—this is Nietzsche's moot point. And with this, the whole pre-Socratic vista of public philosophy becomes suddenly available where Heraclitus is Nietzsche's justifiable hero.

Is it not because Heraclitus is the first philosopher of the common (logos)? The common is the most common. "For that reason one must follow what is comprehensive (i.e., what is common for the comprehensive account is common)."[7] ... "Though the logos is common (xunou), most men live as if they had a private source of understanding."[8] Or consider this, "Heraclitus says that the universe for those who are awake is single and common, while in sleep each person turns aside into a private universe."[9] Elsewhere, Heraclitus accuses men of behaving in their waking hours

[4] Ibid., 22.
[5] Ibid.
[6] Friedrich Nietzsche, "Philosophy during the Tragic Age of the Greeks (1873)," in *Early Greek Philosophy and other Essays,* trans. Maximilian A. Mugge (London: T. N. Foulis, 1911), 71–170.
[7] "But although the account is comprehensive, most men live as though they had a private comprehension of their own." Cited in Jonathan Barnes, *Early Greek Philosophy* (England: Penguin Books, 2001), 49.
[8] Cited in Edward Hussey, *The Presocratics* (London: Duckworth, 1983), 39.
[9] Cited in Robin Waterfield, transl., *The First Philosophers: The Presocratics and the Sophists* (Oxford: Oxford University Press, 2009), 38.

as if they were asleep, "It is wrong to act and speak like men asleep";[10] broken down, this would stand to mean that people should not carry with them or must not coalesce the common with that of the privately separate worlds.[11]

"A Becoming and Passing, a building and destroying, without any moral bias, in perpetual innocence is in this world only the play of the artist and of the child ... the play of the great world-child, Zeus."[12] Following this only, we had "we hear and do not hear"—an eternal (un)becoming symptomatic of play. This is named by Nietzsche as the "aesthetic fundamental perception"[13] of Heraclitus. The artist was born and held by his/her culture, and the culture was held by its slaves because without this looking down upon, that is, without this pathos of distance, and subsequently self-distance—as we've noted previously—no artist can originate-willfully, and prosper: "[T]he 'Dignity of Man' and the 'Dignity of Labour'. ... The Greeks did not require such conceptual hallucinations, for among them the idea that labour is a disgrace is expressed with startling frankness. ... Labour is a disgrace, because existence has no value in itself."[14] And here, Nietzsche attaches the question of culture, syncretically, to the Heraclitean force of becoming, and this he does with an enduring force and spectacular candour:

> Becoming. Every moment devours the preceding one, every birth is the death of innumerable beings; begetting, living, murdering, all is one. Therefore we may compare this grand culture with a blood stained victor, who in his triumphal procession carries the defeated along as slaves chained to his chariot, slaves whom a beneficent power has so blinded that, almost

---

[10] Quoted in W. K. C. Guthrie, *A History of Greek Philosophy,* Vol. 1, *The Earlier PreSocratics and the Pythagoreans* (London: Cambridge University Press, 1962), 427.

[11] But Heraclitus, as is usual with him, elsewhere acknowledges that because we live, in sleep the severance and the separation between the senses and the outer world remains incomplete.

> Respiration is left as sole means of contact with the outside source of life, "like a root," says Sextus. We are still taking some part in the cosmic activity, which is presumably why "Heraclitus says" (so Marcus Aurelius tells us) "that even sleepers are workers and co-operators in what goes on in the world."

See W. K. C. Guthrie, *A History of Greek Philosophy,* Vol. 1, *The Earlier PreSocratics and the Pythagoreans* (London: Cambridge University Press, 1962), 430.

[12] Ibid., 108, 113.

[13] Nietzsche, "Philosophy during the Tragic Age of the Greeks (1873)," 111.

[14] Ibid., 4.

crushed by the wheels of the chariot, they nevertheless still exclaim: "Dignity of labour!" "Dignity of Man."[15]

Next, Nietzsche, from exploring the personal principle in pre-Socratic Greek philosophers, now turns his torch to Homer. Here, what is the precise issue? "The important problem referred to is the question of the personality of Homer."[16] In other words, whether the poems of Homer could be reconstructed without reference to the personality of Homer, that is, "treating them as the work of several different persons" or a single author: Homer; or, if there is "one single Homer" or if there are several. Was the person created out of a conception, or the conception out of a person?[17] This is the real "Homeric question," the central problem of the personality posed by Nietzsche. The old material meaning of the name "Homer" as the father of the heroic epic poem was changed into the aesthetic meaning of Homer, the father of poetry in general and like-wise its original prototype that "[t]he design of an epic such as the Iliad is not an entire whole, not an organism; but a number of pieces strung together" [which makes "*The Iliad* ... not a garland, but a bunch of flowers"], "a collection of reflections arranged in accordance with aesthetic rules."

Nietzsche, as the first philosopher of the personal, significantly and remarkably hatches onto the problematic of an array of indefinable individual characteristics (we shall say indeterminacy) in order (not) to define—on this ground—the Homeric personality. This helps us to arrive at and endorse the indeterminacy of the personal, theoretically. Second, Nietzsche's hint on the emergence of Homer as a collective personality:

---

[15] Ibid., 8.

[16] Friedrich Nietzsche, "Homer and Classical Philology," in *The Complete Works of Friedrich Nioetzsche* Vol. III, ed. Oscar Levy, trans. J. M. Kennedy, 1910, available as Project Gutenberg E-Book #18188, Released on April 17, 2006, accessed on August 10, 2008. (all quotations unless otherwise mentioned are from this book; italics when used are in the original; no pagination exist in the document).

[17] While Nietzsche mourns the "conceptification" of persons, in Schelling's treatment of mythology—in particular Greek mythology, this question arises again and dissolves with the following answer, "[T]he oldest language was missing scientific expressions for general principles or causes. The poverty of language has obliged it to express abstract concept as persons, logical or real relations through the image of reproduction. In part, however, they have been so seized by the objects themselves that they strived to also place them before the spectators' eyes, so to speak, dramatically, as acting persons." See F. W. J. Schelling, *Historico-critical Introduction to the Philosophy of Mythology,* trans. M. Richey and M. Zisselsberger (Albany, NY: State University of New York Press, 2007), 26.

his transition from being the poet of particular works to that of the father of poetry in general—on which later Schelling would say: "Homer is not an individual like later poets, ... or others. He designates an entire age, is the dominating power, the principle of an epoch."[18] The personal as the epoch-making principle of the collective person distinguishes the personal from the private in a significant manner; the person then from this vantage point could be the individual person or the collective person The collective person is not necessarily opposed to the public as the case is with the private. We shall axiomatically state these observations later.

# From Greece, Rome, to Modernity: Nietzsche to Schmitt

Departing from the healthy culture of the Greeks as Nietzsche had had it, a brief reference to the Romans (since Nietzsche never engaged much with the Romans) will lead us to comprehend how the private-public consolidation and their transcendence in the hands of the emperor prefaces the theoretical inscription of the personal contra-distinguished from the private.

By aiming to achieve finite ends (or purposes of utility and practical ends) even through Gods, the Romans were the first to bifurcate the communion of religion into private and public and invent Gods for all (utilitarian) ends where "[p]articular ends, needs, powers, appear also as gods. The content of these gods is practical utility; they serve the common good or profit."[19] It brooks a pluralism of a peculiar kind: "The art of baking ranks as something divine. Fornax, the oven in which the corn is dried, is a goddess by herself; Vesta is the fire used for baking bread."[20] "[P]rivate aims, needs, and powers also appear as Gods, because [fulfillment in] the human sphere is the fulfillment of God."[21] In the wake of serving finite ends, having presupposed the "existence of an immediate [contingent]

---

[18]  Ibid., 18.
[19]  G. W. F. Hegel, *Lectures on the Philosophy of Religion,* trans. Rev E. B. Speirs and J. Burdon Sanderson (London: Kegan Paul, Trench, Trubner, & Co. Ltd, 1895), II: 305.
[20]  Ibid., 306.
[21]  William Terence Stace, *The Philosophy of Hegel: A Systematic Exposition* (New York, NY: Dover Publications Inc. 1955), 382.

reality," we have the Romans addressing themselves not only to "utility and prosperity" but also to "defect,"[22] "injury and failure:"[23]

> Thus the Romans dedicated altars to the plague, to fever (Febris), to care (Angerona), and they revered hunger (Fames), and the blight (Robigo) which attacked the grain. In the joyous religion of art, this side of religion which consists of fear of what brings misfortune, is put into the background.[24]

Now, this finite scheme of things meant that "[i]n this religion of utility or conformity to end, the end was none other than the Roman State, which, thus, represents abstract power," producing

> the universal sorrow which existed in the Roman world, a sorrow which was to be the birth-throe of the religion of truth. The distinction between free men and slaves disappear in the presence of the all embracing power of the Emperor ... and we are in the presence of the death of finitude, since the Fortuna of the one Empire itself succumbs too.[25]

Now, the ground was prepared, at least to Hegel, for a true universal religion: Christianity. Before this finitude, not understood infinitely, or particularity estranged from universality, could only cry and mourn in sorrow and slumber. "It was the Jewish nation which preserved the idea of God as representing the ancient [abstract] sorrow of the world ... [and uniting it later with the] willfulness of self consciousness ... [which is] ... at the same time bound up with the abstraction."[26] Differentiated into the abstraction of speech and gestures, it takes on a complex attire, more so because in the Greek world gods appear in the hands of the artificer, and with the Romans they tend to appropriate a semblance of reality with utility. In Greece, "just as it is essential for a statue to be the work of human hands, so is the actor essential to his mask,"[27] that is, essential to his persona, the role "the unconscious self of the actor coincides with what s/he impersonates, just as the spectator is completely at home in the drama performed before him and sees himself playing in it."[28] This phenomenon

---

[22] Hegel, *Lectures on the Philosophy of Religion,* II: 307.
[23] Ibid., 306.
[24] Ibid., 307.
[25] Ibid., 322.
[26] Ibid., 323.
[27] G. W. F. Hegel, *Phenomenology of Spirit,* trans. A. V. Miller (Delhi: Motilal Banarasidass Publishers, 1998), 444.
[28] Ibid., 452.

could be deployed to instigate and put in place the fact that the persona, unlike the private that conveys disjunction with the collective present, or the present as configuration, retains a refreshing sense of integrity and, well, if one may have it, ambiguity. However, this is displayed most forcefully in the comic predicaments (or comedy) where he/she wears the mask only to tease it open, and expunge a reality hidden away—as if from the "spectator consciousness" (this is Hegel's phrase). While in tragedy, the fate is that what engulfs the ordinary consciousness in the actor in the abundance of consciousness and hinders it pitifully; in the comedy, the fate is dedicated to the self-control and strong self-persuasion posed by the actor who—purportedly—is in immense command of the self. "This self certainty is a state of spiritual well-being and of repose therein, such as is not to be found anywhere outside of this comedy."[29] This is damaged the moment "it raises itself out of this content, and its levity refines it into a 'person', into the abstract universality of right or law ... which disembodies ... and imparts to the spiritless self, to the individual person, a being that is in and for itself."[30] (The being that is in and for itself is the private individual—though disregarded here—elsewhere will be theorized by Hegel as the abstract personality becoming concrete.) What for comedy is laughable, for this consciousness it becomes unbearable plight; the skeptical consciousness becomes unhappy consciousness where suddenly a knowledge of the loss (of self-certainty, God, even the knowledge of all this) appears with its burden, so unbearable that

> [i]t has lost both the worth it attached to its immediate personality and the worth attached to its personality as mediated, as thought. ... The statues are now only stones from which the living soul has flown, just as the hymns are words from which belief has gone.[31]

The unhappy consciousness, in its emergent mode, as in the Roman phase—pictured in Hegel—is nearly the modern consciousness. Now, the empty, empirical destiny leading to the disappearance of the individual, "finally found a personal representation in the power of the Emperor, a power which is arbitrary and takes its own way, unhindered by moral considerations."[32] In fact, here in Roman hands, we have, albeit for the

---

[29] Ibid., 453.
[30] Ibid., 454.
[31] Ibid., 455.
[32] This segment, though tangentially, was pursued in Chapter 2 as having prefaced the history of the personal in divisions: private and public.

first time, the person of the emperor who imbibes both the private and the public and then transcends both of them by a feat of sheer, arbitrary will. And here we also do have welfare in its ancient, personal form:

> [A]s far as personality is concerned, it is the character of the person, the subject, to surrender its isolation and separateness. Ethical life, love, means precisely the giving up of particularity, of particular personality, and its extension to universality—so, too, with friendship. In friendship and love I give up my abstract personality and thereby win it back as concrete. The truth of personality is found precisely in winning it back through this immersion, this being immersed in the other.[33]

Now, if this is in a sense the most humane, and not a philosophical (a dialectical one for instance), resolution to the problems with which we've been grappling pace Hegel, Schelling, or Adorno, then we must leave it at this to enter our main text. We shall recount through the book, often, how the personal, through the sieve of friendship and love, escapes the juridical apparatus of sovereignty, or as discussed later (in Chapter 6), how charity or philanthropy manifestly, or immanently, are forms of giving as love, in contrast to the bourgeois welfare state that tries to adopt and temper the narrative management of emotional differences, according to a logic of its own; but does it succeed? The self-referential, internally packed detour of the means and ends of welfare resembles the excessive gift structure of charity or benevolent giving. If we tend to think in terms of subjectivity, then love is far from abstract subjectivity since "love is indignant if part of the individual is severed and held back as a private property".[34] If love is to lose oneself in the other, love is intersubjective—even objective, but not impersonal. Similarly as self in its immersion into the other—in order to lose itself,[35] or subsequently to have already lost it, it is ethically objective in a severe personal manner—not in terms of the self–other opposition, since the self–other are united in the person in love—and having escaped all juridification, all measuring meters—the event is personal. Even though they "are in connection with much that is dead" and "external objects belong to each of them ... in

---

[33] G. W. F. Hegel, *Phenomenology of Spirit*, 427–28.

[34] G. W. F. Hegel, "Love," in *On Christianity: Early Theological Writings,* trans. T. M. Knox (New York, NY: Harper Torchbooks, 1961), 302–08.

[35] "'I love you', a declaration where 'I' is posed only by being exposed to 'you'. That is to say that the heart is not a subject." See Jean Luc Nancy, "Shattered Love," in *A Finite Thinking,* ed. Simon Parks (Stanford, CA: Stanford University Press, 2003), 245–74.

the course of their multiplex acquisition of property and rights,"[36] death hardly could separate them since "in the child their union has become unseparated."[37] But in modernity as we know, the predicament being invested and littered with property rights must bring the lovers in its fold. And if we are to go by Hegel, even common ownership must remain singular in its exercise—if not solitary—but a short remark flowering in the middle of a sentence is more suggestive in its embodiment. He says when the right to the possession of property remains undecided, "the thought of this right would never be forgotten."[38] And now, if we are to account for modernity in its full, and still throbbing genealogy, we ought to be convinced by this stumping observation: the thought of the right or—if one is more prone to foreground it—of private property right, despite its abolition or sacrifice, remains pervasive in thinking. Marx's indictment that everything in Hegel is derived from, and stays at the level of thought is, thus, a hearty misnomer. It is not right as a thought but the thought of this as a right. Even a hundred years after, it springs a surprise and resurrects itself incessantly out of all debris against the joint curse of "pain and perish"; thought, of course, is a determination.[39]

It is curious though why besides love, friendship—which is another paradigmatic personal relationship outside the margins of legislation or juridification—does not hold Hegel's attention for long. There is already an array of the literature, particularly in the anti-liberal camp, as to how "friendship" (or fraternity) and its opposite "enmity" lies at the root of all political vigor and strife. No wonder that in modernity, where the personal is (mis)understood to be just a temporal derivate of despotic kings, it will be allowed only to stay back as the silent synonym of the private, and its separate identity foreclosed.

> It is not surprising, therefore, that liberal individualists tend to relegate the practice of friendship (and its norms) to the private sphere, where citizens as private persons are free to establish amicable relations with whomever they chose regardless of whether their friends are fellow citizens.[40]

---

[36] Hegel, *On Christianity*, 308.
[37] Ibid.
[38] Ibid.
[39] "Personality expresses the concept as such; but at the same time the person enshrines the actuality of the concept, and only when the concept is determined as a person is it the Idea or truth." See G. W. F. Hegel, *Elements of the Philosophy of Right*, trans. H. B. Nisbet (UK: Cambridge University Press, 1991), 317.
[40] Jason A. Scorza, "Liberal Citizenship and Civic Friendship," *Political Theory* 32 no. 1 (2004), 85–108. But while Emerson in 1844 wanted that "citizens might someday

But this telos to displace the personal to the home of the private, and keep the pubic secure in modernity, how does it happen and why, or, do we have a different story to tell? Carl Schmitt—one of the dreaded theorists (philosopher and jurist) of such a disclosure—summarizes it too well:

> The modern idea of the state, according to Krabbe, replaces *personal force* (of the king, of the authorities) with spiritual power. "We no longer live under the authority of persons, be they natural or artificial (legal) persons, but under the rule of laws, ... [t]his is the essence of the modern idea of the state." They agree that all personal elements must be eliminated from the concept of the state. ... For them, the personal and the command elements belong together. All these objections fail to recognize that the conception of personality ... a distinctive determination of which individual person or which concrete body can assume such an authority cannot be derived from the mere legal quality of a maxim. ... What matters for the reality of legal life is who decides.[41]

Who decides? With this resounding sentence, we had prepared ourselves to enter into impersonal modernity (Chapter 1), and we saw for ourselves the truth-claim that it percolates for itself and others.

The philosphical trajectory is clear. But to construct a theory out of this philsophical history that Nietzsche outlines, and the way we advanced its rigors through the ages—down to Schmitt—is the present challenge. The aesthetic perception the personal entails (where the artistic language pervaded by metaphors) is opposed to a dialectical formality (of a scientific, merely logical language). The indefinable individual characteristics (because the person can never be exhausted by a catalogue of characteristics) that meet or are available in the person, and finally the collective personality of a poetic name (where Homer stands for a whole poetic race as well as that which is Homeric) foregrounds our theoretical approach to the personal as not private, and not necessarily against the public or the collective.

---

'exercise towards each other the grandest and simplest sentiments, as well as a knot of friends, or a pair of lovers'," this was not an invitation for "personal" friendships or love to run riot. "Emerson distrusted personal friendships because they are 'based on qualities of personality [which] hamper men in their efforts to 'merge' with all'." See Jason A. Scorza, "Liberal Citizenship and Civic Friendship," *Political Theory* 32, no. 1 (2004), 85,101. Emerson's advocacy is for democratic connectedness. Love and friendships are inherently anti-democratic.

41 Carl Schmitt, *Political Theology: Four Chapters on the Concept of Sovereignty*, trans. George Schwab (Cambridge, MA: The MIT Press, 1985), 22, 29, 31, 34 (italics mine).

Thus, having interpreted Nietzsche to have provided us with the indeterminacy of the person/personal and the collective personality or (the aesthetic name) of a person, we could brace ourselves to theoretically extrapolate the lessons of such an enterprise.

# III

## Personal as Pre-private: A Theoretical Detour

Putting Nietzsche aside for a while, notice that when we were revisiting the etymological meaning of private and public in the previous chapter, we did not refer to the person or personal. But if we had done so, personal-private difference would be restored even in that. Person deriving from old Latin *persona* meant mask, particularly one worn by an actor; personal also derived from the same persona and metaphorically, if extended, it could stand to mean many more things: "Persona means the actor's mask through which his dramatic tale is sounded. Since man is the percipient who perceives what is, we can think of him as the persona, the mask, of being."[42] Now one reason for wearing this mask was to enable the audience to identify the character's personality who—because of the distance— could not always traverse it visually. Therefore, while private meant (often) a solitary existence removed from the public life—as in *privare*—person or personal grew up in response to a collective audience—in communicative complicity. Armed with this one insight as a flicker, now we are able to expand on the distinction theoretically.

Here we are approaching then a theory of the personal. But because the personal appears lost in the private, what has been, quite declaratively, central to my work is the distancing of the personal from the private since, having been embodied in the private, it is used interchangeably with the private as a similar register of opposition to the public. So before we begin, let us rehearse, at the cost of uneasy boredom, the standard usages that private and public have assumed: Public in the West is built into the optic of the "public sphere" where public opinion is formed through the mediation of publicity forms and is connected to certain forms of representation, deliberation, and political authority. Private (sphere) follows by entailing

---

[42] Martin Heidegger, *What is Called Thinking?*, trans. J. Glenn Gray (New York, NY: Perennial, 1976), 62.

things that are not to be publicized in a particular sense. Private is in opposition[43] to the public in the sense it suspends the formal equality of all before law and entails things that will not be shared with the public; in fact, it opposes and excludes the public and what wonder that the family organized around private property, sex to that of correspondence, and conversation over telephone give a content to the private and privacy.

So we begin by exploring the personal-private difference and then chart it vis-à-vis the public to complete the triangle.

Let us then try at first to validate the personal-private difference by deploying the best contemporary classic discussion of privacy.

W. A. Parent's landmark paper titled "Privacy, Morality, and the Law"[44] published in the journal *Philosophy and Public Affairs* is memorable for many reasons. One of them is, of course, that he demolishes here all the classic comfortable notions (some of which I've used above) of privacy we had taken for granted. Here is a short synopsis of his destruction: First, "[p]rivacy consists of being let alone." Parent argues,

> [There are] innumerable ways of failing to let a person alone which have nothing to do with his privacy. Suppose, for instance, that A clubs B on the head or repeatedly insults him. We should describe and evaluate such actions by appeal to concepts such as force, violence, and harassment; [not the violation of privacy].[45]

---

[43] But it would be instructive to remember that we have two models here: one that of private/public opposition, another of "complimentarity." The second view goes thus: "There is only one public ... regime of injunctions which is observed at a variety of levels. Only one of these levels is properly private. ... To conclude, the private and the public are not contrary principles in modern times but are mutually reinforcing." See Dipankar Gupta, "The Domesticated Public: Tradition, Modernity and the Public/Private Divide," in *The Public and the Private Issues of Democratic Citizenship,* ed. Gurpreet Mahajan (New Delhi: SAGE Publications, 2003), 56–73.

For Gupta, private is an expression-setting of the public where the latter does not lose itself even after it had undertaken the task of expressing itself in multiple settings. I shall concentrate more on the oppositional part rather than the part that is complimentary. However, as is evident, both the paradigms remain trapped in the public/private binary. (This is just a self-defending caveat in order to avoid the complaint that my definitions are unimorphic and purposive in as much as I persistently harp on the fact that the private is opposed to the public. This is approved even by Habermas when he argues that the private/public binary is schematically and foundationally oppositional. My supplement elsewhere in this work has been the attempt to trace this binary to its pre-semiotic, which is the person).

[44] W. A. Parent, 2003, "Privacy, Morality, and the Law," *Philosophy and Public Affairs* 12, no. 4 (2003), 269–88.

[45] Ibid., 272.

Second, "[p]rivacy consists of a form of autonomy or control over significant personal matters." Parent wonders at the example of a person

> who voluntarily divulges all sorts of intimate, personal, and undocumented information about himself to a friend. She is doubtless exercising control. ... But we would not and should not say that in doing so she is preserving or protecting her privacy. On the contrary, she is voluntarily relinquishing much of her privacy. People can and do choose to give up privacy for many reasons.[46]

Third, "[p]rivacy is the limitation on access to the self." Parent retorts by saying if by access we mean physical proximity or an exemption from snooping or surveillance, then solitude or peace could be more viable alternatives. But is peace or solitude privacy? No.

> [Because] it confuses privacy with the existential conditions that are necessary for its realization. To achieve happiness I must have some good luck, but this does not mean that happiness is good luck. Similarly, if I am to enjoy privacy there have to be limitations on cognitive access to me, but these limitations are not themselves privacy. Rather privacy is what they safe guard.[47]

Now having demolished nearly all of the received definitions of privacy, Parent comes out with a terse formulation of his own definition of privacy that survives, and I think quite plausibly, the above objections: "[P]rivacy is the condition of not having undocumented personal knowledge[48] about one possessed by others. A person's privacy is diminished exactly to the degree that others possess this kind of knowledge about him."[49] Parent adds, "What I am defining is the condition of privacy not the right of privacy."[50] Let us just take hold of the word personal in the given definition. What is personal here is that it is a prior condition of privacy.[51] The personal may

---

[46] Ibid., 273.

[47] Ibid., 275.

[48] Parent excludes from his definition documented personal information available in public or institutional records.

[49] Parent, "Privacy, Morality, and the Law," 269.

[50] Ibid.

[51] Our reversal must be a reminder, and an able testimony, to those who would try and reinstate privacy as a precondition of the personal where love appears as the consequence of self-entitlement—where self is nearly a private possession. The argument is on the brink of the comical: How could I lose myself in you, unless I *have* myself in the first

provide the private or privacy with a content, but personal is not privacy. Nothing can be the condition of something unless it is different from that which is being provided with the condition by courtesy of the former, or unless we are ready to mess up, in the most unphilosophical manner, the precondition of a definition with the definition itself.

Now, if we are correct to argue the personal as the theoretical (and not only historical) precondition of the private, let us expand this to a full formulation by bringing in the public to complete the triad.

1. *The Personal is Phenomenological, the Private/Public is Juridico-Political:* We are aware of the criteria for public and private. Private/public are stable categories that are defined by legal-juridical indexes and people go to court for redress if they feel violated.[52] But genuine (and not forged) personal matters such as that of love or/and friendship[53] cannot be legislated and

---

place? But this is not without the dose of common sense where "you have *stolen* my heart" suddenly rings quite literally true!

> Equally fundamental to the development of an individual's moral and social personality is the capacity to form important, intimate relationships involving love, friendship, and trust. These relationships require the spontaneous relinquishment of parts of one's inner self to another, inspired by certain kind of attitudes. This capacity for sharing presupposes secure possession of those features of self in the first place. Privacy, and the sense of self and the title to the self that it engenders, thus constitute necessary conditions for love, friendship, and the ability to modulate important but less intimate relationships.

See Ferdinand Schoeman, "Privacy: Philosophical Dimensions of the Literature," in *Philosophical Dimensions of Privacy*, ed. Ferdinand Schoeman (Cambridge: Cambridge University Press, 1984), 1–33.

This forgets the basics where the self or the sense of having a self is the effect-structure of a prior order of the symbolic (mooring) that comes from the outside or the community (recall the liberal-communitarian debate) or one could say, nowhere. In this sense only, the "I" for Lacan is an empty speech in everyday life, "speech alienated in language, subjugated to its imaginary deformation." The opposite, Lacan is correctly cited to say "*Full speech* is the founding medium of the intersubjective relation." See Lorenzo Chiesa, *Subjectivity and Otherness: A Philosophical Reading of Lacan* (Cambridge, MA: The MIT Press, 2007), 39–40.

[52] In this sense, let us not be misled by what goes on by the name of personal laws; they are but remnants of private or customary law.

[53]

> The concrete act of the person can be understood as a mere sum or a mere construct of such abstract essences no more than the person can be understood as a mere interconnective complex of acts. Rather, it is the person himself, living in each of his

are not subjects of litigation. There is a unique uncertainty and indeterminacy associated with the decision or the destiny of a person in these cases (nobody knows whether A loves B—even B does not) that makes it a phenomenological[54] notion and not a political one.

2. *The Private is Opposed to the Public, the Personal Is Not:* Personal, unlike the private, is not necessarily opposed to the public. I might choose somebody to be my lover; it's my personal choice and I might want to declare my choice to the public. This makes love a personal relationship, and not a private one. Consider more examples: When "personal attacks" are made in politics, they may not intrude into somebody's sacred domain of privacy but are essentially directed against a person, and in this sense they are personal attacks. I have a personal opinion, and who can stop me from uttering it to the TV interviewer? But consider sex; it is private in the sense that I cannot choose to have sex in the public. Or consider private property that is famous for its exclusion of the public.

3. *The Persons/Personal Are Not Spheres Like the Private and the Public:* The interesting point is, while public/private spheres are categories that are tied to certain phenomenon, "personal" is a category that is peculiarly tied to the "person;" there is no "sphere"[55]

---

acts, who permeates every act with his peculiar character. No knowledge of the nature of love, for instance, or of the nature of judgment, can bring us one step nearer to the knowledge of how person A loves or judges person B; nor can a reference to the contents (values, states of affairs) given in each of these acts furnish this knowledge. But, on the other hand, a glance at the person himself and his essence immediately yields a peculiarity for every act that we know him to execute, and the knowledge of his 'world' yields a peculiarity for the contents of his acts.

See Max Scheler, *Formalism in Ethics and Non-Formal Ethics of Values*, trans. Manfred S. Frings and Roger L. Funk (Evanston, IL: Northwestern University Press, 1973), 386.

[54] Phenomenology is the discourse of subjective, "pure" experience bereft of presuppositions and pre-existing categories. As a foundational science, it posits, as Derrida is fond of describing it, a principle of principles.

[55] Just consider the special meaning that Habermas alludes to the italicized word here, "The principle of the public sphere, that is, critical publicity, seemed to lose its strength in the measure that it expanded as a sphere and even undermined the private realm." See Jurgen Habermas, *The Structural Transformation of the Public Sphere: An Inquiry Into a Category of Bourgeois Society*, trans. T. Berger (Great Britain: Blackwell Publishers & Polity Press, 1996). And from the quote itself, I guess, it becomes clear as to why, while Habermas previously deployed the word sphere to refer to the personal sphere of the monarch, the use was distinctly unhappy.

that is or ought to be explanatively employed here. (Sphere, etymologically, is referred to an area of activity and public/private arenas refer to a collection of actions, whereas the personal refers to the agency of these actions.[56] We may be fathers in our private sphere and officers in the public office, but a person is not simply a father or an officer. We might perform our public or private actions but a person cannot be reduced to these actions. He is both a father and an officer and more. A dangerous mafia outside may be a caring father at home. Him combining these irreconcilable roles or differentiating them in the agency of his person and the way he does it constitutes the personality or the personal agency of the person (see Case Study One and Two [later in this chapter] in lieu of a conclusion for a clarification on this).

4. *The Personal Is Both Private and Public and/or Beyond:* Let us remember that in Indian law, the personal is defined as anything referring to a person—they may be private matters or public affairs. In this sense, personal is both public and private. A person at times is a private person or assumes public roles. But as he/she belongs to both, it can be as well argued that he/she belongs exclusively to neither. Or again, he/she belongs to both by virtue of crossing both these floors time and again, and as such the personal becomes a third not reducible to the two other registers. It is impossible to reduce it to private/public functions because it is able to grasp and escape both limits at the same time.

---

[56] Therefore, if at times we are to call pain private, I guess we are victims of a politically contaminated use of an expression—that is, one might hazard, our liberal pain and not pain itself. While meditating on the metaphysical relationship between "work" and "pain," consider this from Heidegger, "If anyone would, indeed, dare to think through the relationship between 'work' as the basic feature of being and 'pain' ... Then pain would be the most intimate of gatherings." See Martin Heidegger, *The Question of Being*, trans. W. Kluback and J. T. Wilde (New York, NY: Twayne Publishers, 1956), 69–71. But this deep subjectivity, in order to be successful, should be located in the person and not the sphere that is private (and some having ascribed, after an incorrect beginning where pain was privately and inalienably owned and epistemically known ("no one else can have MY pain"—"which only I can know") to a no-ownership theory of pain (ending though in a theory of inner "avowal"—but that's a different story). In this sense I would argue, pain is personal and not private. This would clarify why even if the later—Habermas tried to include the intimate sphere as the third beside the public and the private—could not make any departure. I think Hannah Arendt was right when she focused on the failure of the creation of a deep private sphere or the intimate sphere in trying to resist the rise of the social. This amply shows—I guess—also the limits of the category "intimate" and why it fails to move beyond the liberal binary.

If we are ready to conclude now, then let me hazard that I have so far argued that the personal cannot be subsumed under the private/public binary and have tried to point out that if in particular discourses the personal has been wrongly used as a synonym of the private, it should receive a corrective measure. We could, in a short space here, attempt to deploy the personal as proposed earlier and see for ourselves the consequential import of the same.

# IV

## Case Study (One): "Personal Agency" for "Identity"—Refuting Amartya Sen

In recent times, in India and elsewhere, Amartya Sen has been celebrated for invoking the question of multiple identities that—if reckoned with—would lead to toleration and diversity. I shall propose, along the lines of our argument, that the question of personal agency would be a better substitute than identity as Professor Sen would like to have it. I think what happens here is that a sociological register is being mixed up with a social philosophical one. Role, role taking, hypothetical role taking, role reversal, etc. are all sociological determinants emerging in response to the "functional differentiation" of society; identity is a classical philosophical problem that can be—I'm afraid, appropriated in sociology or social philosophy with an unprofessed naiveté. Put briefly, the fact that I'm a father at home and an officer at the office does not entail I've two identities or multiple identities here (and, therefore, I be tolerant about others). Now (granting this technical mix up a breather), given the classical formulation of identity in philosophy, it is the question of uninterrupted continuity that matters, that is, my sure transition from this role to that role will sustain my identity. This will not be possible with an absolute identification or total immersion in a particular role or else, as we know, a salesman, as if in an economic delirium, will use the language of selling love to his wife at home. This is only possible when there is a lack of identification rather than identification as such, which in fact imparts the power to feign and cheat others (as narrated in Chapter 1, this is "the governance by fraud" that we placed before the "governance by force" or "the governance by consent") as well as subscribes to purposive truthfulness. Now, we can guess why we do not succeed with honesty in daily life; honesty as the practical maxim of truth is based on a total positive, normative identification with a norm or a rule; when it promises rights, it offers them. But Hegel, you'll remember, defined fraud as giving the semblance of rights rather than the rights themselves to the recipient who has the mistaken contention all the while that he is being offered the right thing. This successful and enabling (!) lack of identification could not be a placeholder for the phrase "identity"; one could as well term it disidentity or nonidentity. What we are rejecting then is an absolute lack or an absolute identification with a particular role, and given our everyday life, we master or learn to master more or less the manipulation or maneuver of these and "continue" without interruption; our corresponding success or failure depends much on this.[57] Now, the question is, who does this? I'll answer: the person. And if it is that, then I'm perhaps right in using personal "agency" (where identification, disidentification and the maneuver is present in their rational and/or irrational combinations) and not personal "identity."

Identity when reduced to such sociological questions of functional role assumptions, has also given rise to other misunderstandings a la Amartya Sen: for instance, toleration emerging from multiple identities (!). The answer is that if there is a constant lack of identification with each of my roles (well again, wrongly, "identities"), there is a constant disidentification at work (and why not) with other similar or dissimilar people. Now to what extent this would be tolerated or not is an empirical question and cannot be solved philosophically or predicted sociologically.

---

[57] This observation seems to be confirmed by Jon Elster, who in his (edited) classis study *Multiple Selves* comments, firstly on voluntary incomplete identification:

> The tripartite self is at the core of Freud's anatomy of the mind. Actually this conception amounts to saying that the person tries to mediate between the long-term and the short-term interests, or between the private and the public man. The autonomous individual *does not* want to identify fully with any of these extreme strivings." (31, italics mine)

Secondly, on the invitation to maneuver: "Although only one *person* is in charge, he is challenged by semi-autonomous strivings that confront him as alien powers. To get his way, he may have to resort to ruse and manipulation." (p. 31). See Jon Elster, "Introduction," in *The Multiple Self*, ed. Jon Elster (Cambridge: Cambridge University Press, 1986), 1–34. [Pages as indicated].

## Case Study (Two): Personal Identity and Unknowability—Adopting Rakhi Sawant of Indian Popular Culture

Now, the pious and engaged, attentive interlocutor will ask, "Well if you are correct in saying that though identity could be posed to study continuity (I'm a feminist outside and a masculinist inside—but still it is me and I'm either and neither of them), personal agency is a better, theoretically correct replacement of identity, when would you pose the question of identity?" And here—thanking this serious reader—I'll give her an example of where both these moments are present but where one will fail in order to give way to another: Rakhi Sawant is a famous actress with an arguable taste for roles in films and comments in her everyday life. In an interview to the *Times of India* in 2007 she narrates about an absolutely disagreeable or uncomfortable thing she had to do at the age of 13 in order to save her penniless ailing mother. And now, after having seen the ways of the world, she thinks there is nothing wrong in exposing or indiscriminate chance encounters. But at her own home, she says, she is in absolute command; there she wears no revealing dresses and allows no fickle person to come near. Now, if I say she combines these well in her personal agency, one will have to agree; I will go further and argue that her transition from this to that is carried well—she is self-conscious, aware, and her ego is intact—and this is the minimal identity trait that could be included as an element of her person-al agency. But now if I ask a substantive identity question: Rakhi, who are you? Are you the one who does dirty dancing and sells sex at high prices? Or the one who will not allow sex seekers inside your house (whose interior, you say, you have made all by yourself)? Rakhi will say, "Yes all of them and none of these: my identity cannot be reduced to any of these even though it runs through all of them."[58] Then, who are you Rakhi? "I don't know, I've never asked myself this question."

---

[58] Faced with the existence of an apparent plurality of selves—as in Rakhi's case here, how the principle of the person could be used to patiently undertake the narrative management of differences—as we've outlined above, here is an welcome endorsement: We need to firmly identify "the person with one of the selves, on the basis of that self's unique capacity to form higher-order intentions about the other, we can use the preferences of that self to construct the meta-ranking of the person." See Jon Elster, "Introduction," in *The Multiple Self*, ed. Jon Elster (Cambridge: Cambridge University Press, 1986), 13.

Now, whether we shall allow this classical formulation of identity to settle in its unknowability or following modern governmentality, its impossible and false enumerability is the question. So far as this present work is concerned, empowered by the indeterminacy of the personal as a signified, it will concur with the first option for reasons already espoused, and will be elaborated further.

## Concluding Remarks

The transcendent unknowability of the personal, it could be argued, does it not become knowable in objective spirit? In fact in 19th century Bengal, these questions—among other—were debated profusely by Brajendranath Seal: one of the questions being the "objectively valid" possibility of an "external personality."[59]

> For, if subject and object be related as unit and irrational surd, one personality is as incommensurable with another as an irrational surd with an imaginary expression! And if the intuition, or perception, of another personality be thus purely subjective; if self cannot transcend its own plane of existence, what becomes of the great sacraments of religion and society ... of Love and Sympathy, of Faith and Hope, of Reverence and Dependence, of prayer and communion?[60]

So, in love, prayer, dependence, and charity (though Seal notices the abandonment of "old charities"[61]), we see the personal as "crossing over" in denial—as if of the private tinge of what Seal calls "over-subjectivity and individualism."[62] This concurs with what I've been arguing till now.

The second step is only a bit further from this, and in the next two chapters, I shall be interested more in the second point Seal makes: the reality of the external personality. This interrogation will merge in his denomination of modernity as entailing an "objective criticism" of life leading to

---

[59] Brajendranath Seal, "The Neo Romantic Movement in Literature (1890–91)," in *New Essays in Criticism (1903)*, (Calcutta: Papyrus, [1903]1994), 13–84.

[60] Ibid., 36.

[61] Ibid., 38.

[62] Ibid.

estimating and appraising things and institutions according to the measure in which they fulfill the end or law of their own being, or reflect the regulative idea of their type or pattern, and not according to the measure of their adaptation to our subjective desires, or individualistic appetite.[63]

Institutions as external personalities with a spirit of their own: what does it entail? Is the spirit contradicted at any point in time? How consequential is it, then? We shall deal with some of these questions in the next chapter.

---

[63] Ibid., 43.

# Part Two

# Engaging the Personal: Modernity, Legality, and the Practice of Helping

# 5

# Personal in Colonial and Postcolonial Modernity: From Natural Personality to Personality of Organizations

Inspired by our exploration and finding—particularly in the previous two chapters, we can safely and securely opine—it is now common knowledge that the essence of modernity is the public/private divide, and the failure to find its way beyond the dichotomy. I have argued that the personal is not a synonym of the private and, thereby, not the antonym of the public either.

In this chapter, I deploy this paradigm by investigating how the indeterminate, whimsical, and, thus, in a sense transcendent status of personal giving or helping haunts, and in a way subverts the founding of public and determinately rational welfare schemes. The founding aim of this chapter is to propose a theoretical matrix by which the transition from old age charities may be compared to the new forms of helping in modernity—colonial modernity in particular. This is done through re-invoking (apart from the well-known Bankimchandra) a long forgotten 19th century Bengali neo-Hegelian of colonial Bengal and re-inscribing the vagaries of his interpretive reading of the first modernizer of India: Rammohun Roy. Hegel is relevant, being the first philosopher of modernity and a major theorist of civil society. In fact we have here Hegel's proposal to institute civil society through "intelligent" forms of public helping, and we know that the colonizing project in its modernizing periodization was an experiment in instituting forms of civil society where a neatly forgotten 19th century neo-Hegelian (Seal) becomes an emblematic icon trapped in this impasse.

Having prefaced our work with the our aims, scope, tools, and rationale, now we are ready to chart the route the chapter will take.

The chapter in its first part and beginning tries to show—through an interpretive reading of Bankimchandra Chatterjee's *Dharmatattva*—how the affirmation of ordinary life generated a secular ethic of social virtue that emerges out of the sieve of religious, virtuous giving, and the central argument that found the modernist turn in helping. Next, it documents how Hegel—appreciating the universal aspects of poverty—had proposed the mediating institutions of civil society to order this transition. It picks up from the first part the conclusion that a secular science of helping emerged with the rejection of religious or a priori competence (*adhikaribhed*) by what has been called an affirmation of ordinary life or everyday life, and it elaborates on how the modern civil society was constructed to control or normalize that threat of arbitrariness and contingency that haunts (Hegel and) our daily life. Hegel's discussion of welfare, charity, etc. in civil society is briefly summarized and studied as a classic case. Civil society in the colonies form the next part. Here, the fate of such a hunt for the universal in 19th century Bengal is examined through the texts of a Bengali neo-Hegelian, Brajendranath Seal. I tediously follow Seal's reading of Rammohun Roy and his discourse of "theo-philanthropic" reform to show how, in colonial modernity, the construction of civil society through voluntary association receives an unexpected twist in the wake of Keshab Sen's astounding reading (when played against Seal's longer reading) of the multipersonal universalism of Rammohun. The specter of the personal demolishes the impersonal, publicly rational (and, thus, in a sense political) edifice of helping forms in the wake of instituting civil society in the colony. The specter of institutional or group personality haunts them all.

In the first conclusion, I try to assemble the observations made throughout this part.

Part II of this chapter (pace Hiralal Haldar—another forgotten neo-Hegelian of colonial Bengal) offers the trajectory of personality of organizations, and group personality, while culling two major case examples from the colonial and postcolonial inventory.

# I

## Helping: The Modernist Turn

In *Dharmatattva,* Bankimchandra Chatterjee (Chattopadhyay)—one of the great precursors of modernity in Bengal (and India)—sets the tone as to how new reified principles of conduct (or dharma) could be laid down in relation to helping. The book stages the old dialogic pattern of conversation between the master and the disciple by which diverse viewpoints become explicit and the speakers inhabit different but same speech worlds. The master begins by distinguishing Western charity from our kindness, compassion, or *daya*:

> The nurture of charity lies in kindness (*daya*) but the word "charity" seems to have caused a confusion. We usually understand charity to mean the giving of food, clothes, money and similar alms. But this is an extremely narrow sense of the term. It's true meaning is abnegation[1] ... "abnegation of all things; even the abnegation of the self ... right up to the sacrifice of one's self interest. ... You must do good unto others till you inflict pain and suffering upon yourself. That is true charity.[2]

Therefore, according to the master in *Dharmatattva,* the intrusion of the Western notion of charity has contaminated our notion of kindness, compassion, or daya. Charity ultimately is based on a principle of self-preservation and economy; self interest is finally protected, while daya or kindness entails a kind of self-division: sacrifice which brings hardship, pain, and suffering. This is required because it

> [i]s the true spirit of charity ... embodied in the Hindu Dharma, in the philosophy of the Gita. Otherwise, for you to give some alms to a beggar when you are pretty well provided for yourself is no charity—though it is a matter of considerable surprise as to the huge number who do not even do this.[3]

The master here rightly makes a distinction between barter/trade and charity—where a reference to Christian notions of charity is visible. The master says that charity for an afterlife in heaven is to "buy a plot of land in heaven and make an advance against its purchase, as it were. This is not dharma, but barter or trade."[4] But to suspend this notion of immanent exchange, the master brings forth a new resolution: he says, we have to choose the right kind of recipient who will receive charity.

---

[1] Bankimchandra Chattopadhyay, *Dharmatattva,* trans. Apratim Ray (1888; repr., New Delhi: Oxford University Press, 2003), 217.
[2] Ibid., 218.
[3] Ibid.
[4] Ibid.

Benevolence to everybody is like trying to remove sorrows of even those who do not have sorrows in the first place. Charity to the wrong beneficiary has other sinister consequences. It creates a class of degenerate people who are habitual beggars; parasites who feed on alms and eke an easy living. According to the Master, the wise ones have become disillusioned with charity in modern days only for such a reason: acts of misplaced charity. Now, to give kindness (or *dharmic* charity) its good name back, we have to perform charitable acts with discretion—"a virtuous discretion which will nurture kindness (daya) and follow the cultivation of right conduct or dharma."[5]

Charity with discretion is marked by the choice of recipients. Two classes of recipients have to be shunned; first, those who project themselves as necessary objects of charity; second, those who will reciprocate the charity-act (like the alms-deed) and will return something in exchange. Therefore, dharmic charity is successful only when it is performed with the sense or notion of rightness[6] and done unto one who has not the ability to reciprocate. Therefore, dharmic charity deploying real kindness (daya) and leading to love and devotion (*prem* and *bhakti*) calls for a positive discrimination and application. To put it simply, in *Dharmatattva*, the disciple enjoins: place, time, and person are important for dharmic charity to be successful. But here the master's intervention is enervating: the master rejects that the above calls for any specific explanation; he instead asks: Are not these considerations built into the very optic of everyday life? "[A]ll acts must be carried out bearing these factors in mind."[7] Now, if we are allowed to mark the transformative moment of the specifically modern notion of helping, that too in a non-Western but colonized culture, we would appreciate that the earlier mentioned is the moment. Rejecting the appeal that required a special application of mind as to who would be the genuine beneficiary of kindness or dharmic charitable benefits, the master in Bankim Chandra decides to give it the parameters of everyday ordinary action—the way we reflectively consider and apply ourselves with reference to time, place, and person. The dharmic charitable act loses its special pre-scriptural injunctional slot and becomes one with an ethic of virtue that is general or nonspecific and, thus, modern. An exemplary consequence of this transformation is immediately available

[5] Ibid.
[6] Ibid., 219.
[7] Ibid.

in the same text by Bankimchandra. If there is a famine in Bengal when at the same time relief is required in Manchester, what are we to do? An ordinary theory of social action will approve us to serve the here and now. The master in *Dharmatattva* similarly does not even require to elaborate on the principle of charity that will automatically unfold out of the mundane. Now, what is this modern ethic of virtue that touches and transforms the principle of charity in so much a radical manner? Alisdair MacIntyre answers: "an essential characteristic of [modern] human selfhood" [is] "the capacity to detach oneself from any particular standpoint or point of view, to step backwards, as it were, and view and judge that standpoint or point of view from the outside.[8] (This is perhaps not possible till customary support and traditions recede to the background. Ensconced within a rigorous framework of duties and scriptural sanctions, this neutrality and objectivity secured by 'stepping back' is not possible. Therefore, we have to assume here the desacralization of social life in Bengal.) However, it is evident that the transformation of charity as 'beyond duty' and/or as virtue, in modernity is subjected to the ethics of everyday virtue as in Bankim's *Dharmatattva*. This is in contrast to both the Christian traditions of charity and the Hindu traditions of *dana* and *daksina*. With the master in *Dharmatattva,* we are ready to undertake a secular heterogeneous notion of reform and social service that actually marked a transition from *seva* to *pariseva* (in Bengali taxonomy) removed from explicit religious claims,[9] or claims which are there to benefit the donor (i.e., "selfless service"), or dana as glorified within the patron-client relationship (in ancient and medieval India).

To resume, what is propagated finally is a kind of social virtue and not personal character-based practice of private virtue.[10] To follow

---

[8] Alisdair MacIntyre, *After Virtue: A Study in Moral Theory*, 2nd ed. (Notre Dame, IN: University of Notre Dame, 1984), 126.

[9]

> The organization of *seva* [or, correctly put, *pariseva* as an amalgamation of particular forms of services] provided by the Ramakrishna Movement between 1895 and 1912 was characterized by the use of public appeals, co-operation with government, public accountability, a move toward systematic record keeping, rational methods of working and a growing involvement in long-term projects; for example, the maintenance of permanent centers for relief operations, schools and orphanages.

See Gwilym Beckerlegge, "Swami Vivekananda and Seva: Taking Social Service Seriously," in *Swami Vivekananda and the Modernisation of Hinduism*, ed. William Radice (New Delhi: Oxford University Press, 1999), 175.

[10] G. W. F. Hegel, *The Philosophy of History*, trans. J. Sibree (New York, NY: Dover Publications, 1956), 66–67.

Hegel, hitherto we have had "personal character" and the "conscience of individuals—their particular will and mode of action;"[11] modes of helping were marked by "the litany of private virtues—modesty, humility, philanthropy and forbearance."[12] Social virtue in Hegel, based on a kind of universality bearing strong Kantian strains, recognizes the objective character of actions and wants while not being founded on "what the agent holds to be right or wrong, good and evil."[13]

Therefore, earlier, we have tried to clarify that it is the ethics of everyday life with an inbuilt sense of self-distancing that forms the essential, decisive moment in the narrative of helping in modernity. Having done that, we are able to anticipate an objection that will be addressed in a later section. Now, the objection is simple; if it is ordinary action or mundane practical activity that provides the parameters of a new modernist helping, there is a danger that it might just succumb to the arbitrariness and unrest of daily life. One is tempted to consider the fact that, given the condition mentioned earlier, such helping will lose all its distinctiveness, being dissolved in fragmented life-worlds or surrender to the systematic disintegration that the everyday life-world of ours suffers from. In such a state, "helping" might just assume "unintelligent" forms, "deception" is a daily occurrence here (these are all Hegel's phrases to which we'll return later in detail), and everyday life is marked by this non-distinction of particularity and universality: anybody wearing the mask of universality gives us a semblance of rights, and we think that we are getting our due and end up being cheated. Welfare of others then requires a systematic treatment rather than just a parochial one; but Hegel will first consider the moment when we are interested in advancing our own interests "regardless" of others, where the arbitrariness and unpredictable unrest of our daily life asks to be tempered. We have arrived at Hegel and his discussion of civil society.

## The Ghost of "Arbitrariness" and "Contingency": Civil Society in Hegel

Civil society as we know in Hegel appears between the family and the state. It includes the economic community in which citizens fulfill their

---

[11] Ibid., 67.
[12] Ibid.
[13] Ibid., 66.

wants or needs, the administration of justice, and, finally, the police and corporation. Outside of the family and the state, the individuals appear as independent persons pursuing their own selfish-private interests while trying to use others as means. In the process of pursuing private ends, inadvertently, common ends are also accomplished. This is the received definition of civil society in Hegel. We are interested in a different strand of this discourse. Civil society in Hegel appears as a realm where, while trying to accomplish particular interests, universal ends are accomplished. There are two points to note here: first, all particular ends require the compulsory presence of other people to be used as means; second, all people end up, though involuntarily, serving the whole community. But civil society being the site where private individuals pursue private ends, the threat of caprice lies open

> [d]ue to the variability of the wants themselves, in which opinion and subjective good-pleasure play a great part. It results also from circumstances of locality ... from errors and deceptions which can be foisted upon single members of the social circulation and are capable of creating disorder in it;[14] civil society tries to temper this "threat" in a manner of its own.

Given that, Hegel argues, "since particularity is tied to the condition of universality, the whole [of civil society] is the sphere of mediation in which all individual characteristics, all aptitudes, and all accidents of birth and fortune are liberated."[15] Thus begins the drama where Hegel seems to have been theorizing civil society as something that normalizes or controls arbitrariness or contingency that pervades our everyday life beginning with the site that is the family.

The discussion is available in his *The Philosophy of Subjective Spirit*[16] where Hegel somewhat categorically (very unlike of him) charts this suspicion. In his view, contingency resides with "individual subjects" or singular souls: "Its mode of being is the special temperament, talent, character, physiognomy and other dispositions and idiosyncrasies,[17] ... it is in this soul that the sphere of contingency is initiated. Individual souls

---

[14] G. W. F. Hegel, *Hegel's Philosophy of Mind, Translated from The Encyclopedia of the Philosophical Sciences,* trans. William Wallace (Oxford: Clarendon Press, 1894), 261.

[15] G. W. F. Hegel, *Elements of the Philosophy of Right,* trans: H. B. Nisbet (1991; repr., Cambridge: Cambridge University Press, 2000), 220–21 (italics mine).

[16] G. W. F. Hegel, *The Philosophy of Subjective Spirit,* transl. M. J. Petry (Holland: D. Reidelberg Company, 1979).

[17] Ibid., 83.

are distinguished from one another by an endless multitude of contingent modifications."[18]

The discussion becomes more effective and illuminating when Hegel comes to the education of children. We are of the view that teaching is best when it brings out the individuality of the child. To Hegel, this is a clear mistake. The teacher "has not the time to do so."[19] Further, it is not necessary either. "The peculiarity of children is tolerated in the family circle."[20] Hegel's conclusion is definitive: "The more educated a person is, the less will his behavior exhibit anything contingent and simply peculiar to him."[21]

Transferring the potential of this insight to charity in relation to the discourse of enlightenment, we find that this is in absolute concurrence with Rousseau's observation on Emile's education. There, charity is a pedagogic virtue without which Emile's education will remain imperfect. In response to the principle of "active benevolence," Rousseau is referring to "an education whose principles engender charity."[22] Charity as a pedagogic virtue and not a religious one imbibes the hunger for the universal that is so peculiar to the Hegelian view of education in schools. Education "irons out" particularities, and, therefore, the kind of charity that grows out of this leveling also, expectedly, is not anything that will be disorganized, unsystematic, and reflective of peculiarities of people. As we've noted before, this is symptomatic of the modern, secular view of helping.

We have been trying to bring out how one of the registers of civil society—education—becomes in Hegel a method to restrain the "accidental subjectivities" and sympathies that personalities of people imply. Briefly put, through education a student will be able to recognize "the universal aspect of the object."[23]

But what about those who will be unable for various reasons to secure education? Directly related to the discourse of helping, this is the second register of an interesting aspect of civil society in Hegel. Hegel anticipates, and rightly so, that the blind play of private interests in the economic

---

[18] Ibid., 85.

[19] Ibid.

[20] Ibid.

[21] Ibid.

[22] Michel Delon, ed., "Charity," in *Encyclopedia of Enlightenment* (Chicago: Fitzroy Dearborn Publishers, 2001), 1: 233–34.

[23] Hegel, *Philosophy of Right*, 226.

community in civil society may push many to the state of degrading poverty. However, other factors are also there. According to Hegel:

> Not only arbitrariness, however, but also contingent physical factors and circumstances based on external conditions may reduce individuals to poverty. In this condition, they are left with the needs of civil society and yet since society has at the same time taken from them the natural means of acquisition, ... they are more or less deprived of all the advantages of society, such as the ability to acquire skills and education in general, as well as of the administration of justice, health care, and often even of the consolation of religion.[24]

And what do "their predicament and sense of wrong"[25] give rise to? It seems Hegel reproduces the historical consensus on the matter: "Laziness, viciousness and other vices."[26] These, in fact, are what Hegel thinks as the "subjective aspects of poverty,"[27] where poverty induces peculiarities in individual subjects. And this requires—derivatively—"subjective help, both with regard to the particular circumstances and with regard to emotion and love. This is a situation in which, notwithstanding all universal arrangements, morality finds plenty to do."[28]

What Hegel is referring to by the name of subjective help is the aspect of sentimental, optional benevolence or private charity led by personal idiosyncrasies. But the Hegelian civil society cannot approve of this, and Hegel admits that: firstly because of the fact that "livelihood of the needy would be ensured without the mediation of work" by being simply dependent on others, which violates the principle of civil society where all are self-regarding persons and, therefore, justly, the burden of poverty has to be borne by poor people themselves; secondly, it is a violation of the self-respect or the dignity of the poor person.[29] Therefore, in consonance

[24] Ibid., 265.
[25] Ibid.
[26] Ibid.
[27] Ibid.
[28] Ibid.
[29] This point that alms degrade men is emphatically available in Kant.

> Better than charity, better than giving of our surplus is conscientious and scrupulously fair conduct and a helping hand in need. ... Alms degrade men. It would be better to see whether the poor man could not be helped in some other way which would not entail his being degraded by accepting alms.

See Immanuel Kant, "Poverty and Charity," in *Lectures On Ethics,* trans. Louis Infield (New York, NY: Harper and Row, 1963), 235–36.

with the primary proposal, Hegel appropriately declares: "But since this help, both in itself and in its effects, is dependent on contingency, society endeavors to make it less necessary by identifying the universal aspects of want and taking steps to remedy them."[30]

Throw in here the fact that Hegel, in this context, goes so far as to say that when I—being guided by my personal idiosyncrasies or "out of love"—give something to somebody and not to the more deserving ones or without inviting the universal to "have a share in the action," I "cheat the universal out of its right."[31] Thereby, what Hegel does is to introduce the concept of objective help that, having discovered the universal aspects of want, institutes public modes of addressing the same. In brief, Hegel is keen to arrive at—following the formal character of his concept of civil society—some principle of helping that will not be contingent, arbitrary, and subjective. What are they? They are a series of examples catalogued by Hegel, "public poorhouses, hospitals, street lighting, etc." But Hegel does not rule out the functions of contingent helping as well—and this is important. "Charity still retains enough scope for action," but

> [i]t is mistaken if it seeks to restrict the alleviation of want to the particularity of emotion and the contingency of its own disposition and knowledge, and if it feels injured and offended by universal rulings and precepts of an obligatory kind. On the contrary, public conditions should be regarded as all the more perfect the less there is left for the individual to do by himself in the light of his own particular opinion (as compared with what is arranged in a universal manner)."[32]

So Hegel's model of helping in civil society is inspired by a kind of public mediation of wants, but the term that he uses for this kind of help is "intelligent." In this last part, therefore, using this description of intelligence, let us try to delineate finally the Hegelian mode of civil society. What Hegel disapproves is the kind of "unintelligent love" that is characteristic of singular, contingent acts of incidental charity. And here to describe the intelligent mode of helping, Hegel connects it, albeit for the first time, with the state: "Intelligent, substantial beneficence is, however, in its richest and most important form the intelligent universal action of

---

[30] Hegel, *Philosophy of Right*, 265.
[31] G. W. F. Hegel, *Phenomenology of Spirit*, transl. A. V. Miller (New Delhi: Motilal Banarasidass Publishers Pvt. Limited, 1998), 255.
[32] Hegel, *Philosophy of Right*, 265–66.

the state—an action compared with which the action of a single individual as an individual, is so insignificant that it is hardly worth talking about."[33] But this rhetoric of disapproval, we must note, had not gained such energy before, because here what Hegel is interrogating is not merely the arbitrary, contingent nature of personal helping, but the sheer existence of such helping through these strong words not uttered ever before; the first part we know, but we shall attend most to the second part:

> The only significance left for beneficence, which is a sentiment, is that of an action which is quite single and isolated, of help in [a situation of] need, which is as contingent as it is transitory. Chance determines not only the occasion of the action but also whether it is a "work" at all, whether it is not immediately undone and even perverted into something bad. Thus, this acting for the good of others which is said to be necessary, is of such kind that it may, or may not, exist.[34]

We are, of course, aware of the solution offered by Hegel and need not rehearse it here. But what might be asked is that, irrespective of the risk of repetition of the first part, what is so new about this passage with which it became incumbent upon us to end this section? Let us offer this as the working summary of this section.

We have been trying to trace how the secular modernist mode of helping inscribed within the restlessness of everyday spirit tries to normalize and temper the arbitrariness and contingency of personal acts of charity through the mediating institutions of civil society. We made a case study of Hegel, where Hegel's proposal is, through state-related, public forms of intelligent helping, singular, isolated, and illusory modes of personal and private modes of helping may become redundant or play a supplementary role—at the most. But it can play a supplementary role only when it has a minimum of positivity granted to it, that is, if it is not an entity (or in Aristotelian terms, a substance) at all, or if it does not therefore have a bare existence, how can it play even a supplementary role? This suspicion emerges strongly with the last paragraph quoted earlier where Hegel is disputing the status of personal and private mode of helping as a work at all because of its illusory nature and the possibility of perversion—in short—of deception. With this, we've returned to the point with which we had begun: deception and the perverted will of the giver. Through

---

[33] Hegel, *Phenomenology of Spirit*, 255.
[34] Ibid., 256.

recommendations of intelligent, public modes of helping what Hegel is trying to do then—apart from normalizing the threat of arbitrariness and contingency—is to introduce some kind of moral world view, which also, as we know, forms the cornerstone of modernity. Hegel is then hunting the universal in civil society and trying to give a kind of fixity to helping processes in civil society so that people are not deceived, the universal is not cheated, and that good works are works and they are good too. Summarily and brutally put, Hegel is trying to depart from the risky terrain of a virtuous theory of personal giving to an impersonal, institutional way of public assistance.

We shall examine in the next section what fate this search finally assumes at the site where civil society, while looking for consumers when "production exceeds the needs of consumers,"[35] has to "go beyond its own confines" or is "historically driven to establish colonies."[36] The next section may, therefore, bear the subtitle "the fate of civil society in the colonies;" the title will be explained in the beginning of the section itself.

## The "Multipersonal" Universalism of Rammohun Roy or the Fate of Civil Society in the Colonies

Though in the penultimate lines of the last section I've quoted Hegel as saying how civil society is historically driven to establish colonies, I've stopped short of saying that this also inaugurates—and we know it does—the postcolonial critique of Hegel. The synopsis of that critique is—in the language of Spivak—Hegel is a strong moment in the "epistemic graphing of imperialism."[37] Apart from Gayatri Spivak, Ranajit Guha[38] has approved of such a critique in his works. Now, it would not be correct, or perhaps even possible, to engage with Hegel in the colonies without referring to the critique; but as it will be shown, I'll not require this critique at all. Not, because I think this critique, by and large, is misplaced. This misplacement emerges handy because its authors consider

---

[35] Hegel, *Philosophy of Right*, 269.

[36] Ibid., 267.

[37] Gayatri Chakravorty Spivak, *A Critique of Postcolonial Reason, Towards a History of the Vanishing Present* (Calcutta: Seagull, 1999), 65.

[38] Ranajit Guha, *History at the Limit of World-History* (Oxford: Oxford University Press, 2003).

Hegel without his system.[39] But the point is not whether Hegel belongs to this or that kind of historiography. If there is anything that Hegel belongs to, it would be a philosophical history that some, including Hegel, have observed as a kind of a priori history, that is, Hegel is said to have provided the transcendental conditions by which the experience of history or us experiencing history becomes possible. Following Gillian Rose, the historical a priori is the precondition of the possibility of actual historical facts or values; "it is an apriori, that is, not empirical, for it is the basis of the possibility of experience."[40] This experience is not dependent on the empirical realities of factual history because the latter kind of material history draws its categories or becomes possible by such already present forms. For instance, we would not be able to make sense of anything called social facts if we did not presuppose the concept of society; similarly, historical facts are nothing without the [a priori] concept of history. "It cannot be a fact, because it is the precondition of" [historical] "facts and hence cannot be one of them: it is a 'transcendent objectivity'."[41] Hegel is, in fact, categorical on this: "the philosophy of history is nothing more than the application of thought to history."[42] This thought in Hegel is the self-activity of the concept which is independent of empirical data: "Philosophy ... is credited with independent thoughts produced by pure speculation, without reference to actuality ... [and] ... forces it [i.e., the latter] to conform to its preconceived notions and constructs a history a priori."[43]

That endorses the perceptive remark made by William Stace that civil society is a logical derivation and not a historical derivation in Hegel.[44]

---

[39] A plain historical approach may be corrected in the following way: Take, for instance, the observation that the Hegelian construct of civil society exhibits exhortations that express Hegel's fear of the *rabble* or the large mass of the poor people. Some with a historical nose smelled in this Hegel's fear of the future industrial proletariat and the communist revolution. It has been recently pointed out how this is mistaken. Hegel's face is, rather, turned toward the past. It is, rather, England's poor law that could be said to have had a remote thematic reference. For some of such corrections see Gareth Stedman Jones, "Hegel and the Economics of Civil Society," in *Civil Society: History and Possibilities*, eds. Sudipta Kaviraj and Sunil Khilnani (Cambridge: Cambridge University Press, 2002), 105–30.

[40] Gillian Rose, *Hegel: Contra Sociology* (London: Athlone, 1981), 14.

[41] Ibid., 15.

[42] G. W. F. Hegel, *Lectures on the Philosophy of World History, Introduction: Reason in History,* trans. H. B. Nisbet (Cambridge: Cambridge University Press, 1987), 25.

[43] Ibid.

[44] William Terence Stace, *The Philosophy of Hegel: A Systematic Exposition* (New York, NY: Dover Publications, 1955), 412.

And the justification of such a logical derivation, Hegel is very clear on this, cannot "come from the world of experience." Because

> [w]hat philosophy understands by conceptual thinking is something quite different; in this case, comprehension is the activity of the concept itself, and not a conflict between a material and a form of separate origin. An alliance of disparates such as is found in pragmatic history is not sufficient for the purposes of conceptual thinking as practiced in philosophy; for the latter derives its content and material essentially from within itself. In this respect, therefore, despite the alleged links between the two, the original dichotomy remains: the historical event stands opposed to the independent concept.[45]

Therefore, Hegel—given his project—should be judged for the correctness of the philosophical journey that he traces for autonomous concepts rather than being faulted for various cultural and ideological, anthropological reasons; we are, perhaps, forgetting his own objections made against such trials. The postcolonials have made Hegel—unlike Marx and for all the wrong reasons—stand on his head "requiring identity of the non-identical. Historic contingency and the concept are the more mercilessly antagonistic the more solidly they are entwined."[46] I think this last reprimand from Adorno forecloses the postcolonial critique[47] that prides itself by placing Hegel on the imperial theatre.

Situated against this the colonial reading of Hegel are Brajendranath Seal and Hiralal Haldar. All of the postcolonial maneuvers were anticipated and included in their writings with better theoretical correctness. But, who reads Brajendranath Seal now? And moreover, who now reads Hiralal Haldar? That there were these 19th century scholars in Bengal who had wanted to "correct"[48] Hegel (Seal) in those strong, sunlit days of

---

[45] Hegel, *Philosophy of World History*, 26.

[46] Theodor Adorno, *Negative Dialectics,* trans. E. B. Ashton (London: Routledge, 1973, 359.

[47] Gayatri Spivak in her more deconstructive moods remarks that there is a lack of fit between morphology and narrative in Hegel (see Gayatri Chakravorty Spivak, *Outside in the Teaching Machine* [New York, NY: Routledge, 1993], 209). But, if that is so, then Hegel's historical narrative should be assumed to have been belied by his abstruse and complicated logical machinery or morphology; in other words, Hegel could be shown to have been opposing his own historical conclusions. Among those who are known as "postcolonials" and have engaged with Hegel, it is, to my mind, only Partha Chatterjee who has been able to avoid this trap by not trying to *historically* address Hegel. See Partha Chatterjee, "Communities and the Nation," in *The Nation and its Fragments* (New Delhi: Oxford University Press, 1994), 220–39.

[48] Brajendranath Seal, "The Neo Romantic Movement in Literature (1890–91)," in *New Essays in Criticism (1903)* (Calcutta: Papyrus, 1994), 13–84.

Hegelianism or had argued with an original neo-Hegelian philosopher (J. E. Mactaggart) over the correct interpretation of the absolute[49] is absolutely forgotten now. Forgotten, yes, but strangely. If these weak days are marked by a certain post, postcolonial-postmodern or whatever, it cannot be denied that what we are debating or contemplating is modernity. Then let us point out that Brajendranath Seal has—besides elaborations and formulations— explicit observations to make on modernity, literary modernism, and other similar things. In the 19th century, it was Seal (and I think he was the only one in that) who had defined modernity as the criticism[50] of social life or the discovery of the individual with a single scheme of life. And a hundred years after, Charles Taylor in his classic contemporary study[51] would extend such theses and establish them beyond doubt. But the despair remains. So far as the theoretical discussion of modernity is concerned, I think Bankimchandra Chatterjee is definitely interesting, but Brajendranath Seal or, more than him, Hiralal Haldar is rigorous.

But to debunk the postcolonial readings of Hegel through his colonial readings is, for the present occasion, not central. It is rather to reiterate what we had told in the beginning of this section: to engage with Hegel or Hegelese in the colony, we may justifiably (for reasons elaborated earlier) bypass the postcolonial critique of Hegel.

Let us return—with this knowledge—to Hegel and the philosophical fate of civil society in the colony where we had left ourselves. Now, if deception is one moment that Hegel wants to encounter through the formal equalization of public assistance and corporations, is it not coincidental that Brajendranath Seal, while writing a treatise on Raja Rammohun Roy—the alleged "father" of modern India and meditating on his inner history, writes how Roy "divides mankind, in Voltaire's (and Volney's)[52] fashion,

---

[49] Hiralal Haldar, *Hegelianism and Human Personality* (Calcutta: University of Calcutta, 1910).

[50] Also, "an objective criticism, appraising things according to the measure in which they fulfill the law of their being, or reflect the regulative idea of their type or pattern." See Brajendranath Seal, "The Neo Romantic Movement in Literature (1890–91)," in *New Essays in Criticism (1903)* (Calcutta: Papyrus, 1994), 57.

[51] Charles Taylor, *Sources of the Self: The Making of the Modern Identity* (Cambridge, MA: Harvard University Press, 1989).

[52] Dilip Kumar Biswas, a Rammohun specialist, disagrees with Seal. He opines that instead of Voltaire et al., it was Roy's engagement with Islamic discourses where one might seek the sources of this comparison. See Dilip Kumar Biswas, *Rammohun Samiksha* (Kolkata: Saraswat Library, 1983), 62.

into four classes—those who deceive, those who are deceived, those who both deceive and are deceived, and those who are neither deceivers, nor deceived."[53] If we link this with the Hegelian argument on civil society, then we shall be examining how the principle of deception instituted through the haze of multiple particularities and personal idiosyncrasies, gets normalized or controlled through what Seal calls a "principle of organization."[54] Seal—who thinks this element of deception is more psychological than historical[55] is seeking in Roy not personal principles but a "principle of organisation" to emerge in civil society. (Whether this could be called a principle of reform is another debate.) And it emerges from his argument that the later Rammohun (more organizationally inclined) perhaps for this reason holds Seal's interest longer, "In later life he more and more directed his studies from doctrines to institutions, and his efforts from Polemics to Reform." Thereafter, having begun with a "comparative study of religions," he ended up making—a "comparative study of social institutions."[56] But what is ironical and interesting, as well is a common theme running through the large literature on Rammohun Roy, is the study of the personality of Rammohun Roy in terms of virtues or character. (Even in Seal, Rammohun appears first with his inner history and then in terms of external social history.) William Adam lecturing at "Boston, U.S.A. in 1845" says: "Philanthropy is a Christian virtue not found in Asia where Raja adopts it with exceptional skills and virtue of personal conduct, and then 'gave a character to ... age and country'."[57] Now, if this argument is accepted, then it has implications for our future argument. We know from our extensive discussion of Hegel's civil society that from a personal virtuous theory of philanthropy in civil society and in order to forego its subjective deceptive consequences, Hegel was proposing an objective, "intelligent," structural theory of public assistance. Seal, by proposing a "principle of organization" for Rammohun is going in the same direction—but only apparently; the tale will be told—much against their intentions—through the narrative registers rejecting which civil society emerges. Curiously enough, this virtuous reading of Rammohun's

---

[53] Brajendranath Seal, *Rammohun Roy: The Universal Man* (Calcutta: Sadharan Brahmo Samaj, 1933), 10.

[54] Ibid., 2.

[55] Ibid., 10.

[56] Ibid., 8.

[57] William Adam, *A Lecture on the Life and Labours of Rammohun Roy*, ed. Rakhal Das Haldar (1879; repr., Calcutta: Sadharan Brahmo Samaj: Calcutta, 1977), 3.

persona will elicit an interesting debate, and the debate will also take an interesting turn with Keshab Sen entering the frame.

We have talked about the discussion of personality that is a running theme in the discourses on Rammohun. And in such discussions, what is endlessly repeated is the diverse, pluralistic nature of Rammohun's personality, and as per a virtuous theory, it is held that Rammohun simply transferred these virtues to the social field. But even then a problem persists and this, I'll argue, is crucial. Seal says,

> As I have said elsewhere, Raja Rammohun Roy was a Brahmin of Brahmins. He was also Mahomedan with Mahomedans, and a Christian with Christians. He could, thus, combine in his personal religion the fundamentals of Hindu, Christian and Islamic experiences. In this way he was, strange to say, multipersonal. But behind all these masks[58] there was yet another Rammohun Roy, the humanist, pure and simple, watching the procession of Universal Humanity in Universal History.[59]

And the problem of wearing "so many masks, personae, on the public stage in bewildering succession"[60] was evident: "After his death, Moslems claimed him for Islam, and Christians for Christianity. But still others are puzzled. Was he all things to all men?"[61] Now being all things to all men is the realm of deceptive particularity. Seal's mask argument pejoratively revokes the complaint—if he was all things to all men, what was he? How did he have a personality? How would work, to use Hegel, be truly work or good? Seal's answer is equivocal, "And yet in playing so many parts he kept his personality intact and integral."[62] How? "These historic cults and cultures had been fused in one discipline of Universal Humanity in his soul. ... But the centre of centres in himself was beyond them all. ... He thus showed how universal Humanity in future may realize in individual synthesis of life. ..."[63]

So in Seal, the answer finally is that the multipersonal universality of Rammohun ultimately meshed to produce an individual synthesis of

---

[58] Basing myself on the mask or *persona* and the *aesthetics* of Hegel, I elaborate elsewhere (not in this work) how the figurative character of charity (made memorable by the Pascalian saying that charity is not figurative), which civil society tries to suppress, opens up, through the bursting of allegories in poetry and painting, an immense number of interesting readings.

[59] Seal, *Rammohun Roy*, 37–38.

[60] Ibid., 24.

[61] Ibid., 26.

[62] Ibid., 27.

[63] Ibid.

life, or what Seal elsewhere terms as an individual with a scheme of life. Where is the principle of an impersonal organization—so very crucial to the founding of an active civil society—that Seal had proposed earlier? Instead, as our detour shows, it is the principle of personality or personal principles that masquerade as the real principles. In institutions, they are just externalized, or all institutions are just internal—in this sense. This becomes evident when Seal appears onto the discussion of Brahmo Samaj. Seal says, "The Raja's social model, the Brahmo Samaj was but a faint external replica of the universalism he had raised in his own person. ..."[64] Nothing could be more explicit a statement, and nothing could be more telling about the failure of the principle of organization that was destined to found civil society in the colonies where the ills of the old society was to be purged to arrive at modernity. And the first ill would have been, as per Hegel too, the transitory, contingent character of personal benevolence, even if that dawns the mask of "multipersonal universalism." And in the face of this failure, Seal's other compensatory exhortations that Rammohun was a believer in "natural rights of man" or that he spoke "oftener in terms of happiness than of rights, 'common good' over 'contract'"[65] does not help him recover from the thematic failure of his project.

But Keshab Chandra Sen's arrival at the scene to answer the same question gives an interesting direction to the impasse—though it cannot solve it. In fact, Sen's answer is more conducive to Seal's initial hypothesis, which is also the hypothesis of civil society. The question as we know was pretty simple, and Keshab Sen knew it. According to Sen, the Raja's "ruling idea" of mind was that in trying to promote "the universal worship of the One Supreme Creator," he had become "a member of no church and yet of all churches."[66] Now, to answer this problem, Sen gave altogether a different twist to the debate. He did not, unlike Seal, explore the "inner history" or the universal content of religions personified in the Raja, rather he opined that

> The trust Deed of the Samaj premises contains, we believe, the clearest exposition of his idea and will, it is hoped, if duly appreciated, settle all

---

[64] Ibid., 25.

[65] Ibid., 30.

[66] Keshub Chunder Sen, "The Brahmo Samaj, or Theism in India," in *The Golden Book of Rammohun Roy*, ed. Saroj Mohan Mitra (Calcutta: Rammohun Library & Free Reading Romm, 1997), 164–73.

contested points regarding that illustrious man's religious convictions. It provides that: "The said message or building, land, tenements, hereditaments and premises with their appurtenances should be used, occupied, enjoyed, applied and appropriated as, and for, a place of public meeting of all sorts and descriptions of people without distinction.[67] [And with a tendency to] "the promotion of charity, morality, piety, benevolence, virtue and the strengthening the bonds of union between men of all religions persuasions and creeds".[68]

Now, what is the advantage of Keshab Sen's interpretation over Seal's? How would it be charted against the problem of activating a civil society in the colonies? How would it solve the contingent particularity of personal and private helping, philanthropy, charity which haunts even such a philosopher as Hegel?

I think in Seal we've had a virtue-based personalism, and institutions emerge from that only. Seal does not—in an attempt to solve the debate on positions of Rammohun—take recourse to an intensive analysis of relevant organizations; rather, he assumes that they may be solved by an analysis of the inner history or psychological principles—in short, the personality of the Raja himself.

Keshab Sen, in order to resolve the dispute over taking positions in social life by a personality (Rammohun), does not engage with the internal ideological riddles and ripples growing and dissolving in the internal psyche of the personality. He, instead, is taking recourse to the trust deed of an institution, which he thinks "will settle all contested points." The institution will prove the personality. With this, we've arrived at the "principle of organization" originally promised by Seal and which is outside the arbitrary principle of personalities and personal choices. With this also—so far as helping, etc. are concerned—it is the institutional realm that will be decisive.[69]

To hazard a quick recap, in the present section, we've observed how it was required of Hegel to propose a kind of helping that would override the transitory, contingent, and arbitrary character of personal and private charity. State-related public assistance was Hegel's solution, which he thought recognized the universal, objective character of wants and poverty.

---

[67] Ibid., 169.
[68] Ibid., 170.
[69] Later, the arrival of social work as the science of helping with a large body of services and provisions, expert knowledge, regulation of institutions, and an absolute disapproval of personal and private charity that may be conjectured, was along these lines.

But civil society—driven by its "inner dialectic" to go for colonies— provides an interesting and complicated story in the colonies. We engaged with the career of the "father" of "modern" India—Rammohun—and saw that he—as per the interpretation of Seal and a host of others—sought to appropriate this "universal" in the contingent, virtuous particularities of his personality. This is in absolute violation of the principle of civil society (and, thus, modernity) classically conceived by Hegel. With Keshab Chandra Sen's interpretation of the deceptive "multipersonal universalism" of Rammohun, the impersonal institutional principle is somewhat restored.

## Concluding Remarks

The story of secular modernist-objective-intelligent helping that is symptomatic of Hegelian civil society then fails in the colony. But this was not a conscious maneuver. In fact, the attempt was to concur always with the paradigmatic registers of modernity. The impossibility of a theory of an alternative modernity, I think, lies here. It can be shown, therefore, why self-conscious attempts to find an alternative modernity are perhaps bereft of such a possibility, partly because there the unconscious narrative—against all the intentions of its agents—will tell a different story. What I'll examine in future is this tensed dialectic. It might seem that the story I'm about to tell is a long story of failure. I'll comment on the theory of this failure later.

For the moment, let us reiterate that though the institutional interpreta- tion of Keshab Sen has been endorsed in the chapter as auguring well with the principles of civil society, I've resisted the temptation to show how even this falls a victim to the personal and how even through this failure provides a model to think beyond the limits of public/private divide.

The second proposal shall be pursued in the subsequent, upcoming part of this chapter, but let us necessarily anticipate the fate of the so-called institutional interpretation of Keshab Sen. Again, to reiterate what Sen had proposed, irrespective of the vagaries and contradictions of one's personal character, we need to look forward to the personality of the organization from which the personality of the person may be inferred. But Keshab Sen stopped short of the dangerous possibilities of such an interpretation. The institution embodies a separate personality—a personality of its own— which stands apart from its members—even apart from its founder. This is close to granting it the (now available)[70] status of juristic personality or personality embodied in institutions and sanctioned by law—which becomes real through a trust deed, legal oath, undertaking, or activity. And when after a few years a split became imminent over old/young rivalry in Brahmo Samaj, this truth that institutions have personality of their own assumed body. The irony of this was that no amount of "multipersonal universalism" was universal enough to grasp and contain all the members irrespective of age, creed, caste, etc. though the trust deed had declared so.[71]

Therefore, with the "multipersonal universalism" failing and personalism's triumph with even institutional personality invading, is not our interpretive grid able to account for not only our past but also present history? Now, to claim legitimacy and contemporary relevance of this interpretive paradigm which is I think better suited to chart the (albeit failed) transition of helping processes from old age charities to social work, I shall claim a final example. Belur Math (the official headquarter of Ramakrishna Mission) had a publication in 2003, which is also an official treatise on consciousness raising and organization of the Ramakrishna Mission and sister organizations. The author—a leading monk of the math—declares:

> Every organization behaves like a living being. For this reason every establishment or organization may be called—an impersonal personality ("*nyarbyaktik byaktitvo*"). In the larger context of society, the individual image that any organization bears, is its impersonal personality. If we imagine a radiant backdrop, a backdrop that influences and attracts the larger society behind that impersonal personality, it must depend on its members'

---

[70] It is interesting and contextually exciting to note that a history that attempts to document charities and social aid in Greece and Rome requires to inform us in a chapter titled "Charities and Legal Personality" (See A. R. Hands, *Charities and Social Aid in Greece and Rome* [Great Britain: Thames and Hudson, 1968], 17–25) about the way modern charities "are generally institutions existing in their own right; ... independently of the continued existence of the particular body which may be administering it at any given time" (p. 17). But this modern inheritance, it may be noted, does have a very relevant pre-history too.
"The establishment of permanent endowments, administered by trusts of this nature was notably encouraged by the Elizabethan Act of charitable uses in the post Reformation period, ... similar to those which in the Middle Ages had been granted by the Ecclesiastical Courts to charities..." (pp. 17–18).

[71] Given the current conjuncture of discourses on what some call "globalization," it is time we rehearse these lessons.

renunciation, liberality, purity, truthfulness, neutrality, perseverance and the will to pursue *seva*. And all these virtues are results of genuine love for Sri Ramakrishna. And to render this a better image what is necessary is, a genuine social welfarist agenda or a developmental model.[72]

Nothing could be a better deployment of the interpretive paradigm we had been proposing. In 2003, the notion of institutional (impersonal) personality and the virtuous theory of religious origin shared a peaceful co-existence; seva is just one among many personal virtues of the monk, and the schedule of social welfare is invoked to improve upon the current image made up by such incidental conjunctions. What is not answered is how the universal would bear the burden of such personal particularities. The failure that was inaugurated in the 19th century, then, continues unabated. Our interpretive graph is successful in rendering this trajectory transparent.

So, apparently, what we had thought of agreeing with the registers of civil society (or modernity) failed to sustain the universal conferred upon it. With everything failing, as Hegel remarked, pathos not only becomes joyous but is a work of art. But, as I had mentioned before, the theory of this failure will tell that we are perhaps not wrong in choosing our addressee. It is Werner Hamacher who endorses such obsessions in the following manner.

Hamacher argues that modernity is founded on failure. If what we called the pre-modern or tradition (those much debunked words), had not failed, then modernity would not have come into being. In this sense, it is ridiculous to say modernity reflects an incomplete project because then the pre-modern could be said to have been similarly incomplete. Therefore, modernity not only has failure as its foundation, it is its lifeline "because it recognizes itself in the collapse of the old, modernity must make failure into its principle. Modernity must fail in order to stay modern."[73] When we want modernity to succeed, we want it to disown its basic premise and, thus, wishing for its annihilation.

Are we convinced now that by their sheer failure, the likes of Rammohun, Brajen Seal, Keshab Sen, and all others have given

[72] Swami Sarbagananda, *Bhavprachar O Samgathan* (Kolkata: Udbodhon Karyalaya, 2003), 44, (italicized words are in English in the original) in Bengali.
[73] Werner Hamacher, *Premises: Essays on Philosophy and Literature from Kant to Celan*, trans. Peter Fenves (Cambridge: Harvard University Press, 1990), 294.

modernity its tonic? They were not modern because they had succeeded in overcoming "tradition"; they were and still are modern because they had failed. And this failure; when recounted, is, at par with the Hegelian premises, reading returning to itself.[74] It is evident why—after nearly hundred years have elapsed after Brajen Seal or Hiralal Haldar—we've not stopped reading Hegel; we'll never stop writing Hegel too.

# II

# Group Personality and the Personality of Organization

*Human personality is a colony rather than an abstract entity.*

—Hiralal Haldar

In this part, as announced in the previous sections, we shall explore the personality of organizations as an instituting principle of an alternative modernity in the colony that have become historically definitive and have continued to stay with us. Here, we shall try to think it through Hiralal Haldar—another neo-Hegelian and a contemporary of Brajendranath Seal.

Some years ago, my attention was directed to the phenomenon of multiple personality and the problem arose in my mind: How is this fact to be harmonized with the Idealistic theory of the unity of the self ...[75] a flood of new light was, for me, thrown upon the pages of Hegel. I discovered that Hegel, after all, does not teach that the Absolute is a unitary personality. His real theory is that the Absolute is a unity differentiated into persons. It, in one word, is the organic unity of selves—the very thing that multiple personality is! I found a solution and my difficulties were over.... Early in 1909, I read for the first time, Dr J. E. McTaggart's *Studies in Hegelian Cosmology*. I was greatly delighted to find that he also concludes that the Absolute is a unity differentiated into selves. ... But though I agree with Dr McTaggart in thinking that the Absolute is a unity differentiated into

---

[74] Werner Hamacher, *Pleroma—Reading in Hegel: The Genesis and Structure of a Dialectical Hermeneutics in Hegel,* trans. N. Walker and S. Jarvis (London: The Athlone Press, 1998), 9.

[75] Hiralal Haldar, *Hegelianism and Human Personality* (Calcutta: University of Calcutta, 1910), iii.

persons, my differences with him are serious. I hold that the Absolute is a self conscious unity of its constituent selves, while Dr McTaggart is of opinion that it is an impersonal unity of persons.

Yet, this is but too terse a formulation of what Haldar had attempted and the suggestive consequences that it entails. Let us follow Haldar as he uncovers his argument.

According to Haldar, McTaggart's major and most original contribution becomes visible when he interprets Hegel's absolute idea—which is spirit "necessarily differentiated"[76]—as (reality) being a unity differentiated into a plurality where "the parts have no meaning but their unity, while the unity again, has no meaning but its differentiations."[77] This entails that "the unity must be completely in each individual, yet it must also be the bond which unites them."[78] This should be the illustrative ground of the absolute being a unity of persons ("where the parts have no meaning but their unity"), yet is itself not a person ("the unity ... has no meaning but its differentiations") and, thus, lacks a sense of an indivisible unity symptomatic of a finite personality—"which is all the personality of which we have experience."[79] In other words, self-conscious unity of impressions demarcated by the requisite cognitive mapping gives the person his/her unity that differentiates him/her from all others (excludes what it includes); the absolute resolutely grants each person his/her personality, but being the precondition of all differentiations, whom shall he/she differentiate himself from? To reiterate, unity is exclusively a person's, but multiplicity he/she shares while being with and among others ("multiplicity, though it belongs to him, belongs also to the outside reality with which he is in connection")[80] McTaggart elsewhere cites the example of a citizen who is a citizen only in his/her relation to other fellow citizens; if we take the latter away, the former becomes nonexistent; while this is not the case with the state, "the state has a multiplicity within itself, and can be conceived without reference to anything external."[81] The multiplicity that belongs to the person—that is in his/her external relationality, is disavowed by

---

[76] Hiralal Haldar, *Neo Hegelianism* (London: Heath Cranton Ltd, 1927), 428.
[77] Ibid.
[78] Ibid.
[79] Ibid.
[80] J. E. McTaggart quoted in Haldar, *Neo-Hegelianism*, 430.
[81] J. E. McTaggart and Ellis McTagart, *Studies in Hegelian Cosmology* (1901; repr., Cambridge: Cambridge University Press, 1918), para 80.

the person by which the self-conscious unity becomes perceptible (excludes what it includes); but having had no outside, the absolute cannot indulge in the same to become a person. Elsewhere, McTaggart is more forceful and drives in the force of another example "the element of unity is the father, the element of difference and multiplicity the son, and Spirit is the One-in-many, the unity realized in its own differentiation." To be a person, the absolute has to be either father or a son; he is not; in fact he is "all in every part."[82] "The absolute is the full reality—the differentiated unity, or the unified differentiations. And there is nothing which is in any way outside this, or which in any way be distinguished from this."[83] McTaggart's central example in the main part of his arguments revolves around the college "I know that I can 'I am'. I know that a college cannot say 'I am'.[84] "It does not follow from this, however, that the absolute is a person. It might be said of a college, with as much truth as it has been said of the absolute, that it is a unity, that it is a unity of spirit, and that none of that spirit exists except as personal. Yet the college is not a person. It is a unity of persons, but it is not a person itself."[85] McTaggart argues in a similar vein, The absolute is a similar unity of persons but in itself not a person but "a far more perfect unity than the college."[86] Having foregrounded his argumentative article thus, McTaggart is succinct here, "If, for us, the sense of self is not in this element of indivisible unity, I cannot tell where it is. The absolute, as we have seen, cannot have this element of indivisible unity. And, therefore, it cannot have the personality that we have."[87] Elsewhere McTaggart elaborates on how this is more impossible: all individuals are finite selves marked by a consciousness of the nonego or not I,[88] but the absolute sustains in itself both the ego and

---

[82] Haldar, *Neo-Hegelianism,* 429–30.

[83] J. E. McTaggart, "The Personality of the Absolute" in *Studies in Hegelian Cosmology,* http://www.marxists.org/reference/archive/mctaggart/cosmology/ch03.htm, para 70; accessed on July 13, 2008.

[84] McTaggart and McTagart, *Studies in Hegelian Cosmology,* 57. Interestingly, McTaggart uses the neuter pronoun "it" rather than the masculine "he" in order to avoid giving the absolute a personality.

[85] Ibid., 58.

[86] Ibid.

[87] Ibid., 83.

[88] This line of reasoning could be refuted easily by using a slice of Hegel himself, very relevantly cited by another author working on Hegelianism and personality in the 1880s; this is where Hegel seems to be arguing that anything expressed through language has to be universal:

the nonego and, therefore, cannot be reduced to any of these. McTaggart concludes: "Our conclusion then is that personality cannot be an attribute of a unity which has no indivisible centre of reference, and which is from all points of view (as the personalities we know are from one point of view) all in every part."[89] How does Haldar struggle with this and emerge after overpowering it fully—or even a strand of it—if we want to consider? Let us proceed point-by-point in recovering Haldar's refutation of McTaggart.

Haldar begins by taking hold of the unity argument—summarizing first and then reconstructing it. For McTaggart, Haldar states,

> [The absolute is] a real unity, an harmonious and coherent whole. All finite selves which are its differentiations are included in it. It is not above and beyond these differentiations but in and through them. The relation of each finite self to the Absolute is organic. The whole is in each part and is equal to the part. Now if the whole, in so far as it is in the part, is personal and can say "I am"; how can the whole itself be impersonal?... The part is the whole and if it is self conscious, so must the whole be. If my eyes see a thing, I see it; if my ears hear a sound, I hear it; so if the Absolute is a person in me, it must itself have personality.[90]

Subsequently, Haldar addresses the "college" clause of McTaggart, which is given as:

> Moreover, if the Absolute is to be called a person because it is a spiritual unity, then every college, every goose club, every gang of thieves, must also be called a person. For they are all spiritual entities. They all consist exclusively of human beings, and they all unite their members in some sort of unity[...] Now we call ourselves persons, but no one, I believe, has ever proposed to call a football team a person. But if we now call the Absolute a person, we should have no defence for refusing the name to the football team. For it shares its imperfection with human beings, and its want of a direct sense of self with the Absolute.[91]

---

[w]hen I say "I," I *mean* my single self, to the exclusion of all others; but what I say, namely, "I," is just every other "I," which in like manner excludes all others from itself ... *All other men have it in common with me to be "I"*.

See Andrew Seth, "Hegelianism and Personality," (1887) in *G. W. F. Hegel: Critical Assessments*, ed. Robert Stern (London: Routledge, 1998), 20–40.

[89] Ibid., 84.

[90] Hiralal Haldar, *Hegelianism and Human Personality* (Calcutta: University of Calcutta, 1910), 31.

[91] McTaggart, *Hegelian Cosmology*, 86.

Haldar retorts with generous fervor:

> The analogy between the college or a foot-ball team and the Absolute is by
> no means self-evident. Subordinate unities like the college or the football
> team exist for temporary and particular purposes and can be formed or
> dissolved without the least advantage or detriment to the essential nature of
> their members, but all such subordinate unities presuppose and are grounded
> on the unity of the Absolute, apart from which nothing can ever exist.
> A football team is a union of its members in so far as they are sportsmen and
> has no bearing on their life in other respects. So a college is a combination
> for purposes[92] which cannot be realised without it and the members of it,
> considered as interested and concerned in the execution of these purposes,
> have no being apart from it, but as individuals with other capacities and
> functions they have no relation to it. The relation, however, of the Absolute
> to its constituent individuals is different. It is a union which makes not this or
> that phase of their existence but the whole of their existence, including their
> existence as inter-conscious members of it possible. It is the precondition
> of and is realized in the interconsciousness of individuals it unites, and is
> ipso facto a conscious unity. ... The unity of the football team is no other
> than the community of purposes of the sportsmen. The unity of the college
> consists in the common academic interests of its members. So the unity
> of the Absolute is, besides other things, the continuity of consciousness
> involved in the inter-consciousness of the selves that constitute it.[93]

In response to the McTaggartian objection that personalities are based on a
fundamental distinction between the ego and the nonego reflexive of finite
persons, where as the Absolute has no outside nonego ("there is nothing
which falls outside the absolute, it cannot have such a consciousness,

---

[92] Coincidentally, this debate, or better the terms of the debate, in due course seeped into
the discourse of various other famous neo-Hegelians such as Bradley and Bosanquet and
instead of the limited debate on the absolute, it brought into its horizon group personality
and group mind. Bosanquet in particular goes far enough to argue that

> All the institutions of a country, so far as they are effective, are not only products of
> thought and creations of mind: they *are* thought, and they *are* mind. ... An Oxford
> college is not a group of buildings ... it is a group of men in the sense of a group of
> minds. That group of minds, in virtue of the common substance of a uniting idea, is
> itself a group mind. ... here is a college mind, just as there is a Trade Union mind, or
> even a "public mind" of the whole community.

See Ernst Barker, *Political Thought in England 1848–1914* (London: Oxford University
Press, 1951), 60–61.

[93] Haldar, *Hegelianism and Human Personality*, 33.

and cannot, therefore be a person"[94] to constitute itself as a personality[95]), Haldar has a rigorous argument to make:

> The essential condition of self-consciousness is the opposition and not the externality of the non-ego. ... The Absolute, of course, has nothing outside it from which it can distinguish itself, but from this it does not follow that within it there is no non-ego in distinction from which it has the consciousness of self. ... In the Absolute, all its differences are united but not lost. They retain their fundamental characteristics. The Absolute which says "I" in each of its determinations, has self consciousness in so far as these egos are brought together in its unity. Their self-consciousness is its self-consciousness.[96]

Now, so far as the ego-nonego distinction is considered, and because it bears with it traces of a psychological register, putting aside the debate on the absolute, and pressing upon more on the college consciousness, the emergence of the group personality with a group mind (we shall pursue this more forcefully within a while) is evident from Freud—our psychoanalytical ally in this journey. Following Le Bon, Freud describes, to begin with, the group as a "provisional being" that, though being formed by heterogeneous individuals, projects a homogenous character in the wake of a racial unconscious and that "puts them in possession of a sort of collective mind which makes them feel, think, and act in a manner quite different from that in which each individual of them would feel, think, and act were he in a state of isolation."[97] The individual acquires new characteristics, attributed by Le Bon and cited by Freud, first, automatic irresponsibility, caused by the disappearance of conscience; second, contagion where the transmission of the acts and sentiments of the group to the individual leads to the submission and sacrifice of individual interest to collective interest; and third, the vanishing of conscious personality while being submerged in a state of hypnotic fascination marked by a loss of individual will and discernment and acquiring, thus, an "unconscious group personality."[98]

[94]   Haldar, *Neo Hegelianism,* 429.

[95]   "For we certainly can never say 'I' without raising the idea of the non-ego, and so we can never form any idea of the way in which the Absolute would say 'I'." quoted in Haldar, *Hegelianism and Human Personality,* 34.

[96]   Ibid., 34–35.

[97]   Sigmund Freud, "Group Psychology and the Analysis of the Ego" in *Civilization, Society and Religion,* trans. James Stratchey (New Delhi: Shrijee's Book International, 2003), 12: 89–184.

[98]   Ibid., 97.

However, Haldar, having had no Freud at his disposal, in neo-Hegelianism, inadvertently, tries to trace precursors to this thinking by engaging with a number of neo-Hegelians. Here, he has turned his torch on Bernard Bosanquet.

> The illusion that we are separate and self-centred arises only when we are at our worst. In the best moments of our life, when, for example, we fight on the same side or sacrifice ourselves for a great cause, we cease to be mutually repellent units and are fused into one harmonious whole. ... Human beings are not merely legal persons or mutually exclusive selves. The presupposition of them as personalities possessing rights is the social spirit, which is itself not the final form of individuality but one of its sub-forms."[99]

Haldar could anticipate the argument of the anti-communitarians of today who would argue in favor of a liberal unencumbered self not grounded in a reproducible sociality. Haldar quotes Bentham at his best: "There is no hard and fast distinction between it and its environment, it is the inwardness of the environment. You cannot say where self ends and environment begins."[100] And finally comes the demolition of privacy and the private to which we've made references in concurrent, yet valuable repetition throughout this section:

> [H]owever private and incommensurable feelings may be, they are never complete by themselves, but imply a universal objective content. ... The pure privacy and incommensurability of feeling as such is superseded in all possible degrees by the self-transcendence and universality of the contents with which it is unified.[101]

This universalism, as we've predicted, while making a reference to Andrew Seth's discussion of Hegelianism and personality, is linguistic. But the concept-metaphor "self-transcendence" is important. It refers to the communicative a priori of each linguistic content in enunciation. This also grants infinitude to limited selves in interaction, and this contamination makes duties or rights (in)finite and impure: "The finite selves are independent beings at arms' length with one another, although connected by relations of right and duty. It is not realized that they are also infinite, and are therefore always beyond themselves ("pure duty"

---

[99] Haldar, *Neo Hegelianism,* 265.
[100] Ibid., 267.
[101] Ibid., 271.

and "whole rights" can never be fulfilled)."[102] Haldar reveals Bosanquest's idea of state action as public action not to be judged "by the same standard as private action" and, thus,

> [c]annot be identified with the deed's of its agents, or morally judged as private volitions are judged. Its acts proper are always public acts, and it cannot act as a state, [or] act within the relations of private life in which organized morality exists ... Moral relations presuppose an organized life; but such a life is only within the state, not in relations between the state and other communities."[103]

This is rightly in consonance with the Hegelian idea that the state is an organized ethical entity subsumed under objective spirit. But this is, at the same time, a caution against too readily presuming as the medieval jurists of group personality did that since all other associations exist as autonomous and sovereign besides the state, state sovereignty is a mirage rightly to be denigrated[104]; it is just another association, of probably a limited life.[105] And in this view, Haldar is correct in arguing that group persons as parts could well be persons within the wholesome personality of the state—where the state lives in all them, singularly, and yet simultaneously.

## Haldar–Mactaggart Debate: The Theory That Was Lost to It

The debate, strangely, does not impact or even impinge upon the notion of fictitious or legal, juristic personality that was available since the Middle Ages.[106] Even if St Paul was indicted, in a book, for having "invaded"

---

[102] Ibid., 274.

[103] Ibid., 294.

[104] "But sovereign your state no longer is if the groups within itself are, thus, self-governing. Nor can we doubt this polyarchism." See Harold J. Laski, *The Foundations of Sovereignty* (London: George Allen & Unwin Ltd, 1931), 169.

[105] The word *life* comes italicized because it has been conventionally important in such discussions where the "personal identity" of institutions is in question, "[w]e must, surely, accept the point of view of Lord Haldane when he argued that 'the test of the personal identity of this church lies not in doctrine but in its life'." See Harold J. Laski, *The Foundations of Sovereignty* (London: George Allen & Unwin Ltd, 1931), 160–61.

[106] While Haldar's predecessor Brajendranath Seal with whom we amply engaged in the previous section did acknowledge this—though in too cryptic a manner—strangely

a land that was not his own, it had strengthened the idea of the church owning the land, but the ownership having had to be effected by the Saints and "as the saint retires, the idea of the church is spiritualized; it becomes a person, and, we may say, an ideal, juristic person."[107] Maitland offers Professor Dicey's famous view with a tinge of irony in which Professor Dicey had said,

> {A} body of twenty, or two thousand, or two hundred thousand men bind themselves together to act in a particular way for some common purpose, they create a body, which by no fiction of law, but by the very nature of things, differs from the individuals of whom it is constituted.[108]

But if a natural person does not identify the group as someone other than himself/herself, would it be the same as him/her? In other words, he/she would identify in absolute similarity or difference, and the difference for that matter would be vouched for by the simple mechanism of a legal operation, by a founding law—whereas we know even law could be natural. There could still be nature, but it is something other than natural. We could name it for the moment as cultural and leave it at that (since we've discussed culture and cultural collective persons for long). In our context here, let us pick up Maitland's invocation of group personality. On group personality, similarly, Maitland has this to say:

> If the law allows men to form permanently organized groups, those groups will be for common opinion right-and-duty bearing unit. ... [G]roup personality is no purely legal phenomenon. The law-giver may say that it does not exist, where, as a matter of moral sentiment, it does exist. If he wishes to smash a group, let him smash it ... but if he is going to tolerate the group, he must recognize its personalit[y].[109]

---

Haldar missed out on this completely: Invoking the role of groups and communities as "*intermediary bodies between state and individual*," Seal exhorts' [w]hile there is *community in the individual*, likewise there is *the individual in the community*. In each and everybody's individual-life, *group personality* and *individual personality* are manifest and the two are required equally. It is incumbent to accommodate individual autonomy within group personality." See Brajendranath Seal, *Bangla Rachana*, ed. Tapankumar Ghosh (Kolaka: Patralekha, 2013), 39 (translation mine; italicized phrases are originally in English).

[107] Sir Frederick Pollock and Frederic William Maitland, *The History of English Law* (Cambridge: Cambridge University Press, 1952), 500.

[108] Dicey quoted in F. W. Maitland, *State, Trust and Corporation,* ed. D. Runciman and M. Ryan (Cambridge: Cambridge University Press, 2003), 63.

[109] Ibid., 68.

This concept was forcefully invoked by Maitland to explain 19th century Europe, and while Maine's description of status to contract has become standard taxonomy in sociological, political, or social philosophical circles, Maitland rejects it in favor of an astounding new twist—to which we shall bear—even if it is a temporary testimony: "[t]he line of advance is no longer from status to contract, but through contract to something that contract cannot explain, and for which our best, if an inadequate, name is the personality of the organized group."[110] But is it not a striking coincidence that Ambedkar, and before that Sister Nivedita, would invoke such a concept—sometimes in its exact coinage—to describe colonial and postcolonial moments of institutional ego? So far as the subversion of universal forms of impersonal civil society is concerned in the colony and the post-colony, our thesis has been, and that which has been lost sight of is the invocation of a group personality, and legal or juristic personality to do away with both the impersonal and private. But in the case of Nivedita, while it comes through the curious metaphor of the civic personality of the city, it cannot, and I hope it does not, wish away an essential contractarian tradition mooted in the Rousseaun form as its silent precursor. In the most significant part where he delineates the social contract (or compact), he begins by ushering into the phase where

> Each of us puts in common his person and all his power under the supreme direction of the general will; and in return each member becomes an indivisible part of the whole. Right away, in place of the particular individuality of each contracting party, this act of association produces a moral and collective body, composed of as many members as the assembly has voices, and which receives from this same act its unity, its common self (moi), its life, and its will. This *public person*, which is, thus, formed by the union of all the individual members, used to be called a city, and now is called republic or body politic.[111]

---

[110] Ibid., 69. This is a heady and swift departure from the view that "the language of contract was unable to generate a sovereignty that was single. Instead, sovereignty was permanently divided between the two parties to the contract of government, the people and their rulers, each of whom, as partners in contract, had rights against the other." See David Runciman, *Pluralism and the Personality of the State* (Cambridge, UK: Cambridge University Press, 2003), 38.

[111] Jean-Jacques Rousseau, *The Social Contract and The First and Second Discourses*, ed. Susan Dunn (New Havan, CT: Yale University Press, 2002), 164 (italics mine).

This foundational epithet outlining the "public person" will be clarified, and will become distinctive to us the moment we catch up with Nivedita and her preoccupation with the civic mind in the colonial predicament.

## A Colonial Case Example: Sister Nivedita's Civic Mind[112]

Sister Nivedita begins by contrasting the epic spirit of Mahabharata and Ramayana by noting the contrasting "pervading interests of the Mahabharata"[113] that are "heroic and national, those of the Ramayana are mainly personal and civic." Nivedita finds that

> There is nothing, in all Indian literature, of greater significance for the modern Indian mind, than the scene in which Hanuman contends in the darkness with the woman who guards the gates, saying, in muffled tones, "I am the city of Lanka. We have here what is the fundamental need of the civic spirit, that we should think of our city as a being, a personality, sacred, beautiful, and beloved."[114]

To Nivedita, this was the "habit of relating himself instinctively to his home, his sovereign, and his group."[115] The city is then an extension of the person and his/her family. "What we call public spirit is simply the reflex in a given personality of the civic consciousness. That is to say, public spirit is the expression of that character which is born of constantly placing the ego, with the same intensity as in the family, in a more complex group."[116] Nivedita, of course, ends up with a question: "What, then, is the fundamental bond that welds so many and various elements into the single, communal personality?"[117] And her answer is simple yet very, very complex and farfetched; she approaches the answer first by denying the two dominant spatial metaphors of industrial capitalism—which she finds are of "pathetic significance" in this respect—"the railway station

---

[112] Taking cue from Nivedita's work referred to here, elsewhere, I develop the notion of the group personality of the caste (caste personality), caste culture, and case counselling.
[113] Sister Nivedita, "The Civic Ideal," *The Modern Review* 3, no. 1 (1908, January), 1–42.
[114] Ibid., 2.
[115] Ibid.
[116] Ibid., 3.
[117] Ibid.

and the general post office [which] form features of the central Place"[118] in the Europe of her times, and her condemnation here is cutting: "How eloquent is such an arrangement of the fact that home has been abandoned, in favor of a world of going and coming: a temporary foothold for the bird of passage!"[119] Now, after this denouncement comes Nivedita's answer as to what is the bondage that reaps the civic mind, "Does it not lie in the equal relation of each of these to the common home? There is no motive in life like the love of the dwelling place."[120] This "idealizing of the abode" that Nivedita holds up as the citizens' "surpassing sanctity"[121] is much more than the iconically separate, strewn "private" homes[122] of each of us—distinct, separate, and splendid in their isolation. Like Rousseau, as cited in the beginning, and who held for all the contractarian, right reasons, "houses make the town, and ... citizens make the city,"[123] Nivedita has in mind the "civic building" under "civic ownership" clearly modeled after the commune "the communal palace, the property of all" being "the home of the whole community"[124] (which, according to her, transcends the family and the caste) clearly represents the consolidated civic mind in its breadth and depth: "The scavenger who serves well the civic ideal of cleanliness is a better citizen than a Brahmin, if the latter serves only himself."[125] The civic group mind and the personality of the city coinciding—or even becoming one—with the common and the public (and more extravagant in Nivedita's denouncement of the private) remains unsurpassed in its power and force. But anyhow, Nivedita, in this endeavor—even if not wide in receiving support—is not alone.

Since it was also the time when the new found theory of societies, associations, and registered bodies had started creeping in our colony, it would be instructive to examine in brief a now forgotten classic that tries to delineate—in agreement and disagreement with Nivedita—why *samgha* is not a commune but still is a spiritual collective. If we could connect the

---

[118] To Nivedita, the *place* is not simply a demarcated space "the *Place* (French, proplahss) is the visible evidence of the civic unity)." See Sister Nivedita, "The Civic Ideal," in *Civic Ideal and Indian Nationality* in *The Complete works of Sister Nivedita* (Calcutta: Advaita Ashrama, 1996), IV: 205–325).

[119] Ibid., 217.

[120] Ibid., 213.

[121] Ibid., 214.

[122] Ibid., 212.

[123] Rousseau, *Social Contract*, 164.

[124] Ibid., 216.

[125] Ibid., 212.

theory of life-community (in Chapter 3) to what Matilal Roy is espousing in *samgha tatva*,[126] then the links are apparent: "In Bengal the word samgha has begun to have come in popular reckoning. ... Many have asked for a descriptive brochure delineating the rules, by laws, activity-catalogue [etc] presupposing that samgha is just another name of an association."[127] Roy surmises, and quite emphatically, that the samgha is not only not an association or similar to that of a registered society but also not a commune in the Western style (with this his disjunction with Nivedita is evident); the Indian theory of samghas is not a page from the West's communism.[128] Curiously, Roy extends the family (modeled upon the "union of eternity" between wife and husband)—where "two lives are continuously connected in a pure relation ... not disrupted by earthly force, and not terminated by death [...] since it is not a fanciful construction for the meeting of ends." Thereby distinguishing the samgha from the purposive, (*abasthachokre*) or situational mechanization of forming a society or a voluntary group, Roy designates the former as "a life-theoretical (*jivan tatva*) manifestation of spontaneity; it is fundamental, real-nature."[129] Here, instead of work, emphasis will be more on penance[130] requiring the whole of one's self to be symbolized collectively, where the collective as a symbol is the sole, definitive object of worship.[131]

Leaving this here, we might not be surprised when—marking the temporal episode of the colony and the post colony—B. R. Ambedkar while addressing the notion of the collective in fragments also departs rigorously from the concept of the voluntary group; yet he forcefully, and reasonably so, resists the idealized union conjectured to have been present in a mythical life-community. For Ambedkar, marriage being a stratified (intra-caste) event can hardly act as a model to forge a unity, and this time his polemic will be directed against Gandhi, who seemed to have imbibed in himself much of the indigene spirit that Nivedita or Roy self-persuasively advocated and called for a unity with the ruse of the broader narrative of the struggle against the British. Ambedkar's fatal question is, even if we have a good caste-couple, would they be able to overcome,

---

[126] Motilal Roy, *Bharatiya Samgha Tatva* [Bengali] (Kolkata: Prabartak Publishing House, 1932), 1339 (B.S).

[127] Ibid., introductory chapter, diacritically marked. (not available in the current type set).

[128] Ibid., introductory chapter, diacritically marked.

[129] Ibid., introductory chapter, diacritically marked.

[130] Ibid., 5.

[131] Ibid., 8.

or would they be able to chasten by their forbearing, the personality of the collective that will be discriminatively domineering? Let us find the answer for ourselves.

## (Post) Colonial Case Example: Ambedkar's Caste as Corporation

Ambedkar has been considered, despite retaining a handle over various other significant texts (say, from the philosophy of revenue to the principle of money in banking), a classic theorist of the caste group. While addressing the theory of caste, Ambedkar introduces the kindle of an organized, "involuntary [social] group": no voluntary membership, but "subject to social regulation and traditions over which he has no control of any kind."[132] But here is that catch:

> The significance of a separate name for a caste lies in this—namely, it makes caste an organized and an involuntary grouping. A separate and a distinctive name for a caste makes *caste akin to a corporation* with a perpetual existence and a seal of separate entity.[133]

Now, while social groups (Ambedkar seems to be referring to occupational groups) and their occupational classification has been used to designate castes in India, Ambedkar thinks, this is clearly confusing—even misleading.

> [Social groups (potters, washermen, intellectuals)] in other countries ... have remained as unorganized and voluntary groups while in India they have become castes because in other countries the social groups were not given a name while in India they did. It is the name which the caste bears which gives it fixity and continuity and individuality. It is the name which defines who are its members and in most cases a person born in a caste carries the name of the caste as a part of his surname. Again it is the name which makes it easy for the caste to enforce its rules and regulations.[134]

---

[132] B. R. Ambedkar, "Caste and Class," in *The Essential Writings of B. R. Ambedkar* (New Delhi: Oxford University Press, 2002), 99–105.

[133] Ibid., 02. (italics mine).

[134] Ibid., 102–03.

The norm becomes productive in as much as the offender cannot impersonate by other caste surnames and, thus, legal identification becomes easy, but along with it, it is opportune for social or corporate jurisdiction helping to "identify the offending individual and the caste to whose jurisdiction he is subject so that he is easily handed up and punished for any breach of the caste rules. This is what caste means."[135] Meaning apart, if we are to study the caste system we have to observe caste in interactive relation with other castes. An interesting departure would be to consider following Ambedkar's suggestion that the character of caste corporation would project a different personality than the constitutive caste members. And what kind of traits would the members imbibe or alter? They would be in relation to one another (endogamously) and also in relation to other caste members outside the group. (All world is a caste ridden world to them; the rest may appear as "alien,"[136] or we might surmise, religion begins (to our rescue) at this point, where castes end: *mlechha* for instance is a religious imbrication). Ambedkar answers this question while trying to refute Gandhi's emphasis on personal character and (proposed) spiritual mimesis; by aping great spiritual leaders (like Chaityanya), everybody could transform himself and transcend caste. Ambedkar's point is simple. No outside specific individuation can work in the face of a domineering, and claustrophobic group individuation or—deriving from above, if we may—group personality.[137] For a low caste member, any other caste neighbor would be construed as a higher or lower, or better or worse but not a good man.

> [H]ow can you accept the personal character to make a man loaded with the consciousness of caste, a good man, i.e., a man who would treat his fellows as his friends and equals?. ... A high caste man cannot be a good man in so

---

[135] Ibid., 103.

[136] B. R. Ambedkar, "Reply to the Mahatma," in *The Essential Writings of B. R. Ambedkar* (New Delhi: Oxford University Press, 2002), 311.

[137] Group personality and its reality are seen to have been debated and followed with interest in such a journal as *Mind* even as late as in the year 2008. In a masterly review of the book *The Reality of Social Groups* by Paul Sheehy, David-Hill Ruben rightly describes the moral status of groups in terms of group rights or as objects of moral evaluation, and most importantly as standing for "concerns, evaluations and policies [as] directed at individuals considered together as *them*. Furthermore some of an individual person's own claims can only be made ... as *our's*." See David-Hill Ruben, Review of *The Reality of Social Groups* by Paul Sheehy (Ashgate, 2006), Mind, Vol. 117 (No. 467), July 2008, p. 154.

far as he must have a low caste man to distinguish him as high caste man. The best of men cannot be moral if the basis of relationship between them and their fellows is fundamentally a wrong relationship. To a slave his master may be better or worse. But there cannot be a good master. A good man cannot be a master and a master cannot be a good man.[138]

Learning from, and imitating Chaitanya would fail—pace Ambedkar— because the caste's group personality would not allow it; this is a point we've already made. That is—so to say—its reality. But caste as a corporation must justify some artificiality or fictionality[139] even while we want to explain this instance, and do justice to the legal fiction theorists. Risking some oddness, we could buy from Bentham (who is a pioneer-philosopher of the theory of fictions) to make the point. Caste is a determinate, real entity when it applies with sanction to the caste members "now or before in existence.... It is as much a fictitious entity, considered as applied to all or any one or more of those individuals which, with that same specific character belonging to them, are considered as about to come into existence."[140] It would be interesting to interpret Ambedkar's malady, in view of Gandhi's suggestion, as having to generate co-evally the "not yet" with those who have already been (i.e., those who are "not yet" are urged to ape those who are "no more" or, future asked to chase the past), and second, the "real" (those who have been present, in Bentham's language "determinate") being applied to fiction (future "indeterminate") without readiness and, thereby, we might conjecture, as the case is, not work because of its imminent logical fallacy.

---

[138] Ambedkar, "Reply to the Mahatma," 311.

[139] Ordained by Thomas Hobbes, there exists to date an important distinction between artificial and fictitious personality (which we've decided to override for the sake of brevity):

> For unlike fictitious personality, artificial personality is not contingent upon government, if only because government itself is contingent upon the authorization of atleast one artificial person—the person of the sovereign, without whom there can be no civil society ... A sovereign is a man, or assembly of men, who, having been authorized by a group of natural persons, has the *Right* to *Present* the person of them all, *(*that is to say, to be their *Representative*). Artificial persons make fictitious persons by providing representation for something incapable of representing itself.

See David Runciman, *Pluralism and the Personality of the State* (Cambridge, UK: Cambridge University Press, 2003), 10–11.

[140] Jeremy Bentham, *Bentham's Theory of Fictions*, ed. with introduction C. K. Ogden (London: Kegan Paul, Trench, Trubner & Co., Ltd, 1932), lix.

But how was Ambedkar's "caste as corporation" theory received in social sciences in postcolonial India? A similar account, if we are able to locate it, might diminish some of the formers' defamiliarizing effect and introduce more diversity, even authenticity. Though this particular interpretation was not referred to, but the question of castes as group persons did feature in the writings of at least one lone sociologist from Bengal: Benoy Kumar Sarkar. Deriving from Panini's cryptic grammar, Sarkar designated samgha as having meant "organized bodies" (*puga, vrata*, etc) of the Buddhist Asia.[141] In fact, the aforementioned puga "as a particular class of *samuha* ... were made up of those who lived at the same place, but belonged to different social orders, the so-called castes, and followed different professions."[142] Having addressed and included the castes, Sarkar wants to term these samuha organizations as "artificial civic bodies" where *gana, sreni and varga*—as illustrating and imbibing in them the "juridical concept of a corporate person or one-in-the-many"[143]—were little instances of the Greek polis.[144] Clearly such an ascription, and quite anachronistically at that, that is, adducing the taxonomy of legal fiction of juridical persons to institutions or associations of ancient India, is largely because sociology in India was at the earliest stage during that time, a disciplinary hyperbole, indebted to—and Sarkar is obliged to acknowledge it at last—Gierke and Figgis. This makes his endeavor even if not a correct one, yet a historically important exercise in terms of predicative, conceptual labor.

## Concluding Remarks

Though now, we could comfortably rewind back to revisit the break-up of the Brahmo Samaj in colonial civil society where the organization seemed to have assumed a spirit of its own and had started to interminably scare even its founder. The Haldar–McTaggart debate foregrounded the personality of associations and was stretched to its discursive consequence by Nivedita and later by B. R. Ambedkar—to name two iconic few among

---

[141] Benoy Kumar Sarkar, *The Political Institutions and Theories of the Hindus: A Study in Comparative Politics* (Leipzig: Verlag Von Markert & Petters, 1922), 31.

[142] Ibid., 32.

[143] Ibid., 44.

[144] Ibid., 31.

many others who deployed group personality to a heightened argumentative effect. That personal could not be sacrificed to an impersonal civil social modernity, and second, remained determinately obstinate to resist the private in the latter's aggressive inward journey, is a fact in place we ought to reckon with.

# 6

# The Personal in Practice: Charity, Altruism to Social Work

*Historically speaking, social work has struggled in its development between perceptions of its task as friendship and art or as profession and service.*
—(Chris Rojek et al, 1988: 18)

All the so-called "personal" modes of helping—from charity to benevolence—were to be set aside in favor of the structural motors of objective, impersonal, and rational-universal forms of assurance. If this was dinned into us by the first philosopher of modernity (for whom, for the first time, modernity was a problem as Habermas rightly credits him with) and the first philosopher of the modern mode of helping, Hegel, then we have demonstrated with fervor that this did not actually happen, or it happened only as an upper narrative, as a presumptive declaration or an appearing feat. Even the institutions paraded, in ghostly apparitions, as collective persons. However, the preparatory evolution and arrangement of things, in terms of the apparatus of the modern state, pointed squarely to the fulfillment of an objective administrative desire. This coincides with our observation that despite the overt willingness to comply with the meters of visible modernity, things had gone wrong somewhere else. However, the declarative desire to abolish the personal by enumerating it, instead of theoretically stating this in a singular way and critiquing it, let us try to illuminate it by the force of a last example. In this, the Hegelian foreboding has been taken a step further where Benoy Sarkar, the speaker, talks—for the first time perhaps—of social insurance, grants for the unemployed and tax-based poor relief—all specific welfare state instruments.

# I

## From Personal to Impersonal, Objective Forms: A Socio-historic Declaration

In 1936, Benoy Kumar Sarkar—a pioneering Indian sociologist and social historian with considerable mastery over German language and German social philosophy—was comparing Hitler Germany's system of Winter Help and the Indian practice of *daridra seva* or care for the poor. While Winter Help was an occasion—on which—to help their suffering poor masses, "Germans would spend during the six months of winter (October to March) nearly 370 million—in Indian currency."[1] Sarkar was aware that daridra seva (seva has had its strongest original lineage[2] in Vaishnavism of medieval Bengal) was re-popularized in the 19th century by Swami Vivekananda—the founder member of Ramakrishna Mission and famous for his so-called American conquests.[3] Sarkar in his lecture wanted to propose a modernist departure for such a project. To begin with, Sarkar illuminatingly and provokingly traced the origins of Vivekananda's "service to the poor is service to God" dictum to that of (another German) Fichte's formulation in which the slave appears as a personification of the Holy Ghost.[4] This striking and disturbing comparison apart, one of Sarkar's agenda was, of course, critical. While invoking Fichte and elsewhere locating Vivekananda's message as complicit with the emergence of the person and individualism in modernity, here Sarkar was clearly dismissing daridra seva as being based on an old model of care or charity[5] for the poor. For Sarkar, social insurance (*samaj bima*),

---

[1] Benoy Kumar Sarkar, "Daridranarayner Samaj-shastra," in *Samaj Vijnan* [Bengali] (Calcutta: Chakraborty Chatterjee Company Limited, 1938), 59–80.

[2] Etymology will be explored for its semantic and semiotic connections later in the chapter.

[3] Vivekananda's success in the USA has often been described as a conquest—so much so that we find the pragmatist William James quoting Vivekananda, Romain Rolland, and Maxmueller, and later Christopher Isherwood writing about him.

[4] Sarkar, "Daridranarayner samaj-shastra," 59.

[5] Sarkar's evaluation and much of the 19th century controversies reminiscent of the Poor Law debate (Sarkar does mention Poor Law once on page 64) debunked charity (in Sarkar's language *daan khairat*, page 64) as old fashioned, "undisciplined," "unruly," and destructive of the self-empowering capacities of the poor; but another trajectory—of which Sarkar seems to be unaware—attempted to derive the theory of self-help surprisingly from charity itself. Thus, a historian quotes from the Charity Organization Report of 1884,

grants for the unemployed (*bekar bima*), and tax-based poor relief[6] (*daridrya-kar*) were the methodologically driven modern (the latter having undergone a revival) versions of a transformed and enlightened helping (we've explored why and how, long before Sarkar, Hegel had termed this "intelligent" helping). Now one of the strong reasons why Sarkar thought that this model had become defunct was based—this time—on a French comparison. Quoting Ferdinand Tonnies, Sarkar dubbed the giving of alms (*mustibhikka*) as an expression of community or *Gemeinschaft* through *atmiyata* (kinship and relationality), *sahajogita* (cooperation) and not (civil) society[7] or *Gesellschaft*. Now why Sarkar thought so is crucial: his argument was that, in the giving of alms, there exists between the donor and the recipient an immediate (*sakshat*) and, in a sense, personal (byaktigoto) relationship; but, in state-organized helping endeavors, what is evident is an impersonal procedure marked by a (quasi-commercial) "regimentation regarding transaction of goods," a "centralized" rational effort (*juktijog*) moved by the force of an "associational collective."[8]

This is the catch! By plotting the personal and the filial as against the public and the rational, it is evident that Sarkar was referring to the arrangements that have been subsumed today under the rubric of civil society with the phenomenon being now predicated as "welfare." Sarkar thought that in a capitalist society, the former has exhausted itself and is absolutely anachronistic unless it is absorbed by civil social forms of institutionalized public helping. In fact, he also tends to find a middle way by suggesting that in the manner of Nazi Germany's Winter Help project, social organizations and institutions in Bengal such as the Ramakrishna Mission, the Indian Congress, Corporation, Municipality, and Bangiya Sankat Tran Samiti, in order to arrive at "modernity" (*adhunikta*), they need to deploy such methods of helping where voluntarism (in the form

"We have to use charity to create the power of self-help." See Kathleen Woodroofe, *From Charity to Social Work: In England and the United States* (London: Routledge and Kegan Paul, 1962), 23.

[6] Although tax-based poor relief has had 16th century linkages, Sarkar detains the public "tax," part of it to project it as a state-linked modern form of assistance. See Sarkar, "Daridranarayner samaj-shastra," 64.

[7] Though in Sarkar's use of the term, Gesellschaft appears as *society,* a more correct, updated rendering of Tonnies—also close to what Sarkar tends to mean by society—is *civil* society; See Ferdinand Tonnies, *Community and Civil Society,* trans. Joe Harris and Margaret Hollis (Cambridge: Cambridge University Press: Cambridge, 2001[1887]).

[8] Sarkar, "Daridranarayner samaj-shastra," 79.

of voluntary donation) meets centralized procedural, public rationality.[9] As we shall find, what Sarkar in 1936 was proposing, in fact, was the paradigmatic proposal of modernity itself, and it was first articulated by Hegel (discussed extensively in the previous chapter). Surprisingly, in 19th century colonial Bengal—as we shall see—the tensions of this thematic schism in the realm of helping was energetically articulated in the domain of "reform" (for Brajen Seal, for instance, it was "theophilanthropic" reform, and the social work–social reform alliance was instanced in the fag end of the previous chapter). By launching an internal attempt to reform practices through voluntary associations and related agenda, it was modernity through civil society in the colony—the deploying of the universal through civil social institutions and activities. Sarkar is revoking the proposal in 1936 in quite a similar way in order to arrive at modernity. The arrival then must have been deferred. Why? Where is the account of the episodic rivalry between (allegedly) personal-particular and public-universal forms of helping? What is at stake in the case of a wronged or a right, a successful or a failed transition? In this, let us recall that what Benoy Sarkar considered as the most important was the "era of Ramakrishna–Vivekananda" and we shall, as also in the previous chapter, address this event more than anything else to illuminate our observation, partly also because it is quite an impossibility to address all agencies from the Municipality to Bangiya Sankat Tran Samiti. Charted against the growing consolidation of social work in various stable forms—which were allegedly imported ones (e.g., Vivekananda's Ramakrishna "Mission" which smelt of Western "missionarism" and was, thus, critiqued by Ramakrishna's other disciples)—the departmentalization of child welfare and as such the gradual governmentalization of welfare provisions, which first assumed canonical forms in England later to be found in India[10] and Bengal, would become visible.

But this conflict between daridra seva or selfless, personal care for the poor (person) and ameliorative attempts at systemic (impersonal!) poverty, how could they be neighboring phrases in Sarkar's oeuvre?

---

[9] Ibid., 80.

[10] The emergence of Poor Laws in Elizabethan England could be seen from this vantage point. And Sarkar's critique seems to bear a smell of that. The relevance and influence of Poor Laws on debates on crisis and philanthropy in India could be seen in the instance of the emergence of famine codes where the governmentalization of the Indian state could be seen to have happened. Further, while the famine event gave the colonial state broaden its grasp, the people turned population responded adequately to concur with it:

Georg Simmel—one of the seminal social philosophers of our times—
expended considerable energy on the issue, and he would be of immense
relevance here.[11] Simmels' prominent problematic is the way the state of
being poor or poverty as an objective condition came to be increasingly
thematized, and a remote "purely social, centralist teleology"[12] appeared
in the wake of the "modern abstract form of welfare."[13] Here, grants
for the unemployed, which Sarkar mentioned in his speech, is in place
for the following rationale.

> The support granted by the English labor unions to their members during
> unemployment was meant not so much to bring about an alleviation of
> individual want as to prevent the unemployed from working too cheaply
> out of need and, thus, depress the wage rate of the whole work force.
> From this meaning of welfare, it becomes clear that, while it takes from
> the prosperous and gives to the poor, it still in no way approaches an
> equalization of these individual positions and that its idea will not at
> all overcome the tendency for the differentiation of society into rich
> and poor.[14]

A few more passing words on this labyrinth that is marked by a
supposedly personal care for the poor and the bureaucratic administration
of social services: welfare. This is curious because Sarkar—as mentioned
before, while marked his own era as the "Ramakrishna Vivekananda era"
in continuity—could be seen to have opined for impersonal services with
difficulty. Therefore, the apparently irreconcilable phrastic neighborhood
of apparently opposed paradigms is not impossible. It could also be

---

Thus, within three decades after the advent of officially-sponsored famine relief, the
state's professed ideology and benevolence had been internalized by its subjects who
started citing back the rhetorical claims of the state. ... In popular perception the burden
of responsibility for famine relief progressively shifted from the indigenous elite to
the state. ... In the case of any calamity, relief seekers would increasingly flock to the
collector's office instead of the *havelis* (mansions) of local patrons.

See Sanjay Sharma, *Famine, Philanthropy and the Colonial State, North India in the Early
Nineteenth Century* (New Delhi: Oxford University Press, 2001), 232–33.

[11] Simmel, "The Poor Person," in *Sociology: Inquiries into the Construction of Social
Forms,* trans. A. J. Blasi, A. K. Jacobs, Mathew Kanjirathinkal (Leiden, The Netherlands:
Brill, 2009), 2: 409–42.
[12] Ibid., 414.
[13] Ibid., 413.
[14] Ibid.

inferred that Vivekananda's insistence on recipient autonomy and distrust of one-way service provisions—excepting the moment of *daridra narayan seva*—derived largely from the materialized instrumentality of idealized services they suffered in the hands of the missionaries. It is necessary to underline this kinship—heterogeneous as it may have been—between Vivekananda's pained tryst with the missionary moment and the ground of his own discourse. In fact, conversion through social (welfare) services was another symptom that he had to reckon with, even in order to mark his departure.[15] Vivekananda would often voice his disagreement with this later turn or the paradigm of conversion so evident in various Christian attempts.[16] But with a difference.[17] So the social critique—even if in the form of a reversal—was already there in place, well before Vivekananda had effectively arrived at the site. Amalesh Tripathi very rightly notes a curious turn in the latter's critique—which is grounded in the radical religious pluralism of Ramakrishna: if all religions are true,

---

[15] This anxiety was not unfounded. For some who would be interested in a plain, narrative social history of facts and not the history of concepts, such information could be exemplary: After 1814, the English and the Dutch missionaries instituted a few schools much to the credit of Priest Robert May and Captain James Stewart. When Stewart died in 1818, he left 36 *pathshaalas* and 3,000 students. In 1832, Incorporated Society for the Propagation of Gospel in Foreign Parts—an organization for the "spread" of Christianity—took its reigns. "By 1954 in the whole of India under the aegis of National Christian Council, 46 colleges, 448 High Schools, 553 Madhyamik schools and 103 Teachers Training Colleges were there. In 1951 42 Colleges, 474 High schools and 4362 Primary Schools belonged to the Roman Catholics."

See Bhabatosh Dutta, "Banglar Jagorone Missonarir Daan," in *Unish Sataker Bangalijiban O Sanskriti*, eds. Swapan Basu and Indrajit Choudhury (Kolkata: Pustakbiponi, 2003), 92–94.

[16] Vivekananda's exhortations would make passing references to the impasse generated by this conversion through welfare: The "practice of gathering of orphans by Christian Missionaries after famine ... was subject to government regulation after the Famine Commission of 1880 and the enactment of Famine Codes to the effect that such philanthropy was not to set the stage for attempts to convert the young from their religious faith."

See Gwilym Beckerlegge, "Swami Vivekananda and Seva: Taking Social Service Seriously," in *Swami Vivekananda and the Modernisation of Hinduism*, ed. William Radice (New Delhi: Oxford University Press, 1999), 168.

[17] So far as the debate on conversion through welfare by the missionaries was concerned, already "in 1843 Debendranath Thakur, Radhakanta Deb, Raja Satyacharan Ghosal, Ramgopal Ghosh decided at a meeting that similar to that of the priests, free schools for the education of the children would be opened. A school by the name of Hindu Hitarthi was subsequently opened." See Beckerlegge, "Swami Vivekananda and Seva: Taking Social Service Seriously," 100.

where does the successful validity of conversion lie?[18] This is, in fact, Vivekananada's true question and real suspicion. Did he explore the question adequately? The answer is beyond the scope of this chapter, but let us note emphatically that it was Vivekananda and his Ramakrishna Mission that not only advocated strict book-keeping for money housed and spent in and for the math, his was a call for autonomy and self-enabling of those helped through education. But in him, it was not plain and secular social work but rather various helping modalities existing in a peculiarly combined form. An intelligent offshoot of this experiment was Sister Nivedita—whose notion of civic personality we've explored in the last chapter, and also Belur math's recognition of institutional personality in a published book of recent origin. The examples could be multiplied and merit a separate case study.

However, in our context, as it is evident, there were a number of mediations that followed the rejection of the old forms of daya or daan, alms-giving or charity, to which even a secular social scientist Benoy Sarkar is referring to, and those that were rejected by Hegel, too, in the last chapter, and those that we find in heterogenously mixed forms in the Ramakrishna-Vivekananda' discourse. Now, what are they? We shall examine the so-called (classically) personal forms of helping—here for the first time—to arrive again at contemporary times.

## Other, Supererogatory Forms of Helping: The Problem

No doubt, our stories of ourselves and our times are replete with theories of transformation in our commitment to political obligation: there lies the new, contractual legitimacy of the constitutional state—in the consent of the people. This narrative is full of tracts that tell of obligatory acts: what we or others are supposed to do or what we compulsorily owe each other in the form of rights and duties. But there has always been a class of acts that were considered beyond obligations or duty: classically, these were acts of supererogation[19] that included such diverse events as "saintliness

---

[18] Amalesh Tripathi, *Italir Renaissence, Bangalir Sanskriti* (Calcutta: Ananda Publishers, 1996), 87.

[19] David Heyd, *Supererogation: Its Status in Ethical Theory* (Cambridge: Cambridge University Press, 1982), 142.

and heroism, beneficence (charity, generosity, gifts), favours, volunteering, supererogatory forbearances, and finally pardon (forgiveness and mercy)." Being nonobligatory, optional, and requiring extreme voluntarism, in moral philosophy, these are called permissible acts in the sense that they are not obligatory or compulsory but if somebody is willing to perform them, they are, however, not prohibited. In other words, "*permissions* are those acts which we are at liberty both to do and not to do. They are acts which violate no obligation or natural duty."[20] These are, so to say, peculiar acts beyond the realm of rights and duties; beyond the contractual extent of the modern state. Charity having had its origin in agape or Christian love, *philanthropia* or voluntary doing or the whole baggage of "meritorious" social services via Greece, Rome, and others (the first alms house was established in Massachusetts in 1662), was attached to the destitute, poor, orphans or the handicapped and the diseased—coalesced in the famous Poor Laws in England that later became instrumental in defining the form that the helping services have presently assumed. The statement that permeates discourses on poverty and charity is: alms, charity, pardon or mercy could not be claimed as a right by the possible beneficiaries. Now what is significant is that with the modernist turn that accumulated in the welfare state, welfare came to be included in the inventory of rights as a social right. Being translated into the language of risk, insurance, and entitlement, supererogatory acts underwent a complex rebirth. They could not be claimed as a right by the accidental, and not targeted, beneficiaries. Further, in the instance of risk—for example, classical supererogatory actions such as heroism or saintliness would entail exposure to risk, while the modern welfare state wants to mitigate the riskful hazards—a life-period entails for a person. It is not easy to reconcile the two positions. Have supererogatory acts become impossible and, thereby, does that entail that the increasing erosion of insurance under post-welfare modernity, since it exposes citizens to risk without offering them the opportunity to exercise their choice in being so, while in supererogatory actions, they are self-chosen, heroism is only personal. The problem that can be posed is, subsequent to their posing as rights, how would they be made to address the classical question that they can never be made to resemble rights or duties. Let us state this more simply: How can that which is not obligatory upon us to undertake—the

---

[20] John Rawls. *A Theory of Justice* rev. ed. (Oxford: Oxford University Press, 1999), 100 (italics mine).

acts which we are free to take or abandon and, thus, signifies our free will—be radically transformed to become obligations in modernity? This is more so because welfare state being a version of the liberal capitalist state does allow us to maximize our own gains at the cost of others, but still while it does not elicit a maxim that doing good to others or helping others in their pressing times is compulsory upon us at our level, it tends to shift and take the duty upon itself by imposing an indirect burden upon the citizens in the form of taxes to benefit a part of the population but even not a part because social rights could be claimed by every citizen. (It universalizes that which was sectional or prudential.) Therefore, it may seem that while voluntary, casual, (inter)personal help may not still) be claimed as a right in a welfare state, a help that originates from the people to the state in the form of taxes and relief funds, and then again filters down to the citizens[21] can, of course, be claimed as a right and, when failed, grievances and agitations, and use of other political instruments of the citizens (overturning the government through franchise) are all the more justified. But the state is still the expressed will of the people realized in the transitory establishment of the government. If that is so, then it is the people helping each other through the public mediation (or else, the personality) of the state that have fallen under social rights (and corresponding duties).

But to address the present tense of the formation is not to paper over a long and resounding past. Today, to write a genealogy of the helping services vis-à-vis social work is to imbricate oneself in the modern rational legal and bureaucratic bargain that lays claims to some form of politico-economic relief and reservation. But, interestingly, disapproving social reform or social services or welfare, it is social work that has come to stay. Social work is the disciplinary, secular, and scientific institutionalization of helping that also claims the benefit of a specific body of knowledge. (The international standard definition of social work is the science of helping others to help themselves.) Surprisingly, in India, there exist narratives of the careers of political or legal obligations and

---

[21] The problem of taxes from the populace and for the populace cannot but end in such a fiasco where the pulls of particular individual and group needs had to balance themselves against the universal pressure of social rights and taxation: "taxes can have a depressing effect on the economy, even when most of the money collected flows back—by and large and in the long rub—to the people from whom it was taken. And that is roughly what happens when the entire population is included in the scheme." See T. H. Marshall, *Social Policy* (London: Hutchinson University Library, 1965), 180.

even some on the violation of such obligations—political or otherwise—but a philosophical genealogy of that which lies, supposedly, beyond obligations or duty (and interpretable on its own terms) is definitely missing. Yet this apparent self-congratulation confronts a difficulty while encountering existing and even contemporaneous attempts that are based on a category mistake: their complaint is that helping practices legitimate (inclusive of past and future) domination through techniques of apparently positive and beneficial persuasion. Those who receive gifts (today they are services) are put under an obligation of unconscious reciprocity. Foucault thinks it was in the 19th century that social workers emerged, armed with the disciplinary techniques of normalization to engage in the affairs of others.[22] The transition from charity to social work is then seen as hegemonic: to repeat, the helping methods, allegedly, have had been instrumental in making domination tolerable, masking its alliance with ideologies and interests. This I mentioned as a category mistake since those actions of helping that are supposedly beyond obligations cannot be interpreted within a framework delineated by obligatory rights and duties. In other words, when in a (modern) welfare state,[23] the right to receive social welfare benefits becomes a welfare-right or a social right, we are contaminated to the extent that it becomes perhaps obvious that we tend to appropriate or interpret other helping modalities too as political discursive formations; in other words, succumb to the much-rehearsed juridico-political notion of sovereignty. But the mistake is to seek permission or permissibility in terms of consent or optionalism through the sieve of obligation; in other words, to seek to understand, using the prescriptive language of rights and duties or contract, acts beyond the realm of rights and duties and contract. What is at stake is a failure to grasp an internal critique that contributed toward the evolution of

---

[22] On meddling with the affairs of others, unlike Foucault, Alisdair MacIntyre grants the credit to benevolence, "Benevolence in the 18th century is assigned very much the scope which the Christian schemes of the virtues assigned to charity. But, unlike charity, benevolence as a virtue became a license for almost any kind of manipulative intervention in the affairs of others." See Alisdair MacIntyre, *After Virtue: A Study in Moral Theory*, 2nd ed. (Indiana: University of Notre Dame1984), 232. But Foucault's objection to this formulation could be as to whether such an intervention, without disciplinary mechanisms of knowledge, was at all an "authoritative" one.

[23] As stated earlier, although "tax-based poor relief" has been traced to 16th century England (see Marjorie K. McIntosh, "Poverty, Charity, and Coercion in Elizabethan England", *Journal of Interdisciplinary History*, 34, no. 3 [2005]: 459), Sarkar wants to retain the public "tax" part of the method and, thus, use it as a state linked modern form of assistance. See Sarkar, "Daridranarayner Samaj Shastra," 64.

ancient charity/benevolence or religious philanthropy via governmental welfarism to universal social work moods and methods. This internal or immanent critique would take hold of a different register than the usual historical accounts (giving linear details of the "Jewish Charitable Bequests and Hekdesh Trust in Thirteenth-Century Spain"[24] or such as "The Earliest Hospitals in Byzantium, Western Europe, and Islam"[25] or plain politico-ideological accounts that see welfare as surveillance or claims to care as hegemonic charted in either Foucauldian or Gramscian terms. Universal, but still which assumed strange but understandable forms in the will to universalize through the act of colonization. What is at stake is a failure to grasp an internal or immanent critique that contributed toward the evolution of ancient charity/benevolence or religious philanthropy via governmental welfarism to the now nearly universal social work moods and methods, and the corresponding status of the personal and truth-claims to its purported erosion. The mentioned frameworks fail to make the change visible. But to write such an instant genealogy would mean taking account of specific juridico-legal or the particular kind of technological transformation historically achieved by the helping services. Here is a paradigmatic example. Classically, we know that it is to benefit the humankind that charitable services like orphan houses were allowed; in a dispute in 1971, an Indian court judged (in Ahmedabad Rana Caste Association vs CIT (1971) 3 SCC 475 at 477-78): "To serve a charitable purpose it is not necessary that the object should be to benefit the whole of mankind or all persons in a particular country or state. It is sufficient if the intention to benefit a section of the public as distinguished from a specific individual—is present." Later, this was considered wide enough to include even singularly religious purposes that may be assumed to have had interesting, even sinister consequences. A charitable purpose, according to Indian law, while subscribes to the big three-pronged relief of the poor, education or medical relief actually, while enumerates them under "charitable uses and trusts," includes even the maintenance of sick and wounded soldiers; repair of bridges, sea banks, and highways; marriages of poor maids; and helping a poor inhabitant in case he is unable to pay taxes. This is nearly an echo of charitable uses catalogued during Elizabeth I in England, which included (just notice the frank, nearly

---

[24] Judah D. Galinsky, "Jewish Charitable Bequests and Hekdesh Trust in Thirteenth-Century Spain," *Journal of Interdisciplinary History* 34, no. 3 (2005): 423–40.

[25] Peregrine Horden, "The Earliest Hospitals in Byzantium, Western Europe, and Islam," *Journal of Interdisciplinary History* 34, no. 3 (2005), 361–89.

mimetic similarity) "the repair of bridges, ports, havens … churches … and highways."[26] Close to charity, "[i]n the eighteenth century, for example, when state intervention was at a minimum, philanthropy ['although the giving a man does is personal'] concerned itself with a much wider range of subjects than it does today." And the inventory is close to charity with items running from "reform of prisons and lunatic asylums" to "the abolition of slavery."[27] Then, we are very ambiguously poised and it is quite unsettling to try to delve into the differences and similarities of the structures of helping with the personal element as it were with them and as we've reconstructed in this book. It is time we look into their lexical form, and if possible—content.

# II

## Etymology: Charity, Philanthropy, Altruism Among Other Structures of Helping

When we indulge in word-original or etymological endeavors, it is not to enter into an originary moment of beginning. But rather, to explore how a concept-metaphor, apropos its own travelling trajectory, has or has not come to resemble its own being or has or has not come into its own. This is what Derrida calls the realm of the "proper." Etymology is not philology, although it could be suspected to preserve certain strains of the latter, which could well be accommodated within our current text, that is, if "it is the examination of the structure of language prior to the meaning it produces,"[28] then we have two other significant times: language at the time of meaning and language after the time of meaning. Now, before we chart the word-genealogical disputes, let us hint at the problematics that will be assumed by helping. A scholar who even dares to disagree with Benveniste as to the right rendering of *daan* in English seems to locate the oldest use of helping in Rig Veda. Indra being requested for *ugramavah*, "help or furtherance," which is characterized as *ugra*—this adjective being etymologically and semantically related closely to *ojas*,

---

[26] Woodroofe, *From Charity to Social Work*, 18–19.

[27] Ibid., 19.

[28] Paul De Man, "Return to Philology" in *Resistance to Theory*, ed. Wlad Godzich (Minneapolis, MN: Minnesota University Press, 1986), 21–26.

a "power substance" that is most characteristically possessed by Indra; (the same deity is besought to impart his *ojistha, mada*—"his most effective and powerful rapture or excitement to those praying").[29] This is also not to miss the point that what has been asked from the deity is that which is most appropriate. Help in the Bengali taxonomy is *sahajyo* standing for not very compatible predicates: first, that which preserves a sense of helping (*sahaybhav*); second, the act of helping (*sahay karma*); third, an act of assistance (*sahayak daan: sahayatakaran*).[30] *Karuna* (pity) includes repentance, mourning, request, and humility.[31] Daya, apart from its usual associationist liaison with karuna meaning pity, means wishing well for the world (and this is close to the current "welfare," which originally meant good journey) the way one wishes well-being for oneself.[32] The word seva had a specific 19th century resurgence in the hands of the disciples of Ramakrishna that belongs to a particular form of culturo-religious comportment. The plain etymological grounding of the word delivers an array of meanings that range from washing, nursing, eating, and *onusthan kora/palan kora* (to celebrate, to host, or to observe) to enjoying.[33] *Sevak*—meaning the provider of seva—stands for a diverse set of objects such as worshipper (*pujak*) to servant (*paricharak*); *paricharja* means care, and in this sense seva would be, as we've already named it, selfless care, even the gift of care. The Bengali lexical ordering for *upokar* (doing a favor or doing good to somebody) itemizes, apart from the above two meanings, the sense of enjoyment (*bhog, upbhog*) and also a cosmetic act for the subject in the literal sense of dressing or beautifying oneself (*prasadhan, mandan, almkaran*).[34] In the Western tradition, even in continental philosophy, as it is well known by now, it is the word gift that is doing the rounds—which we could situate close to the word help and explore the consequences. Let us begin with Benveniste. (Jean Lallot gives a good synopsis.)

> Greek has five words which are commonly translated uniformly by "gift."
> A careful examination of their use shows that they do, in fact, correspond

[29] J. Gonda, "*'Gifts' and 'Giving' in the Rigveda*" (Sadhu Ashram, Hoshiarpur: Vishveshvaranand Vedic Research Institute, 1964). Reprinted from *Vishveshvaranand Indological Journal* ii, no. 1 (1964, March), 6.

[30] Haricharan Bandopadhyaya, *Bangiya Sabdakosh* (repr., 1988, Kolkata: Sahitya Academy, 1966), II: 2211.

[31] Ibid.

[32] Ibid.

[33] Ibid,. 2260.

[34] Ibid., I: 417.

to as many different ways of envisaging a gift—from the purely verbal notion of "giving" to "contractual pre-station imposed by the terms of a pact, an alliance, or a friendship," or a "guest-host" relationship. The gothic term gild and its derivatives take us back to a very ancient Germanic tradition in which the religious aspect ("the sacrifice"), the economic aspect (a mercantile association), and the juridical aspect (the atonement of a crime) are closely interwoven. The varied genealogy of the words ... on the one hand disclose the practice of "potlach" in the Indo European past, and on the other hand show how the ancient notion of "prestigious expenditure" became attenuated to mean 'expense, damages.'"[35]

Benveniste, in fact, has a complex hierarchy in store for this order: He ponders over how even trade or exchange could be seen as "disinterested gift."[36] "In this light exchange appears as a round of gifts rather than a genuine commercial operation."[37] As stated earlier, in Greek, there are five distinct terms which are uniformly translated as "gift": (a) The first form is "dowry" or gifts brought at the time of marriage[38]; (b) The second sense entails praise for "gift" as "a means of establishing advantageous relations"—following which is an historical abstraction: "'giving' is good, 'robbing' is bad";[39] (c) The third sense entails a distinct sense of "the actual gift" and "the act of bringing or presenting a gift." And as a derivative, "the name of the thing or the person to whom it is given" is sustained; in other words "the thing which is presented, the present which serves as a recompense";[40] (d) In the fourth sense, it appears Benveniste wants to convey the gift a la Homer as an "effective accomplishment of an idea, which may also, but not necessarily, be materialized in an object," for instance when a gift is promised in the future made possible by a "nominal transposition of the verbal form in the present tense ... in the future."[41] (e) The fifth notion invokes the previously stated notion of trade as "disinterested gift" but goes beyond it; it is a gift qua contractual pre-station, imposed by the obligations of "a pact, an alliance, a friendship, or a bond of hospitality; the obligation of the ... guest, of the subjects towards their king

---

[35] Emile Benveniste, *Indo-European Language and Society*, trans. Elizabeth Palmer (London: Faber and Faber Limited, 1973), 53.
[36] Is the modern notion of impersonal helping a variation on this theme?
[37] Ibid., 53.
[38] Ibid., 54.
[39] Ibid., 54–55.
[40] Ibid., 55.
[41] Ibid., 55.

or god and also the pre-station implied by an alliance."[42] If it is friendship that forms the background culture (a la Rawls) of a contractual obligation, then it augurs well in consonance with our predominant thesis (stated in Chapter 3) that the private requires the personal as its precondition. This also seeps in the Germanic and Gothic inventory—where it stands for the institutional notion of the Guild as money and gild as tax which engendered "institutions with both an economic and religious character ... [ ] ... fraternities united by economic interests but apparently also by a common cult."[43] It would do well to remember that cult in Hegel has a similar resonance—where it is said to unite several things: for instance God and humanity and my or your participation in it irrespective of subjective personality.

The anthropology of helping through giving or Marcel Mauss and his "theories" of the gift have attracted tumultuous responses from everywhere including Jacques Derrida, for which it is necessary to put in place—even if briefly—Mauss' contribution and meditate on his intervention—and what implications it might have for our work. Mary Douglas thinks that Mauss' famous work *Gift* makes one single big point, "There are no free gifts; gift cycles engage persons in permanent commitments that articulate the dominant institutions."[44] In fact, throughout the book, Mauss tends to make this point again and again. While as Douglas points out that "charity is meant to be a free gift, a voluntary, unrequired surrender of resources"[45] or what was, according to Malinowski "spontaneous, pure of ulterior motive." But the truth according to Mauss is that "the major transfer of goods has been by cycles of obligatory return of gifts." Because according to Mauss, and in contrast to the master in *Dharmatattva*, unreciprocated gifts weaken solidarity and demolish courtesy: "The invitation must be returned."[46] But while the custom of gift exchange endorses the fact that "[w]e possess more than a tradesman morality,"[47] the allegory of barter underlies the whole process. But while Mauss discusses the survival of gift principle in the wake of classical Hindu Law, he is far from accurate. Romila Thapar

[42] Ibid., 57.
[43] Ibid., 58.
[44] Mary Douglas, "Foreward," in *The Gift: The Form and Reason for Exchange in Archaic Societies,* trans. W. D. Halls (London: Routledge, 1990), ix.
[45] Ibid., vii.
[46] Ibid., 65.
[47] Ibid., 65.

thinks that "daana for merit echoes—the Buddhist notion of charity or daana. The idea may therefore have come from Buddhist sources,"[48] while Mauss restricts himself to the Brahmanas as the recipient of gifts and the corresponding complexities. From Thapar, another corrective could be borrowed still. The different existence of dana (gift) and *daksina* (gift by extension) in the Vedic text, which "are by no means synonymous,"[49] have not been addressed by Mauss. But even Thapar cannot contend that the elaborate emphasis on the *pratigrahita* (recipient) of dana in the Hindu system will be done away by the master in *Dharmatattva,* which is the specific modernist turn (we've discussed in an earlier chapter).

Charity[50] has been derived from the English "dear" signifying both "dearness of price as well as affection";[51] the affective mood has been more reinforced by its associational, predominant use "in the context of the Bible ... [where the Greek agape meant in translation] both love and charity[52]. ... Charity was then Christian love, between man and God,

---

[48] Romila Thapar, "Dana and Daksina: A Form of Exchange," in *Cultural Pasts: Essays in Early Indian Genealogy* (Delhi: Oxford University Press, 2000), 5.

[49] Ibid., 522.

[50] On a historical mode, it has been observed,

> Charity is a complex of ideas and practices rooted in Christianity, particularly in the reformed Protestantism of the English settlers; it was reinforced by the heritage of Catholicism and Judaism brought by immigrants in the nineteenth and twentieth centuries. Charity expresses an impulse to personal service; it engages individuals in concrete, direct acts of compassion and connection to other people.

See Robert A. Gross, "Giving in America: From Charity to Philanthropy," in *Charity, Philanthropy and Civility in American History,* eds. Lawrence Friedman and Mark D. McGarvie (Cambridge: Cambridge University Press, 2002), 29–48.

[51] Raymond Williams, *Keywords: A Vocabulary of Culture and Society* (London: Fontana, Croom Helm: London, 1976), 45.

[52] A more conservative estimate disagrees with this view and disconnects *agape* from *eros*: with *eros* which is on the human side "there is no way that leads to God. There is only a way for God to come to humans, and that is *agape*. In other words, there is simply no connection between *agape* and *eros*" (p. 282). But there are a host of other philosophers who do take Eros and friendship into account and opine that in the wake of love of God, all worldly love, affective attachments do emerge purified. Some moral theologians contend, "Personal goodness exists when someone is truly loving (charitable). Mere rightness of acts does not necessarily indicate personal goodness. One could perform an ethically right or wrong act for a variety of reasons, not all of them loving" Bernard Hoose, "Charity" in *Routledge Encyclopedia of Philosophy*, Vol. 1. ed. Edward Craig (London: Routledge, 1998), pp. 280–82.
See 'Charity' (280–82) in *Routledge Encyclopedia of Philosophy,* (reference to be completed).

and between men and their neighbours."[53] Now, if there is a wordly sense of *philos* that persists in philanthropy, then

> it is used reflexively to indicate a special bond with something rather like the English word "dear" … [I]n addition to the reflexive "dear" usage, philos was used to describe bonds of friendship. […] The verb philein also took on the meaning "to kiss," as a kiss was an action that signified a reciprocal agreement between friends.[54]

But while the Aristotelian and early Greek heritage tends to suggest that "[p]hilanthropia is the attitude of a kind and considerate person, even if she lacks material resources … and can be displayed without the transfer of material resources," later Greek connotations brought in the sense of a "definite favor done by a superior to an inferior."[55] In fact, at this stage, the distinction between charity ("charity is benevolence as manifested in provision"[56]) and philanthropy is basically the burden of property and resources—without which charity cannot be performed—while philanthropy is possible.[57]

---

[53] Williams, *Keywords,* 45–46.

[54] Vincent Lloyd, "On Gillian Rose and Love." *Telos* (volume not mentioned) no. 143 (2008, Summer): 51.

[55] T. H. Irwin, "Generosity and Property in Aristotle's *Politics,*" *Social Philosophy and Policy* 4, no. 2 (1999): 37–54, in *Aristotle: Critical Assessments,* ed. Lloyd P. Gerson (London: Routledge: London, 1999), IV: 164–81.

[56] Ibid., 165. But is it, really? Dealing in social historical facticity, and that which has come to stay with us, philanthropy is the use of "wealth to rethink and remake society." See Judith Sealander, "Curing Evils at Their Source, the Arrival of Scientific Giving," in *Charity, Philanthropy and Civility in American History,* eds. Lawrence Friedman and Mark D. McGarvie (Cambridge: Cambridge University Press, 2002), 217–39.

[57] This is, of course, refuted if one has to follow John Winthrop's classic "[a] model of Christian charity" revived by the puritans in which charity could take such forms as a gift of 'good advice, a kind word, or an exhortation to piety,' offered by anybody to a neighbor in need. A poor man could be just as charitable as a rich one." See Robert A. Gross, "Giving in America: From Charity to Philanthropy,'" in *Charity, Philanthropy and Civility in American History,* eds. Lawrence Friedman and Mark D. McGarvie (Cambridge: Cambridge University Press: Cambridge, 2002), 32. In a similar vein, the notion of abstract gift in India, evident in the kinds of *dana* that includes education (*vidyadan*) to labor (*shramadan*), interrupts the notion of financial presence in otherwise popular notions of charity.
    Philanthropy, after charity, in this revisionary discourse, "represents a second mode of social service. Coined as a term in late 17th-century England, it became associated with the Enlightenment, for it sought to apply reason to the solution of social ills and needs … it aspires to aid individuals as to reform society. Its object is the promotion

> Originally connoting "love toward mankind" and hence, synonymous with charity, philanthropy acquired a distinctive meaning in the middle decades of the eighteenth century. Then civic-minded individuals in London seized on ... the joint-stock company—and put it to benevolent ends. Pooling their funds, they came together to form voluntary associations ... [such as Society for the Suppression of Vice (1802)] moved by "an Inclination to promote Publick Good ... practical improvement in the human condition."[58]

Taking this as a historical instance, the spurious and anarchically pluralist mushrooming of societies in 19th century Bengal and elsewhere could be viewed in this light. Moreover, against the broad spectrum of civil rights movement and the praise of Tocqueville, it stood for a progressivist cause for people. The personal element in it, though, thrived furiously: amidst the close neighborhood of Philadelphia, "Teaching a man how to employ and repair a razor, [Benjamin] Franklin could enjoy an immediate relation to the object of his aid and derive direct satisfaction from the results. The practice of philanthropy was not yet an impersonal act."[59]

Altruism becomes contextually more significant here because it was introduced by the sociologist Auguste Comte, and Herbert Spencer vetted the same—where it was urged that it was necessary to move from a self-regarding egoistic social state to another regarding altruistic "social" state where "good of others" would be the object.[60] Originating in mid-19th century, the French word *altruisme*, moved to Italian *altrui* meaning "somebody else" and Latin *alteri huic* meaning "to this other."[61] Whatever, altruism has attracted considerable social and moral philosophical attention. With this original orientation to the other or "else," it is justified that Thomas Nagel now defines altruism as the "recognition of reality of other persons" and "act in consideration of the interests of other person[s]."[62] Now, a brief caveat before we account further: Is it at all possible—in the first place—to be prohibitively blind to the reality of other persons—their existential presence? Or does it mean that when we act

---

of progress through the advance of knowledge". See Gross, "Giving in America: From Charity to Philanthropy," 31.

[58]  Gross, "Giving in America: From Charity to Philanthropy," 37.

[59]  Ibid., 39.

[60]  James Hastings, "Altruism," in *Encyclopedia of Religion and Ethics*, ed. James Hastings (Edinburgh: T&T Clark, 1974 [1908]), 1: 354–58.

[61]  "Altruism" in oxforddictionaries.com, accessed on June 29, 2010.

[62]  Thomas Nagel, *The Possibility of Altruism,* (Princeton, NJ: Princeton University Press, 1978), 3.

in nonaltruistic or egoistic (selfish) manner, we are denying other people a constructivist reality—that is, we act in a manner with an embodied sense as if they do not exist at all; but it is already a philosophical truth pace the communitarians that not only serves my self-interests, but my self could not have come into being without a socialization imputed unto me, or without a language that is primarily not mine—to begin with, it is others or everybody else's. Therefore, first, it is impossible to be blind to the reality of other persons—even if I wanted to use them as a means to serve my advantages; second, to wake up to other people's self-interests is not altruism, too, or cannot be so. The infinite inventory of other people's interests is another instance of an impossibility: they are always in interactive play with my interests, and that is well within their pool of autonomy to have to pursue their own without others' interference. The fact is, when we address ourselves to other people's endangered interests only, and more so when it is not required of us, we could be said to have acted altruistically, not otherwise. But relevant to our present work, the debate is demarcated by the personal principle, though in a curious way. Nagel invokes what he calls a "rational altruism" for which altruism becomes a rational requirement on action, that is, everybody considers him/herself as one among others, and acts accordingly—which becomes later an impersonal principle, an "impersonal judgement."[63] In his words,

> I have tried to show that altruism and related motives do not depend on taste, sentiment, or an arbitrary and ultimate choice. They depend instead on the fact that our reasons for action are subject to the formal condition of objectivity,[64] which depends in turn on our ability to view ourselves from both the personal and impersonal standpoint[s].

---

[63] Ibid., 102.
[64] Accompanying this, Nagel offers an eloquent, vibrant supplement: "When they are wronged, people suddenly understand objective reasons, for they require such concepts to express their resentment. That is why the primary form of moral argument is a request to imagine oneself in the situation of another person." See Thomas Nagel, *The Possibility of Altruism*, (Princeton, NJ: Princeton University Press, 1978), 145. But it is very possible to judge a wrong or an offence, from the third personal standpoint, on the basis of rules, without taking recourse to a second personal substitutive empathy—at least this is one standard view—that justice should not be a personal dressing. "How would you like it if someone did that to you?" (p. 82): For Nagel "the possibility of putting yourself in his place, is [therefore] essential" (p. 83) and this is the rational presupposition of altruism as objective action. Suddenly then, as it is here, a Christian-religious precept, and then a Kantian enactment, is rationally appropriated for a secular, modern comportment.

We stand informed beforehand on the impersonal standpoint; but, what is the personal according to Nagel? "[T]he only personal residue, therefore, which is not included in the system of impersonal beliefs to which I am committed by a personal judgement, is the basic personal premise itself, the premise which locates me in the world which has been impersonally described."[65] Therefore, as a proof of this rhetorical success—which seems to be half-hearted—Nagel while unable to do away with the personal, tends to accommodate it along with the impersonal. However, while meditating on the motivation behind an altruistic act, Nagel, in the early parts of the book tries to seek it, not in desire but rather on formal aspects of "practical reason."[66] One of the most prudent reasons for rejecting desire as motivation—for Nagel—is, besides the fact that it (desire) is not susceptible to rational assessment, the criticism of desire cannot start from desire itself but has to be something other than desire. But this is not too successful, and since he has tried to grant a place to both the personal and the impersonal, he has to confide, "[w]ithout question people may be motivated by benevolence, sympathy, love, redirected self-interest, and various other influences,"[67] but besides this, impersonally—that is, a rational motivation should trump mere self-interest. This is peculiar; Nagel's rational motivation becomes coeval, and is even equal to the content itself: while altruism is the "trump(ing) of mere self interest for others," motivation to do so as per Nagel's version given earlier, is exactly the same. This is absurd—even fallacious! But considering—if he were to go for a personal emotion (for example, love), then the motivating force would not be, by any remote remove, the same as that of the act that is supposed to be a source of it. In order to bring in—with force—the personal, we've pursued throughout the present work plotting it against the private, does Nagel, while invoking the personal, agree with it or, restore it in any viable form? The moment he quotes Moore (of the *Principia Ethica* fame), while Moore is talking about the extractive impossibility of "my good," the excerpt is significant.

> The good of it can in no possible sense be 'private' or belong to me; any more than a thing can exist privately, or for one person only … which if I have it, others cannot have. But if it is good absolutely that I should have it, then everyone else has as much reason for aiming at my having it, as I have myself.[68]

---

[65] Ibid., 103.
[66] Ibid., 15.
[67] Ibid., 80.
[68] Moore cited in ibid., 86.

Nagel seems to construct it as an "objective good," but the way we've reconstructed the personal, and that which goes on to revise Nagel, here, it is not a private good yet it could be a personal one which is not against the public. Further, at a second level, good (as a life-choice question) scarcely can be objective otherwise—even if participatively seen—the notion of the right is what could be objective, universal and consensual; the personal is what again is keen on connecting itself to the issues of the good, while negotiating with the questions of the right, as it can within its own site let the particular and the universal meet: the person, in fact, is such a site from where this distinction has to begin and has to end. Finally, the most damaging scrutiny of this contemporary twist to altruism in Nagel's hand will surmise something very different: If altruism becomes a rational requirement, then how would it remain supererogatory or voluntary, beyond duty and obligation? This is our "personalytic" impasse reiterated.

To contextualize this discussion and make it a bit more relevant to the signs of our time and place, in other words, if we—for the time being— anthropologize a philosophical discussion, and see if our present work can interrupt, displace, and revise the dominant conception there, it might be of some productive, discursive value. In this piece, the well-known Indian political scientist Rajeev Bhargava tends to argue that, given that there is a transition from a hierarchical society to an egalitarian one, as it is has happened in India of the last decade or two, there tends to usher "a period of generalized egoism," where followed by "an attack on altruism" by the lower classes and castes—because they tend to progress and imbibe a "nascent egalitarianism—altruism is debunked since "altruism generates a loss of self-respect, self worth, indeed the very sense of self within the inferior.'"[69] (If somebody recognizes my reality, would it be shame upon me?) Now, these substantive observations of the author—in this strain—will not require of us a critique in repetition, after we have had Nagel with and against us—and perhaps we did score some successful, critical points in the polemic. But a sharp, final, and fatal rejoinder here: first, given the lower castes' competition for reservation and other affirmative action orientation and expectation from the governmental state, it is well within the welfare rationale of other (backward, oppressed, weak, and minority) orientation and its invited "vigil" on them and compensation

---

[69] Rajeev Bhargava, "The Ethical Insufficiency of Egoism and Altruism: India in Transition," in *Indian Democracy: Meanings and Practices,* eds. Rajinder Vora and Suhas Palshkar (New Delhi: SAGE Publications, 2004), 224–25.

for endangered interests; second, caste hierarchies have not become equal or obsolete by any means, a different ranking is taking place where a particular caste consolidation tends to exploit inequality in its favour. This is not egalitarianism; rather, through an understandable electoral arithmetic, their strength of bargaining, and winning at least some relief, is visible. This becomes understandable—not from the above exegesis, rather from Professor Bhargava's comments elsewhere in the essay, which are more promising. When self-interest transcends a particular boundary, it becomes in extension "communitarian egois[m]: or what is called communalism in India. Such communitarian egoism may be focused on the family, the caste, the religious community or the nation. For communitarian egoism, only particular communitarian selves and individuals who partake in it have value."[70] What is being spoken here, if we are to ascribe it the right taxonomy, would be the group personality of the caste or Ambedkar's caste as corporation. Egoism cannot ply unless it is embodied, therefore, caste personality, and it is from it that the members might draw resources, attributes, and characteriological qualities, and where the caste or religious groups' personality might specify, reveal, or project a different conception or will than the aggregate of its members or individual member might want to qualify. Often, the conflict between a member and the group itself, or those who clamor for the right to exit, is understandable from this vantage point. It is also evident from this that the attribution of ego by Professor Bhargava is again a misnomer. How can a member depart from a group ego that is a whole; rather, it is "personality" where ego is simply an element in the structure, and might not be able to account for all the processes and functions.

Now, if we have been able to explore the etymological and essential traits of some of the pre-social work helping structures, let us get down to their genealogy and see how that works.

# III

## Genealogy

We've had Hegel answering this question at length in Chapter 5, and subsequently Brajendranath Seal, Hiralal Haldar, and Benoy Sarkar—all

---

[70] Ibid., 220–21.

speaking in Hegelian resonance, but rising to the occasion only with miscellaneous results. Here, we go on to answer what are the important historical issues involved in the evolutionary act of locating rights that have erstwhile been called nonrights. Historicality apart, there are deep philosophical problems in this where it is argued that a duty to one's own self overrides one's duty to enable the good of others or beneficence, and that it is voluntary (the old paradigm put in a new way). The penultimate stage of our present genealogy is when we see the fruition of such a problematic, with all of us being suddenly exposed to a risk society where there is no social insurance, pension, gratuity, or unemployment grants and where voluntary associations in the form of NGOs run riot with their evident links with global capital! It could be inferred that the well-endowed part of the population is willing to scrap the assistance that was extended to the less "fortunate" or dependent part of the population in the wake of the now defunct welfare state. With this being the case, the results for social work is devastating: if it is helping (equally significant) others to help themselves, then the moment one can help one's own self, the axiological or value-based status that one ascribes to this predicament overrides his/her (i.e., the empowered one's) concern for others; then, is helping of one's own self antagonistic to helping others? Hardly so, and it could be sustained by a specific form of genealogical analysis.

## Pastoral Care: From "Outward Form" to "Inward Help"

Paul Halmos charts our journey from pastoralist to personal-professional forms of social care. But the pastoral tradition has a specific bearing in the European tradition on which he does not elaborate. One, in the form of political rationality; another, in the form of—we can say—cultural rationality. But in both of them, curiously, the personal core thrives. For the first form, it was Foucault who has dwelt at length and has shown how "the idea of the deity, or the king, or the leader, as a shepherd followed by the flock of sheep"[71] who "gathers together, guides, and leads his

---

[71] Michel Foucault, "Politics and Reason," in *Politics, Philosophy, Culture: Interviews and Other Writings 1977–84*, ed. Lawrence D. Kritzman (New York, NY: Routledge, 1990), 57–85.

flock ... in person."[72] is transformed in the political leader is the "shepherd of man."[73] Foucault's insistence on this problem is to reinforce "the power we can call 'pastoral', whose role is to constantly ensure, sustain, and improve the lives of each and every one" reappears in the "welfare state problem" that "has to strike a balance between political power wielded over legal subjects and pastoral power wielded over live individuals."[74] The evolution of pastorship for Foucalut is the evolution of the techno-logy of power. "In Christianity, the tie with the shepherd ... is personal submission to him ... principally, because it is his will ... the sheep must permanently submit to their pastors."[75] For this, personal knowledge of each sheep is required: "the material needs of each member of the flock and provide for them when necessary."[76] Therefore, the knowledge leading to the welfare of the population meshed in the new technology of political rationality embodied in the welfare state. Now, how to link it with what we are calling "cultural rationality"? This rationality led to what Engels called "a settled sentimental Socialism."[77] This entailed a retreat from "trade's unfeeling train," which usurps not only the land but also the values of the people in it;[78] this also impinges upon a difference in as much as the Greek shepherd governs not the land but the flock. In the cultural form of the Arcadian retreat, the land forms an inseparable element alienated by commercial exploitation. "Pastoral is essentially a discourse of retreat which may, as we have seen, either simply escape from the complexities of the city, the court, the present, 'our manners', or explore them."[79] Wordsworth for instance, states here: "Delightful val-ley, habitation fair!/ And to whatever else of outward form/ Can give us inward help, can purify/ And elevate, and harmonize, and soothe. ..."[80] Habitation is of course place, and the town and the city are of course spatial signifiers, and here, as pointed out before, it is a departure from the political rationality of the governmental state; instead, the outward form of natural icons are called to become, transformingly, pieces of "inward

---

[72] Ibid., 60–61.
[73] Ibid., 65.
[74] Ibid., 67.
[75] Ibid., 69.
[76] Ibid.
[77] Terry Gifford, *Pastoral* (London: Routledge, 1999), 39.
[78] Ibid., 46.
[79] Ibid.
[80] Ibid., cited on page 150.

help:" harmonizing the disintegration and soothing in "full complacency," "pleasing rest." The form of the cultural rationality then completes the welfare logic in the inward, self-determining help of social work. This brief trajectory waits an elaboration.

## From Nonrights to Rights in Governmental, Social State

Let us for once retract back to the lesson in the case study of Hegel, where Hegel's proposal was that through state-related, public forms of intelligent helping, singular, isolated, and illusory modes of personal and private modes of helping may become redundant or play a supplementary role—at the most. But it can play a supplementary role only when it has a minimum of positivity granted to it, that is, if it is not an entity (or in Aristotelian terms—a substance) at all, or if it does not, therefore, have a bare existence, how can it play even a supplementary role? This suspicion emerges strongly where Hegel is disputing the status of personal and private modes of helping as a work at all because of its illusory nature and the possibility of perversion—in short—of deception. With this, we have returned to the point with which we had begun. Deception and the perverted will of the giver—which is the personal.

No doubt the theoretical mapping in the hands of Hegel was picked up by social theorists after him (Jeremy Bentham's distinction between "agenda" as the "tasks of government" and sponte acta as the "unplanned decisions of individuals"[81] is a ready instance) who laid the foundation of the welfare state by which we tend to mean today a state-organized endeavor to ensure the well-being of the population against contingencies of life. Foucault called this governmentality and gave a significant turn. He showed that this welfarist turn was not a departure in terms of statist conscience; rather, it was a new way of governing people in which people having become population gaze at power with hope: power becomes positive and the positivity in terms of normativity as well as substantiality because is shared by all, it is, first of all productive, but also deep seated to the extent that it appears as being rootless with sovereignty being

---

[81] Quoted in Asa Briggs, "The Welfare State in Historical Perspective," in *The Welfare State: A Reader*, eds. Christopher Pierson and Francis G. Castles (Cambridge: Polity Press & Blackwell Publishers, 2000), 18–31.

distributed everywhere instead of having a stable center in a single monarch or class. The self-orientation and self-comportment of the people takes the place of an alien power paternalizing from outside. We shall come to Foucault again, but, before Foucault, let us note in passing that his insight was nearly lifted out of the welfare sociology of T. H. Marshall, who in turn shared the vision (with clear originality but little acknowledgment) of the discourse of social work and social workers. In fact, in Marshall we have the first major development of the Hegelian argument wherein the issue of rights as a component of modern citizenship distinctively featured in relation to welfare. We shall see here how the problem of nonrights as rights was presented here and with what consequences for the future. Marshall[82] begins to address this issue by picking up the Speenhaml and the system of poor relief whereby Poor Laws attempted to "inject an element of social security into the very structure of the wage system," and by this maneuver it had become "the aggressive champions of the social rights of citizenship." But—and we need a long quote here:

> By the Act of 1834 the Poor Law renounced all claim to trespass on the territory of the wages system, or to interfere with the forces of the free market. It offered relief only to those who, through age or sickness, were incapable of continuing the battle, and to those other weaklings who gave up the struggle, admitted defeat, and cried for mercy. The tentative move towards the concept of social security was reversed. But more than that, the minimal social rights that remained were detached from the status of citizenship. The poor Law treated the claims of the Poor, not as an integral part of the rights of the citizen, but as an alternative to them—as claims which could be met only if the claimants ceased to be citizens in any true sense of the word. For paupers forfeited in practice the civil right of personal liberty, by internment in the workhouse, and they forfeited by law any political rights they might possess. This disability of defranchisement [disfranchisement?] "remained in being until 1918."[83]

Having thus said, Marshall is perhaps right in commenting: "The Poor Law is not an isolated example of this divorce of social rights from the status of citizenship. The Early Factory Acts show the same tendency."[84]

---

[82] T. H. Marshall, "Citizenship and Social Class," in *The Foundations of the Welfare State*, eds. Robert E. Goodin and Deborah Mitchell (UK: Edward Elgar Publishing Ltd, 2000), 1.
[83] Ibid., 18.
[84] Ibid., 19.

Now, let us evidentially examine for precisions' sake the claims made by Marshall. The exclusion of the pauper is true, but the reason behind the exclusion of the pauper (and not the poor because they could be shown to have evolved as a separate category) Marshall explicates elsewhere. First, being a pauper was a matter of status and not that of contract; this status bore with it a considerable stigma, bringing into its domain of shame the pauper's whole family for the whole of life. Marshall quotes here the principal officer of the Poor Law Division of the local government board, giving evidence before the Royal Commission of 1905–09 who said that the "status of pauper implied 'firstly, the loss of personal reputation (which is understood as the stigma of pauperism); secondly, the loss of personal freedom, which is secured by detention in a workhouse; and thirdly the loss of political freedom by suffering disfranchisement'."[85] Here let us briefly rehearse the paradigms of documentary evidence that could illustrate the force of these terms—"personal reputation," "personal freedom," and "disfranchisement." Numerous examples of loss of voting rights, disreputation, and freedomlessness could be used to augment this observation. In fact, out of "paupers" as an umbrella term, the few "categories of persons who were being gradually extracted … were the children, the old, the sick, and the unemployed."[86] In other words, they emerged from the contagious realm of personal disreputation and personal freedomlessness, and the qualifiers used by Marshall are to a large extent true. But the lack of citizenship was not only personal but in a sense interpersonal as well. Having been invested under the supervision of the Poor Law guardians:

> [T]he guarantee that their needs would be met rested, not on their right to insist, but on the guardians obligation to provide. The only difference between this and charity was that the obligations of the Guardians were legal and those of the purveyors of charity, moral and religious.[87]

Now, this being the state of things, one wonders how the transition to rights from that of loose duties took place? What were the arguments that marked this site?

---

[85] Ibid., 16.

[86] Marshall, *Social Policy*, 35. Prior to this, Marshall notes, how in "the western world there had at one time been a tendency to lump rogues, vagabonds, and paupers together in a single category, and to treat them all in semi-penal institutions," See Marshall, *Social Policy*, 34.

[87] Ibid., 43.

Earlier, we talked about the principal officer of the Poor Law Division of the local government board, who while giving evidence before the Royal Commission of 1905–09 described the pauper in touching terms. But another part of his submission may be invoked here. Here he argues, subsequent to portraying paupers as nonpersons with nonrights, why they are the fittest candidates for rights,

> The pauper, he added, has in practice a right of relief, but his right is not a complete right for the necessary sanctions are lacking ... he cannot sue for his relief, and that is precisely why it was the duty of the State to see that he gets his rights.[88]

So here we have one of the primary enunciations in favor of welfare-right, or as Marshall called them, "social" rights. But still there exist various tracts where the duty, even that of a "public duty" to relieve the poor or take care of those who are unable to take care of themselves', was "admitted, but its source did not lie in any rights possessed by the person relieved", thus, he was still—for instance in England an object of duty and not a subject of rights. But Marshall expressing his surprise at the fact that how can there be remedies without rights[89] quotes from a controversy in which a participant, the Supplementary Benefits Commission wrote in its handbook, "The distinctive feature of the Supplementary benefits Scheme is its discretionary element. ... By definition no one can claim as of 'right' that a particular discretionary power should be exercised in his favour."[90] But Marshall, whose explanation here could be invoked to explain as a kind of justification (he does not maintain such a self-distance) for the emergence of welfare/social rights, states: "If there were no right there could be no grounds for appeal, even if the appeal is only to the discretion of another body. The right to appeal implies that the claimant is the subject of welfare, not merely the object of it."[91] This introduced the welfare state in its theoretical form where the erstwhile nonrights exhibited in supererogatory forms of helping, assumed, amidst suspicion and protest, the body of rights that could be claimed and defended. In other words, from the age of paupers and vagrancy at the break of feudalism, we therefore arrive at the age of insurance, assistance, and

---

[88] Ibid., 16.
[89] Ibid., 89.
[90] Ibid., 95.
[91] Ibid., 96.

social security (in other words, the welfare state about which we've been talking in theoretical terms) about which both the government and the nongovernmental initiatives agreed. Social work in the UK, therefore, is historical for many reasons: articulating the primary methods (case work, group work, and community organization) may be just one of them. But is/was the welfare state able to sustain the spirit conferred upon it? A brief rejoinder will suffice.

## Welfare State Personality: The Luhmannian Critique

It is long since the beginnings of the welfare state—which is now in many countries visibly in a shamble. While the welfare or the social part dries up, the surveillance part extends its sway. This comes in the face of an impossible welfare project and its internalist critique. For Luhmann and his theory of self-referential system reproducing itself autonomously, welfare state or the social state (for Foucault it was the government of the social) poses peculiar problems in the face of, as we shall see, the mechanisms of social work that intend to grant self-enabling powers to the people who are helped. He argues that

> [T]he motivation of those disadvantaged … plays a role [in articulating] the effectiveness of help [and] "This problem is identified but not solved by using slogans like 'helping others to help themselves' [Hilfe Zur Selbsthilfe]. Help, then, has to include a change in the cognitive and motivational structure of personalities, their perception and their intentions. … And this takes the social state to the limits of its capabilities and, morally, to the problem of the justification of its intervention."[92]

This is a vicious circle for the "interventionist state," and it is produced circuitously. I hazard that this problem immanent in helping was first noticed by Hegel in *Natural Law*. Luhmann notes this by confessing that this justification is used to judge claims to being helped. When the entire population—which means all of their interests too—without division as in the olden days, it leads to "the discovery of ever new problems (for the political system)"[93] and ever-growing kinds of thematizations.

---

[92] Niklas Luhmann, *Political Theory in the Welfare State,* transl. John Bednarz Jr. (New York, NY: Walter De Gruyter Berlin, 1990), 22.
[93] Ibid., 5.

But through "law and money," means left to the welfare state, it cannot solve them. Second, while it encompasses all, it cannot secure the support of all. "This contradictory, paradoxical situation—that is, a system whose own operations obstruct their own continuation"[94] relives the spirit of self or auto-referentiality.

But what does this end up in? Luhmann answers this succinctly:

> The idea of welfare as a political goal ... is the exact semantic correlate of political self reference. Self-reference is primarily tautological, Welfare a correspondingly indeterminate principle. Therefore the advancement of welfare can always be a goal of welfare and constitute welfare at the same time ... It has no end.[95] It presupposes itself for the production of its possibilities and problems ... The unity of self-reference and the idea of welfare signify the unity of the recursive closure and thematic openness of politics. Its semantic trappings correspond to the structure that already comes into play with the functional differentiation of the political system.[96]

Welfare being auto-referential and indeterminate, let us see how social work as the precise process of helping people to help themselves tries to temper it in interaction.

---

[94] Ibid., 60.

[95] Two reminders, frankly revisionist, come from Habermas in this regard and we ought to reckon with them: While the welfare state apparatus, through law and administration, or professionalization and scientization of social services tends to implement its programs, it is not a

> passive medium with no properties of its own. On the contrary, they are linked with a practice that isolates individual facts, a practice of normalization and surveillance. ... [While] "its goal is the establishment of forms of life that are structured in an egalitarian way and that at the same time open up arenas for individual self-realization and spontaneity. But evidently this goal cannot be reached via the direct route of putting political programs into legal and administrative form. Generating forms of life exceeds the capacities of the medium of power."

This leads Habermas to a conclusion which is not against Luhmann, "[a] contradiction between it goal and its method is inherent in the welfare project as such." See Jurgen Habermas, "The New Obscurity: The Crisis of the Welfare State and the Exhaustion of Utopian Energies," in *The New Conservatism: Cultural Criticism and the Historians' Debate*, transl. S. W. Nicholsen (Cambridge: Polity Press, 1989), 48–70.

[96] Ibid., 42.

## Consolidation of the Modernist Turn or the Failed Imagination of an (Im)Personalist Social Work

But before arriving at its own phase of civil-social welfarism, social work in India as the most developed, scientific form of helping claims the same 19th century rational, reformist rubric for an impersonal, institutional self. It is necessary to rehearse this tormented trajectory before we embark upon the task of excavating the elemental personal in social work as a structure of helping. That what we had shown as having failed previously emerges with an emblem of success on its forehead in social work, tragically.

So, to begin with and to establish a linkage with the previous chapter for a helping structure such as social work, it would be instructive to remember that canonical histories and historical analyses of social work seem to have been pegging, unanimously, the invention of the social work subject and object to the modernist rational-reformist, liberal, secular humanistic, and welfaristic inheritance. In colonial forms of helping modalities, the same contamination has been emphatically reiterated.

In support of such a sweeping observation, I shall present below a series of such instances where at first I take hold of Murli Desai's heavily used textbook in social work courses[97] and request the reader to notice its structural motors:

> Values such as rationalism, individualism, humanism embedded in European society during the renaissance period, began to take roots in India as well. Besides these values, the reformers were led by the liberal ideals of democracy and democratic procedures in political and social organization, equality, value of education, science and knowledge and the need for rationality in public life.[98]

Plotting this as the "Approach to Social Change," Desai begins, predictably, with Raja Rammohun Roy. The hunch of these histories is clear: To preface the appearance of social work by negotiating modernist reformist movements of the 19th century and harp it as a prelude. To continue this appraisal, Desai apart, here is Sugata Dasgupta—a social work stalwart appropriating and installing this heritage in an exemplary manner:

> The history of social reform movement which began with Raja Rammohan Roy, Swami Vivekananda, Gokhale and others, and the emergence of the

---

[97] Murli Desai, *Ideologies and Social Work: Historical and Contemporary Analyses* (Jaipur: Rawat Publications, 2002).

[98] Ibid., 118–19.

Brahmo Samaj, Arya Samaj, Ramakrishna Mission, Prarthana Samaj, as well as socialist and Gandhian struggles for political freedom, however be logically described as the antecedents of the new concept of social work.[99]

This description, Dasgupta hazards, is apt because they invoked "rights of the individuals," "rational standard of living," "'and pinpointed the obligations of society, including those of scientific services;'[100] these are paradigmatic lessons according to Dasgupta, learnt slowly and procedurally by social work: 'duty' and 'professional responsibility' ... scientific objectivity which is most desired."[101] Now, this is one specific moment we ought not to lose sight of M.C. Nanavaity in a famous essay endorses this claim in these words: "Various religious reform movements that were started as a reaction to the growing influence of Christian missionaries in the country, resulted in the increase in the organized services for the needy."[102] Anticipating Desai's description at least two decades ago, the author delimits the second influence of the reform movements, "[t]he second influence related to the contact with the Western ideas of liberalism, rationalism and democracy."[103]

Consider, for the third canonical instance, a former classic, A. R. Wadia's *History and Philosophy of Social Work in India*.[104] In a chapter titled "Social Work during the British Period"[105] Clifford Manshardt alleges that while

"[t]he early part of the nineteenth century, social reform was linked firmly with religious change. ... [later] men and organizations arose looking at social reforms from a liberal, intellectual and humanitarian point of view ... [leading to] late nineteenth and early twentieth century social work" [which as though being in the shadows of the reform movements] "was largely ameliorative ... relief of the poor, institutions for widows and orphans,

---

[99] Sugata Dasgupta, ed., *Towards a Philosophy of Social Work in India* (New Delhi: Popular Book Services 1967), 12.

[100] Ibid., 12–13.

[101] Ibid., 13.

[102] M. C. Nanavaity, "Origin and Growth of Professional Social Work-Historical Aspects." in *Towards a Philosophy of Social Work in India*, ed. S. Dasgupta (New Delhi: Popular Book Services, n.d.) 20–26 (italics mine).

[103] Ibid., 21.

[104] A. R. Wadia, *History and Philosophy of Social Work in India* (Bombay: Allied Publishers Private Limited, 1968).

[105] Wadia, *History and Philosophy of Social Work in India,* 25–35.

care of the blind, the deaf and the dumb, the establishment of charitable dispensaries and hospitals."[106]

The social work–social reform alliance—genealogically linked—is, perhaps, increasingly clear by now. But while there might be a caveat that Dasgupta and Wadia are a bit dated, it would then be instructive to end this section with a recent author in consonance with the beginning where we had another contemporary author (Murli Desai) vouching for reformist premises contributing to social work. The 19th century, according to Hajira Kumar, brought in "a new generation of social reformer" and a new era marked its beginning with the social legislation of "Regulation XVII of 1829 ... for prohibiting Sati."[107] What was typically wrong with this pre-modernist era? Kumar elaborates:

> Social work profession is not Indian by birth; it should, however, not be considered completely without a past in India. We did have a tradition of philanthropy and intellectual ferment ... but the tradition was basically nonsecular, whimsical, sporadic and according to the choice of the provider.[108]

The reform movements then were symptomatically modernist moments, carving, as if, a reversal and implanting a secular, rational, systematic, and impersonal institutionalization of services and knowledge generating social work in the end. The circle seems to close with this.

Taking cue from the previous chapter, it is clear that I've intended to read and refashion this history altogether. I showed that this claim to systematic, rational and impersonal parameters have had been a complete hoax leading to a failed modernity: the transition was, in actuality, from one kind of personality (organic, individual) to another (artificial, institutional). That being the case, the exemplarity of 19th century reform movements in social work histories assumes a dubious, albeit a mistaken role.

This reading then provocatively goes against a range of social work historians and their conclusions charted before: from A. R. Wadia to Murli Desai; from Sugata Dasgupta to Hajira Kumar and a number of others.

---

[106] Clifford Manshardt, "Social Work During the British Period," in *History and Philosophy of Social Work in India*, ed. A. R. Wadia (Bombay: Allied Publishers Private Limited, 1968), 25–35.
[107] Hajira Kumar, *Social Work: An Experience and Experiment in India* (New Delhi: Gitanjali Publishing House, New Delhi, 1994), 3.
[108] Ibid., 3.

In a mood of affirmative deconstruction again, it becomes evident, cursorily though, how a personalytical approach, thus, is better suited to interpret social work, helping histories including not only bygone ones but also social work to come.

To start again, in our context, would entail revisiting and rethinking social work helping histories through the personalytic sieve: for the moment, I would hazard the following interrogative propositions:

1. How did a failed modernity engender the (modern) structure of helping evinced in social work?
2. How did the hidden, immanent, and personalytical element in such objective, universalist reformist projects (that contributed to the latter's failure) contribute again to the impersonal, scientific professional foundations of social work? (Unless we are ready to argue, social work is also, albeit, manifestly impersonal, scientific, and objective but immanently and self-defeatingly personalist!)
3. The trajectory I've traced is from the individual principle of personality to that of juridical, fictional, or institutional personality; therefore—from personality to personality (this is what I have articulated as the personalytical historiography of early social work). The futuristic history of social work helping histories, in future itself, would, therefore, chart how social work imbibes and projects institutional personality while claiming all the while a rigorous, scientific "pathos"—which might be regarded following Marx (on Bonaparte)—first as tragedy, then as farce.

Now, while these are difficult questions to answer, they might not be difficult ones to ask; the lessons to be learnt are not harder still! They might invade or go into revising and reinterpreting social work histories—while this seems obvious and forthcoming, what might still be pending is how such a proposal would be intertwined with social work practice—understood in a practically mundane but still rigorous sense. I'll squarely close off after hinting at such a possibility.

If any two genealogies might be discerned in the development of professional social work in India, then they might be admitted, only as two insurmountable forms of oppositions; based on the interpretation of Indian social work pre-histories, they are accountable to future social work histories benignly grafted onto social work action—its typologies. Recall the (in)famous conference held in 1964 (in which Jayaprakash Narayan was one of the attending delegates) and the result of which was condensed in the volume edited by Sugata Dasgupta.[109] Inspired by the instance of social reform and the methodology of Gandhian reconstruction, the conference advised social work to abandon social-political indifference and direct social action toward social change. Dasgupta, describing the days of 19th century reform movements as a "resplendent past" and urging social work to "relate itself" to it, declared:

> The professional social worker in India has, however, yet to become a social reformer or leader. … In bringing in the desired changes in socio economic structures and the processes for prevention of some of the problems with which the worker is concerned, the new role would be exigent.[110]

In response, the 1965 UGC report on social work education in Indian universities clearly rejected the advice, arguing that the present day social worker "has ceased to be the social reformer in the old sense."[111] The latter attempt at a synthesis made "social action" into a theoretical-methodological tool to be taught but never practiced.

I think we've come full circle, and the practical relevance of this chapter and its propositions should have become all the more clear: the theme burnt with cold fire and divided social work policy makers and practitioners in the 1960s and the 1970s; the next decades deploy "social action" as a riskless and harmless entry in social work academic textbooks; rarely it pronounces the backdrop of social reform against which it was formulated. While gazing neutrally at this evolution, I'm willing to take no sides for the moment (the politics of social work is a different debate altogether). But while this chapter narrates a caution against Dasgupta's valorization of the essence of 19th century reform movements (where the essence seems to have succeeded); it is too unwilling to concur with the UGC report's dictum that the professional social worker is no more the social reformer in the old Indian sense (which is based on forgetting that civil-social modernity [even the 19th century one] succeeds in and by its failure [see the second part of the conclusion of this chapter]). Their genuine rejection could be that Dasgupta's claims for the reform movements (impersonal, rational, scientific, professional, etc.) were mistaken. But Dasgupta is not alone in this error, as I have pointed out: from A. R. Wadia to Murli Desai; from Clifford Manshardt to Hajira Kumar—the mistake is mirrored, again and again, without respite.

---

[109] Dasgupta, *Towards a Philosophy of Social Work in India*.
[110] Ibid., 12–13.
[111] Desai, *Ideologies and Social Work*, 139.

However, what informs this position again is the (proposed) personalytical critique of the existing historical approaches in social work and their corresponding failure to steer away from committing the double errors. This critique will be taken to its furthest extent in examining social work and other structures of helping specifically with which we've begun in this chapter and reached the limit of welfare. To say the least, we've entered personalist social work, historically.

## Other Structures to Social Work: Does the Personal Reside in Natural Helping?

However, these are some of the elementary, derivative observations based on our previous discussion and the state of social work as of today. But the present challenge is to discover and reinstate the personal in social work despite these declarative, denying, and negative overtures. And here, we could start with a simple and a single question: Does the personal reside in "natural" helping—a rubric still retained by contemporary social work? In social work discourse, a distinction is made between natural and professional helping.

> Natural helping is based on a mutual relationship among equals, and the helper draws heavily on intuition and life experience to guide the helping process. … Professional helping is different from natural helping in that it is a disciplined approach focused on the needs of the client and it requires specific knowledge, values, and skills to guide the helping activity. … In fact, many helping professionals first became interested in these careers because they were successful natural helpers[112] and the found the experience rewarding. Social workers often work closely with natural helping networks both during the change process and as a source of support after professional service is terminated.[113]

---

[112] "'Natural helpers' exist for most families. They are usually friends, neighbours, or relatives that have a relationship with the family not based on the specific needs or problems of the family." See Armado T. Morales and Bradford W. Sheafor, *Social Work: A Profession of Many Faces* (Boston, MA: Allyn and Bacon, 1998 [1977]), 216.

[113] Ibid., 28. So far as the disciplinary viewpoint is concerned, here goes the rejoinder, "However, natural helpers are not a substitute for competent professional help in addressing serious problems or gaining access to needed services." (p. 28).

It is necessary, however, to push the category of natural helping further. Is the phrase so commonsensically grounded? In Freud, one confronts helping only after one has encountered helplessness. Helplessness of man: first, before nature, second, before father, "between the father-complex and man's helplessness and need for protection."[114] Man is first terrorized by nature and then responds by personifying the forces of nature or "personify everything that he wants to understand in order later to control it."[115] Or in other words, the humanization of nature is derived from the need to put an end to man's perplexity and helplessness in the face of its dreaded forces, to get into a relation with them, and finally to influence them.[116] Freud's imaginary antagonist puts in a queer objection (it is Freud thinking otherwise) from which we can debate the natural foundations of helping as whether reflecting primordial conditions of the self or constructed in the background with motives of action. Personifying nature, getting into a relationship with its forces only in order to influence them seems superfluous to the antagonist Freud who argues with the other half. He says,

> [A] motive of this kind seems superfluous. Primitive man has no choice, he has no other way of thinking. It is natural to him, something innate as it were, to project his existence outward into the world and to regard every event which he observes as the manifestation of beings who at bottom are like himself. It is his only method of comprehension. And it is by no means self evident, on the contrary it is a remarkable coincidence, if by thus indulging his natural disposition he succeeds in satisfying one of his greatest needs.[117]

The protagonist Freud gives a fitting answer, but before quoting him let us ask ourselves without letting be examined whether by "natural" we also

---

[114] Sigmund Freud, "Group Psychology and the Analysis of the Ego" in *Civilization, Society and Religion,* trans. James Stratchey (New Delhi: Shrijee's Book International, 2003), 12: 699.

[115] Ibid., 698.

[116] Ibid., 697. Contrast this with the classical philosophical discussion of nature: "What ever forces Nature develops and lets loose against men—cold, wild beasts, water fire—he knows means to counter them; indeed, he takes these means from Nature and uses them against herself. The cunning of his reason enables him to preserve and maintain himself in face of the forces of nature, by sheltering behind other products of nature, and letting these suffer her destructive attacks. G. W. F. Hegel. *Hegel's Philosophy of Nature.* trans. A. V. Miller (Clarendon Press, Oxford, 1970), 5 (italics mine).

[117] Ibid., 697–98.

mean the personification of nature,[118] a relationship with nature, etc. As if natural forms of helping laid bare through certain modes of personification are a response to or a re-living of primordial helplessness in the face of nature; we noted how social work conceives natural helping as residing primarily in the domains of domestic management of sickness and death among others. The point is: is that because it is still the only method of comprehension? Or what is then this mode of comprehension? What mode of comprehension does professional helping entail? However, we return now to Freud's answer: Freud says,

> I do not find that so striking. Do you suppose that human thought has no practical motives, that it is simply the expression of a disinterested curiosity? That is surely very improbable. I believe rather than when man personifies nature he is again following an infantile model. He has learnt from his environment that the way to influence them is to establish a relation with them; and so, later on, with the same end in view, he treats everything else that he comes across in the same way as he treated those other persons.[119]

The first paradox that haunts a practitioner of genealogical criticism while trying to address helping—charting the way professional helping emerged out of its intuitionist modes still interrupting the formers' formations—is the undertaking to clarify helping more than its genealogy, helping rather than genealogy. What is more intriguing is the contemporary co-existence of natural helpers in the days and domains of professional helping, which as a fact has been acknowledged in social work treatises: Helping obviously presupposes the presence of two or more than one: A helps B or A helps B, C, D, and so on. There is also an assumption here that helping perhaps could not turn inward; it is without an active interiority so much so that it will stop functioning the moment the other—the one who receives help is expelled or erased. But social work as the modern instance of helping, albeit which claims to be the disciplinary science of helping, curiously, defines itself as the art of helping others to help themselves. A second order helping? Now, what it is to help one's own

---

[118] Let us not mistake the fact that this notion of personification here is more philosophical than psychoanalytical. Consider this Hegelian excerpt: "But instead of leaving nature as she is … we make her into something quite different. … We give them the form of something subjective, of something produced by us and belonging to us, and belonging to us in our specifically human character." See G. W. F. Hegel. *Philosophy of Nature.* transl. A. V. Miller (Oxford: Clarendon Press, 1970), 7.

[119] Freud, "Group Psychology and the Analysis of the Ego," 12: 698.

self? Better—if asked—is it possible to help one's own self? To ask this question is to engage in a historico-genealogical project where an answer will emerge in terms of possibilities rather than positive certainties. Help is given, offered, and sought; someone helps while somebody receives.

## Personalist vis-à-vis Professional Social Work

Our pursuit of a personalytical history in the preceding chapter made no qualms about having to refute the (proposed) impersonal transition to social work. Here let us, after having made an appraisal of the transition to this stage, attempt to grasp it a bit more theoretically.

The traditional understanding of the person is quite a failure with social work, in as much as, social work—deals with distorted identities and damaged lives: if persons are determined as rational, moral agents with a sense of responsibility, self-conscious, fully formed beings with a scheme of life, then social work has to deal, often, with just the reverse, those who have undergone (a la Nietzsche) "life diminishing" effects, or those who are not even fully formed, or deformed beyond the active "structures of recognition" that is crucial to their identities: the children, the handicapped, the old, the sick and the terminally ill, the prisoner and the pervert (before the social work counselor), the maladjusted, the rapist, the animal, and so on. For social work, "[r]ather, it has to be seen that personhood is socially defined ... through identification and ascription."[120]... "This means that those entities who are accorded the standing of personhood are seen to be entitled to certain kinds of treatment, even if their claim to personhood may be dubious."[121] It might, of course, be acknowledged, still, and lately, that this entitlement is a kind of right, and thereby the Kantian conception of persons as beings with rights is able to stand scrutiny. But the right, as we've allowed to contest with nonrights previously, is here apparently a matter of nonright—the nonjuridico political and the personal (like friends and lovers). The person here is an outcome of the interstitial investment of relations, the in-betweenness of things, a result of narratives. Social work here emerges, as it is evident, as a narrative science of new relations with the stranger at times, and with the unknown most of the time.

[120] C. L. Clark and S. Asquith, "The Person and Moral Agency," in *Social Philosophy and Social Work* (Boston, MA: Routledge and Kegan Paul, 1985, 6–22.
[121] Ibid, 19.

(Who is the anonymous? Like "who is my stranger?") "Modern social welfare has really to be thought of as help given to the stranger[122] [and] not to the person who by reason of personal bond commands it without asking. It assumes a degree of social distance between helped and helper."[123]

Helping people to help themselves or inducing self-help: let us, albeit briefly, inquire into its genealogy.

> Self-help was the Victorian ideal ... fostering a spirit of thrift, independence and self-reliance perfectly in tune with the competitive ethic of the age. ... There were many avenues for self help, most of them approved by government. There were burial and collecting societies, building societies, saving banks and a flourishing co-operative movement. The best known were friendly societies [who had] five times as many members as did trade unions at the same time.[124]

The word "friendly," keeping in view our previous discussion of friendship in the main text, is curious, yet explanative, to say the least. While elaborating on the singular isolation of an individual person, the writer in 1855 elaborates on the kind of circumstance of warm assistance—where he/she is placed—when he/she is a "member" of a friendly society.

---

[122] For the double bind of love as merely erotic one and love as agape or Christian charity, the division that becomes apparent is that the personal, familial bond becomes thinner and thinner, and is extreme when it meets the stranger, provoking us to ask the question, as to how to relate to strangers then—methodologically—vis-à-vis social work, for instance? The assumption that is imminent with Eagleton is the nearest and dearest take on the mantle of assumable priority. But this knowability is murderous, even self contradictory, we fall in love with unknown people (or where knowledge at least is distinctly limited). This unfamiliarity is then translated, and might even breed contempt—in the most proverbial sense–so the knowable threshold of the family is not necessarily the trajectory of the personal. A more promising interpretation in Eagleton is,

> Its not simply a matter of treating strangers as neighbours but of treating oneself as strange—of recognizing at the core of one's being an implacable demand which is ultimately inscrutable, and which is the true ground, beyond the mirror, on which human subjects can effect an encounter.

See Terry Eagleton, *The Trouble with Strangers: A Study of Ethics* (Sussex, UK: Wiley Blackwell, 2008), 60.

[123] R. M. Titmuss, 'Who Is My Stranger'? in *Talking About Welfare: Readings in Philosophy and Social Policy*, eds. Noel Timms and David Watson (London: Routledge and Kegan Paul, 1976), 207–36.

[124] Eric J. Evans, ed, "Aspects of Self-help," in *Social Policy, 1830–1914: Individualism, Collectivism and the Origins of the Welfare State* (London: Routledge & Kegan Paul, 1978), 102–03.

In case of accidents, or unanticipated unemployment, even an industrious individual might go astray, but "[w]henever a liability to any unfavourable contingency exists, the best and cheaper way of obviating its effects is by uniting with others."[125] Similar was the causal case made for cooperatives where—as far back as 1861—the principle amount and the interest on deposits by members and the capital thus raised not only helped provide each member with the bare necessities of life, or at least aimed to, but also shaped a library. The cumulative, programmatic effect of this was put in a picturesque way:

> [I]t may, perhaps, provoke a smile to find ... "social and intellectual advancement" placed[126] in such a close juxtaposition with "groceries, ... drapery goods, clothing, shoes and clogs." But there is a real and very close connexion between these two classes of things.[127]

The role of the friendly societies "formed on the principle of mutual insurance,"[128] other than organizing the usual fraternal recreation and generating creative pastime, was "aimed at protecting members' funds against incompetent actuarial calculations, fraud or other loss."[129] The habit of saving money coupled with a preliminary theory of the provident fund, and "[t]he pursuit of economy and thrift will beget, as a matter of course, self-dependence; and as soon as men became socially independent they also become self-relying and self-supplying."[130] This notion of self-help then, based on a solid calculus of cost and expenditure, emerged to lessen the harsh indeterminacies of fate and uncertainty, contingency, and loss. But the question is: With whom this philosophy of self-help clicked? "[I]t is not surprising that self-help philosophy was more readily accepted among skilled workers and regular earners than among the casual and poorly paid members of the working class."[131] Even a close reading of the self-help classic [*Self Help*] of Samuel Smiles (written sometime after

---

[125] J. Tidd Pratt, "The Principles of Friendly Societies (1855)," in *Social Policy, 1830–1914: Individualism, Collectivism and the Origins of the Welfare State*, ed. Eric J. Evans (London: Routledge & Kegan Paul, 1978), 104.

[126] The author did stitch them together while enumerating the aims of a cooperative society. W. N. Molesworth, 'Co-operation' (1861) excerpted in Ibid., 107.

[127] Ibid., 107.

[128] Ibid., 104.

[129] 'Aspects of self-help', Ibid., 102.

[130] William Lewis, 'Savings Banks' in Evans ed. *Social Policy, 1830–1914*, 105.

[131] 'Aspects of self-help', Ibid., 103.

1840) reveals his overwhelming emphasis on the force of exemplary characters, an internalization of industrious virtues, and courage leading to self-helping individuals to success. This kind of charged personalistic approach was not without its share of politics. "Whatever is done *for* men or classes, to a certain extent takes away the stimulus and necessity of doing for themselves; and where men are subjected to over-guidance and over-government, the inevitable tendency is to render them comparatively helpless."[132]

But despite this complexities of comparative institutionalization, is it not co-incidental that Lord Beveridge's classic *Voluntary Action* while urging that mutual aid "must broaden into philanthropy,"[133] unleashes the burden unto friendly societies' (whom he defines as "a fellowship of men knowing and trusting and influencing one another"[134]), and that will, in its determinate outcome, expand its content and core unto the whole human race, encompassing the whole human society? "So at last human society may become a friendly society—an affiliated order of branches, some large and many small, each with its own life in freedom, each linked to all the rest by common purpose and by bonds to serve that purpose."[135] And this is more so because this warm and unique fraternity blossoms only in voluntary action and voluntary society, which being different from a statutory body "cannot be constitutionally responsible to those it serves, because they are a scattered amorphous and indeterminate body which is constantly changing."[136] Even the statutory services, in this discourse, have been interpreted to fulfill a relational function such as this one: the aim of the statutory services is "the establishment of a proper co-operative relationship between the public and the bureaucracy" where the ordinary citizen learns to regard the official as "his friend and servant."[137] And if anybody has witnessed the organization of relief work, or medical camps, or the spate of friendly football matches between the police and the community neighborhood groups, in India or elsewhere, one cannot but believe in the attempts, from the very surface, or roots, to effect the

---

[132] Samuel Smiles, *Self Help* (repr., 1866; Mumbai: Wilco Publishing House: Mumbai, 2004), 2; italics in the original.
[133] Cited in T. H. Marshal, "Voluntary Action," in *Sociology at the Crossroads and other Essays* (London: Heinemann, 1963), 329–41.
[134] Ibid., 331.
[135] Ibid., 330–31.
[136] Ibid., 333.
[137] Ibid., 332.

construction of civil and professional trust as a prerequisite of underscoring statutory and legal challenges.

## Professional Social Service, Social Work Disinterred

That "trust" is a prerequisite in an apparently, impersonal professional liaison between service-professionals and their clients, is underscored by a seminal sociologist—none other than T. H. Marshall. One of the distinguishing, judging markers of the other, preceding structures of helping vis-à-vis social work, as we've already noticed, is that charity, philanthropy, altruism et al. are not professions, while social work is, and followingly, bound by the professions' own code of ethics and behavioral charter; professional ethics in this sense is that it is regulated by its own criterial norms of practice. Though, as Marshal reminds us, Herbert Spencer "traced their origin among primitive peoples,"[138] Weber, we think, has been more accurate in defining its ascendancy and consolidation against the emerging backdrop of impersonal, bureaucratic, official, "gentleman's" modernity[139] in Western Europe. While the market metaphor seems to be strong in interpreting, and laying down the relationship between the professional and the recipient of his services according to contractual registers, the professional codes brook the same,

> The commodity can be inspected before it is paid for: the service cannot. The principle ... is plausible when you are buying ... a pound of strawberries: it makes nonsense when you are calling in a surgeon to a case of acute appendicitis. ... There are two reasons for this. One is that professional service is not standardized. It is unique and personal. ... The professional man is distinguished by the further fact that he does not give only

---

[138] T. H. Marshal, "The Recent History of Professionalism in Relation to Social Structure and Social Policy," in *Sociology at the Cross Roads and Other Essays* (London: Heinemann, 1963), 150–70.

[139] Consider the fact that "The Law Society came into being in 1739 as the Society of *Gentlemen* Practisers and became the most authoritative of the legal clubs which met in the taverns and coffee houses around Chancery lane" contributing much to the growth of the British public sphere. See Maria Malatesta, *Professional Men, Professional Women: The European Professions from the Nineteenth Century until Today*, transl. A. Belton (Los Angeles, CA: SAGE Publications: Los Angeles, 2011), 27 (italics mine).

his skill. He gives himself. His whole personality enters into his work. ... He is called upon to show judgment and an understanding of human nature, as well as a knowledge of medicine or law. The best service can be given only when the practitioner knows his client intimately, his character, his foibles, his background and his family circumstances. That is why the British Medical Association is now deploring the way in which specialization and institutional treatment are ousting the family doctor from his key position. These essential qualities cannot be specified in a contract, they cannot be bought. They can only be given.[140]

In a sociological enunciation, while this appears as an observation extrinsic to its essence, in social work, this cements itself as a built-in aporia. Whether the NASW (National Association of Social Workers, adopted its formal code in 1960) or the BASW (British Association of Social Workers, in 1976), even though late, it was already common knowledge that "many of social work's first principles or ground rules have been borrowed from medicine: the notions of aetiological explanation, diagnosis, treatment, and the profession's mastery of a body of scientifically valid specialized knowledge[e]."[141] But social work trailed behind medicine in adopting a professional charter of ethics. And when it did, finally, it seemed to suffer from a deep seated ambiguity, or perhaps a lack of clarity, as to what kind of statement it is trying to make. "The principles purportedly underlying the codes are not translated into any clear or complete statement of rights and dutie[s]."[142] While "respect for persons" is a compulsory presence in all charters, how it may be embodied, or violated in specific "technical" practice principles is not stated (despite "non-judgemental attitude, acceptance, client-self determination, controlled involvement," etc). This is more evident when such codes are split into values and corresponding principles[143]—though their philosophical import and predicament, as we clearly know, are completely different—even if catalogued in unison. It is completely at a loss when social workers complain of insurmountable dilemmas faced by them in their everyday functioning.[144] However, why is this so? Just stating

---

[140] Ibid., 154.

[141] Clark and Asquith, "Professional Ethics and Politics," 84.

[142] Ibid., 85.

[143] Frederic Reamer, *Social Work Values and Ethics* (Jaipur: Rawat Publications, 2005), 36–37.

[144] If this has been the complaint of Clark et al. in their famous book, Frederic Reamer (*Social Work Values and Ethics* [Jaipur: Rawat Publications, 2005]) does try to rectify many of these, even resolve ideal typical cases of code conflict. See page 42–164.

them in terms of a contest between personal and professional values, as is so often found in social work textbooks, as evident, is not enough. It is largely because, as Clark and Asquith succinctly tells us, "social work is intrinsically a moral endeavour"[145] (unlike medicine, law or engineering, "in the case of some professions, notably social work and education, the end itself is controversial and difficult to state.[146] It is not just a set of more or less value-neutral technical skill[s]").[147] The paradox is complete when the so-called value neutrality has to be stated as a value in social work's professional code of ethics.

But such an indubitable paradox, now after this detour, should be prescribed in larger terms. A debate is raging in contemporary moral philosophy around the role relative, person neutrality, and the extent of it in public/professional life. Person violation is wrong and immoral, but my participation in a boxing match will require that I must make the other person bleed. My professional role as a soldier requires of me that I throw a bomb from the plane on an anonymous group of men—whom I do not know whether they are civilians or terrorists. What shall I do? Morality—as we've learnt from Habermas—when tied to context specific personal, that is, individual, group, or institutional orientation structures, is ethics. Ethics in the public domain (open to public scrutiny, administration, and legislation), and ethics in the private domain (operative in the general space of private citizens' activity or contractual exchanges) are mediated by the person: if this is correct as explicated in the previous chapters, what we do when we face the above impasse? A superb theorist of professional ethics, Arthur Applbaum, in a classic work, answers: "[Q]uietly withdrawing one's service through resignation or transfe[r] ... 'absolute personal morality.'"[148]

Why resignation and not whistleblowing, public disclosure? Protest? Partly because these role requirements are innate, and apparently presuppose tacit consent on the part of the professional, this does not thrive on the brink of explicit corruption. Such undue permissibility is contingent upon individuals, and, thus,

---

[145] Clark and Asquith, "Professional Ethics and Politics," 86.
[146] Emmet (1967) cited in Clark and Asquith, "Professional Ethics and Politics," 87.
[147] Ibid., 86.
[148] Arthur Isak Applbaum, *Ethics for Adversaries: The Morality of Roles in Public and Professional Life* (Princeton, NJ: Princeton University Press, 1999), 67.

The message of resignation is that this public official[149] can no longer execute this government's policies in good faith, so person and office must part ways. Some one else with different contingent obligations or different reasonable views, could in good faith do the job, for the legitimacy of the government or the policies are not in question.[150]

The answer to our primary question then, in the face of person violation unduly permitted (or at least "not prohibited" otherwise) by professional ethics, the only, and actual inhibitor, is this: Only a post personalist ethics can prohibit person violation, but that it can do only in the face of flexible and fledgling uncertainty. "Respect for persons" as we see now, is deeply and devilishly problematic in social work when left to mere professional yearning to recreate it; only a post personalist ethics can protect it from the normative damage generated by the factual impact of intractable tension or, error.

Its reasons have to be discovered from within this thematic. And a startling observation can act well as a starter. It is perhaps—in social work at least—the veering away of social work practices from the friendly dispensations—which in turn had contributed toward its professional mooring—that could claim responsibility for this attenuation. A look at the debate on the spread of healthcare provision in Great Britain where healthcare that remained "under the control of friendly societies,"[151] now on the insistence of the "elites of the medical profession" who favored the National Insurance Act with the amendment that it separated itself from friendly societies because "wrangling with which had become excessive ... and smacked of socialism."[152] Soon, of course, the NIA ran into heavy weather with the British Medical Association (BMA) asking "its members to refuse to sign any contracts whose provisions differed from those established by the BMA."[153] The professional exclusivity had come full circle.

But this disciplinary nervousness was not warranted and completely out of place so far as the evolutionary history of social work as a "personal service" profession is concerned. The career of one of the founders of

---

[149] In the case of a boxing match, this will be replaced by the figure of the private citizen: individual.
[150] Applbaum, *Ethics for Adversaries,* 255.
[151] Malatesta, *Professional Men, Professional Women,* 47.
[152] Ibid., 47.
[153] Ibid., 47.

social work and its methods—Mary Richmond—is a telling testimony in this context.

Mary Richmond is remembered as one of the founders of modern social work that emerged from the wombs of "organized charity"—a term which was put into circulation by Richmond herself. "[S]he formed a committee on professional organization in 1918 to establish common terminology ... social work and social case work as alternatives to charity and philanthropy";[154] despite these alternatives, let us keep it straight, the persona(list) spirit of social service—as she conceived it—was retained, and the professional stint of the new dispensation was aptly named too: civic professionalism. The last is important because it clarifies a problematic in the context of our discussion for which we invoked her example: personalism (not aptly) pitted against professionalism.

But it was also the end point of a long tryst and a longer journey with charity and philanthropy, which underwent complex transformation in her hands, and during her troubled times. Richmond understood charity as being "expressed through friendship with those in need";[155] "here she echoed Octavia Hill's motto 'no alms but a friend'."[156] This she used in her polemic to argue against public relief: "Richmond believed that public relief was a source of demoralization because of its failure to establish a personal relationship."[157] But even though it failed on that front, it generated—otherwise—personal feelings of the loss of self-respect and loss of pride, instilling instead shame, because public relief is the arrangement of provisions that generated no entitlements for the recipients. "Public relief was further demoralizing, in her view, because it had the effect of supplying a gift, but not a giver."[158] In personal relationship—the gift is "presenced" and has a proper figure—a subjective presence of one who gives; though this view goes against Richmond's opinion elsewhere where she states how the gift has no quality but develops in the process of giving and receiving.[159] If gift(ing) is processual and, therefore, a product of iterability, the presence of the giver in the end, or the beginning of the gift-spectrum is at the most suspicious. The cycle cannot begin

---

[154] Elizabeth N. Agnew, *From Charity to Social Work: Mary E. Richmond and the Creation of an American Profession* (Urbana, IN: University of Illinois Press, 2004), 177.

[155] Ibid., 63.

[156] Ibid., 79.

[157] Ibid., 90.

[158] Ibid., 90.

[159] Ibid., 91.

with him, nor does it end there: it has to be an interminable "economy."[160] However, Richmond's disapproval of giving anonymous gifts to the unknown poor was, thus, well placed since it meant a "disregard of actual needs, and a failure to please the recipient." This went to the extent of receiving funds from advertisers since "it appealed to self interest" rather than to the "better self" of the "philanthropic advertiser."[161] In a similar vein, Richmond differentiated health insurance from "handouts." "She opposed the latter because they could be pocketed, and they carried no guarantee of 'effective living'. In contrast, she saw insurance as a 'gift' that would 'release energy instead of crippling it'."[162]

Against the rising impersonal boredom and burden of helping, Richmond relied on personal social service through friendly societies. "Friendliness and kindliness could 'transfigure and transform' otherwise pauperizing, impersonal relief, whether in the form of money or material assistance."[163] Insisting on personal service, Richmond espoused this as a method which entailed personal family visits, taking of intimate life-history and an understanding of the problem against a broader backdrop; in other words a "thorough knowledge of their lives."[164] Similarly, Charity Organization Society's board of managers "stated its commitment to the 'duties of good citizenship' through 'patient personal service'" and the extension of neighborhood centers.[165]

Here lay the new crunch: this threefold pairing of citizenship, personal service, and neighborhood posed new problems of perception and acceptance. The debate between the economist Simon Patten and Richmond reached a new high in terms of the distinctions that were to emerge a decade or a century later; her model of "personal friend" shifted to the idea of a "good neighbor"[166] as urban, industrial expansion and anonymity made friendship based on personal intimacy difficult, if not altogether impossible. During this intense era, Richmond Wrote *The Good Neighbor in the Modern City* (1907). Patent's critique in the essay "Who is the Good Neighbour?"[167] argued that the duty of "true neighborliness"

---

[160] This comment does not draw upon, or comment on the (now) overgrown literature on the phenomenology of the gift.

[161] Agnew, *From Charity to Social Work*, 90.

[162] Ibid., 127.

[163] Ibid., 91.

[164] Ibid., 97.

[165] Ibid., 101.

[166] Ibid., 137.

[167] Ibid., 139.

existed only in the context of "social similarity" and not reach out across social and class differences. The "service altruism" of Richmond, Patten contended, was out of times with the spirit of a civic participation. As "citizens" the proper work of the well to do was "to provide 'a definite part of their income' and support the work of experts in creating more favourable environmental conditions. Such 'income altruism' would make charity efficacious and replace volunteers with 'trained, paid agents'."[168] This quasi-anonymous tax, operating without direct knowledge of the recipient would be criticized from Richmonds' point of view of "gift." Whereas Patten drew a clear line of distinction between neighbors and citizens, between service and financial generosity, and between improved character and improved conditions, Richmond argued that these pairs represented complimentary forces and called for pairing personal assistance with legislative and professional efforts.[169] In Richmond's own words, "Impartial, enlightened neigbour-love" combining "citizen participation and professional expertise"[170] produced social work as a civic profession; [her] "social diagnosis remained committed to the artistic and personal dimensions of friendly visiting. The latter had entailed the friend's 'art of asking questions' that went 'to the very heart of difficulty'."[171] As a method, as mentioned before, it elicited not only modern social work but its prime method—case work—which has become the transmuted naming of friendly visiting that includes personal case history, the reproduction of social evidence—even counseling. The principles of social case work—for that matter—begins with the "person."[172]

## Friendly Societies Within Colonial Difference

While cooperation, in this technical sense, dates back to the end of the 18th century, with the "first English 'store'" having been founded in 1795,

---

[168] Ibid., 139.

[169] Ibid., 139. In *Social Diagnosis,* however, she treated neighbors as mere machines of information, "and as such, she regarded them as a "synonym for gossip and inaccuracy" distinguished from case workers with expert knowledge and skill; see Elizabeth N. Agnew, *From Charity to Social Work: Mary E. Richmond and the Creation of an American Profession* (Urbana, IN: University of Illinois Press, 2004), 166.

[170] Ibid., 138.

[171] Ibid., 159.

[172] *Helen Harris Perlman,* "The Person," in *Social Case Work: A Problem Solving Process* (Chicago, IL: The University of Chicago Press, 1957), 6–26.

"[t]he Co-operative Credit Societies Act was passed in 1904" modelled upon the "Friendly Societies Act of Great Britain."[173] Through mutual help, lessons were sought in

> [P]unctuality (and thrift ... by demanding regular instalments of share money ... and avoidance of extravagant and wasteful expenditure[174]) to be inculcated in the members and often the direct, instant benefit of a disbursed loan was contrasted against the indirect and long lasting advantages of winning health, literacy, "the avoidance of extravagance or evil habits ... [and] legislation for social ends."[175]

An interesting foray of such cooperative "friendly" societies was into the realm and depth of local "quarrels" arising out of deeply personal reasons, which was, at the same time, instanced as a case of instilling "social co-operation. They require the participation, as members, of almost the entire population of the village if quarrels are really to be prevented ... and save the village from the ruinous cost of litigation."[176] One remembers here Hegel's famous indictment that the more litigation there is in a community, the more flourishing sense of private individualism should be inferred thereof. But why everybody? The argument is, "the true facts are known to everybody", and, thus, the litigational and ceremonial swearing in becomes, in a sense, redundant, and instead of punishment, a novel element of "warning"[177] looms in. While these were some of the active mediations carried out by the friendly societies and their indigene avatars, they were also coeval with the founding and spread of local government regimens in India.

But even if it were to be mentioned by a colonizing official, this observation is not only correct but goes along with the theoretical mapping in the hands of none other than Mahatma Gandhi, who way back in 1909—in a feat of rage against the professionalism of law supposedly mooted by the English—argued the following for a substantive "self-rule" or *swaraj*:

> The Hindus and Mahomedans have quarrelled. An ordinary man will ask them to forget all about it, he will tell them that both must be more or less

---

173 Sir Edward Blunt, ed. *Social Service in India: An Introduction to Some Social and Economic Problems of the Indian People* (London: His Majesty's Stationery Office, 1945 [1939]), 312, 318.
174 Ibid., 337.
175 Ibid., 334.
176 Ibid., 338.
177 Ibid., 363.

at fault, and will advise them no longer to quarrel. They go to lawyers. … The lawyers … will as a rule, advance quarrels, instead of repressing them. Moreover, men take up that profession, not in order to help others out of their miseries, but to enrich themselves. It is one of the avenues of becoming wealthy, and their interest exists in multiplying disputes. It is within my knowledge that they are glad when men have disputes. Petty pleaders actually manufacture them. … Lawyers are lazy people, in order to indulge in luxuries, [they] take up such professions. … It is the lawyers who have discovered that theirs is an honorable profession. Some families have been ruined through them; they have made brothers enemies. … [178]

However, a more basic and perhaps a more damaging attribution is that it is through the English' system of law and the lawyers that the colonial rule has been perpetuated. Gandhi's argument is that the law—in its natural appearance—seems to be delivering justice and, thus, "appears" as just—while all the way it could be based on a natural injustice.

Those who want to perpetuate their power do so through the courts. If people were to settle their own quarrels, a third party would not be able to exercise any authority over them. … It was certainly a sign of savagery when they settled their disputes by fighting. Is it any the less so if I ask a third party to decide between you and me?. … The parties alone know who is right. We, in our simplicity and ignorance, imagine that a stranger, by taking our money, gives us justice.[179]

And finally, in relevant consonance with the collective cooperative spirit invoked just before we brought in Gandhi, it was urged that the lawyers not wanting to "meddle with the quarrels between parties … [would] refuse to be a judge"[180] and would give up their profession and urge the people to do likewise. In conclusion then, we can decisively surmise, that the theory of passive resistance[181] or love-force, as Gandhi liked to call it, and that which had heralded the nationalist predicament in influential forms, betokened the power of self-governing life communities in place of the impersonal-modern, juridical third force.

---

[178] M. K. Gandhi, *M.K Gandhi's Hind Swaraj: A Critical Edition*, eds. Suresh Sharma and Tridip Suhrud (New Delhi: Orient Blackswan, 2010), 51. Italics in the original.

[179] Ibid., 52 (italics in the original).

[180] Ibid., 96.

[181] Though as we all know, Gandhi veered away from his erstwhile theory of passive resistance which seemed to lack an active moral commitment to the theory of *satyagraha* or nonviolence. But love, as Martin Luther King were to interpret Gandhi's legacy, consecrated *agape* and inserted into it a notion of resistance, hitherto absent.

# Concluding Remarks

From ancient forms of giving—whether Indian or Western—to the moment when we listened to the birth pangs and the subsequent constitution of such a modern discourse as social work—all of them, we could briefly hazard, are invaded by the contingency of the hazardously personal: sometimes manifestly, sometimes immanently. The task of a personalytical critique is such a "re-memoration": in contemporary terms, this would be saying in explication that the gift exceeds the act of giving. What invades then is the gift-structure. This becomes pertinent even in today's raving debates on the ethical anonymity of blood donation, surrogacy, or organ donation as gifts—even from the dead.

But if this is the poison, then love or friendship from outside the legal juridical sovereign regimes are also proposed as possible cure. While they are instituted as friendly societies in Europe and even in colonial India,[182] the institutional personality as an endgame is proven. We need to have a phenomenology of institutions, broadly speaking, to stretch this attempt, presently available in a hint only, to its furthest extent. And that is our future challenge.

---

[182] Surveys of "highly personalized" Anglo-Indian charities in colonial South India and the history of *The Friend-in-Need Society* (FINS) founded in 1806 is an excellent case example. See Lionel Caplan, "Gifting and Receiving," in *Tradition, Pluralism and Identity: In Honour of T. N. Madan,* eds. Veena Das, Dipankar Gupta, and Patricia Uberoi (New Delhi: SAGE Publications, 1999), 283–305.

# Epilogue

## *Personal Is Not Private:*
## *Rewriting Modernity for the Last Time*

If modernity is the journey from personality to impersonality, and if we have reversed this, then this is the re-inscription of modernity—perhaps for the last time; more eminently, this lays the ground for a full-fledged philosophical discourse of alternative modernity—still absent.

It is time now, finally, to relate the substantive essence to the method-analytical moods present or absent in the work, for which the primary suspicion could be: this is a personalist work in the last instance, or else, what then has been the use of reiterating "personalytic" at odd times throughout the book? The problem is, to be a personalist, except for the limited Schelerian use already cited, is to incite in others a whole lot of signified that the signifying phrase (personalist) abundantly triggers. That would be trenchantly misleading, or I could have been prevailed upon to introduce a new version of personalism. This seemed excessive, and the current work is not a contribution to the now defunct personalist trends with all its theological gloss (personalists did not dismantle the private). A better alternative would be to call this—as I have done it not too often—personalytical[1] (or, in brief, personalytic), where the category

---

[1] Though the word 'personalytic' in its academic use could be traced to a 1982 article by Anthony Greenwald, but his psychologistic deployment deriving from personalysis has nothing to do with my (post personalist) personalytical form of mediation to be effected in social-phenomenological and legal-political theory, and practice. See Anthony Greenwald, "Is Anyone in Charge? Personalysis verus the Principle of Personal Unity" in *Psychological Perspectives On the Self,* Vol.1, pp. 151–181, ed. Jerry Suls (Hillsdale, N.J : Erbaum, 1982).

personal would have an analytical value and could be deployed to mediate and unpack discourses of politics, social theory, history, culture, ethics, and social work. Allowed and affirmed this way, the personal has never been so aggressive and invasive, and the work has addressed all these discourses in some form or the other. For instance, in Chapter 1, in the domain of politics, I have meditated extensively on the phenomenon of personal attacks, where personal attacks do not always signify attacks on a person's privacy and could thus be distinguished from the notion of privacy as such. There is more to it: personal "pure" politics of dirty hands where the person appropriates the private/public roles and manipulates them, severely. The modern public sphere is rational and refers strictly to an impersonal office dominated by the symbolic rivalry of files while the private and privacy oppose publicity and public scrutiny. The real reason as to why—in modernity—impersonality was called for or the personal was sought to be driven out of the public sphere is already well-known. For a moment, let us recall the two more famous reasons: the first is the anti-absolutist fear of the monarch who was sovereign in person (we pursued this at some length in Chapter 2), and the second is the fear of the incalculable and the irrational—the person steeped in "particularity" and armed with deception and fraud, one who can pursue self-interest monstrously without a market measure. (In this sense, Bataille was correct in stating that the "person" is feudal, pre-modern, and Strawson's idea that the person is "primitive" could be added to it, with a pinch of decontextualized salt; capitalism is the order of "things," and property is that which enjoins or hyphenates persons and things.)

However, in this world neatly apportioned between private and public or property and hegemony, there were philosophies struggling to break free of this domineering binary. While Marxism and Fascism would like to transcend the dichotomy in the modernist transformation of the monarch—the dictator in whom private/public would be personified in an anachronistic unity—a stream of texts could be recalled that had tried in their desperate will to move beyond this liberal paradigm, and failed. So it could be construed as a fight between the illiberal pre-private, pre-public personal, and the liberal democratic fracture. With whom do my determinate sympathies lie?

In social theory—while denying to be subsumed under the private, here—the personal emerges as an originary first. Such a first I've used historically to explore the Gandhian notion of personal integrity as rememorating the monarchical unity of private and public in one person. In culture, I've explored Max Scheler's cultural collective persons, where having previously recuperated the personal as a suppressed

narrative using historical and sociotheoretic tools, here I interrupt it by
thematizing the proposal, especially the Hegelian one that had intended
to found an impersonal civil social modernity through the cultural self-
understanding and unpack the allegedly impersonal fund of cultural stock.
I have deployed it later by using the registers of the various structures of
helping, wherefrom the personal forms—imminent in charity, altruism,
benevolence, and others—have had to be expelled to found welfare and,
finally, social work. The results speak for themselves.

# I

Now, having had a narrative summary-understanding of this text, I may
be allowed to hazard a more thematic conclusion in an algebraically
narrative form.

The personal and private are different, and the mix up is of recent
historical emergence suited to the liberal project. But the coalescence
cannot be done away with as a result of this reconstruction or a reversal
that could be theoretically produced by a finite discovery procedure.
Historically speaking, now there emerge two registers where the personal
is privatively interpellated and the personal is its own self. (The first
algorithm, as I show, is the forged personal. As obvious, the second
register, where the personal comes into its own, is the more interesting
one on which I've spent considerable energy.) But that too has required
a hierarchy of historicity and a canon of culture. Thus, it was perhaps
incumbent upon us to discover and sanction the presence of a third (which
is originally the first) term as an existential qualifier, besides the usual
public/private. That supposedly suspends much of the discursive unrest
and the failed quest reproduced in the vast literature devoted to finding
a way out of the liberal binary. They have ended up in discovering, as I
stated in the Prologue, either an alternative vision of privacy or counter
publics, not realizing that the colonial predicament has left us with an
"immature" private and an "incompetent public," which, in fact, has helped
my endeavor to recover and reconstruct the personal liberated from the
discursive lineaments of the private.

Three major lessons seem to emerge from such an engagement whose
conclusions have been outlined earlier: first, personal is not private—both
in theoretical terms, if we are ready to recover them from their immanence,
and in cultural-historical terms found in manifest display. The privative
personal is a product of historical contamination and liberal investment.

This comes to a significant fruition in a postcolonial community where, in the absence of a corresponding notion to address private and personal separately and *byaktigoto* standing for both of them, it seems useless to posit the private-public distinction in our context and study it in terms of lack or plenitude. We live in the difference that is between byaktigoto (inclusive of personal-personal and private-personal, and the difference in between them), the private, and the personal (as broader rubrics). We inhabit the difference between janta, *jonosadharon* (our nonpublic), and public. Are they also the nonpersons as described in the Weberian grid? While the element of charisma did introduce in Max Weber a moment of the irrational, magico personal, as we have argued in this book, and this goes much against—as a modification of—the general theory of modernity that he was proposing, we tend to go against Weber's proposed predication of Asiatic nonpersonality,[2] where given his protestant graph of ascetic rationalism mobilized in the puritan personality to flourish in an accumulative capitalist spirit, his mourning is only understandable. If in Hegelian terms, private property is a requirement to be a person, and posits personality, then the nonperson is the one who is bereft of, or stripped of, the investment or the inducement of private property. This is in a reversal of Weber—a position, if we are able to manufacture it, we would be too happy to adopt.

Second, to go for a cultural and cognitive self-understanding of this, the observation that the byaktigoto or our personal could be appropriated by the non-"vernacular" domineering-self (such as that argued by Ashis Nandy) would be wrong, even in terms of a specifically periodized cultural history. To agree with Rabindranath Tagore and an episodic narration of Bengali culture, there has had never been a privative-personal or pure byaktigoto in India. (The emergence of the privative-personal and its slow usurpation of the field of the communo-personal in terms of samaj or life-community is the colonial-moment. Therefore, it is not the public appropriation of the personal that has marked the colonial predicament but the private appropriation of the personal.) The study of such "personal" emotions as grief with reference to an emergent public sphere during Rabindranath's times corroborate the polemic. Rabindranath refers to the personal in the samajik or life-communal sense, but his public is also an unmade public (or a nonpublic) to be educated through public programs

---

[2] Sara R. Farris's book *Max Weber's Theory of Personality: Individuation, Politics and Orientalism in the Sociology of Religion* (Brill: Leiden, 2013) treats this in the context of an Orientalist accusation directed at Weber.

of mourning the death of public figures. With an unformed public, the personal becomes more unnoticeable, yet palpable.

Third, with our particular colonial induction, it would be again a large error to generalize the aforementioned conclusions to the point of blindness: as told before, much will depend on the particular kind of discursive site inhabited by us (and personal in legal juridical discourse is not interchangeable with byaktigoto in the cultural or political discourse.) While the legal juridical discourse and the bureaucratic-administrative apparatus do administer various applied notions of the person, public, or private, which bear traces of the Western dichotomy, the political deployments of such categories—that too with the cultural unconscious in action—is bound to be fluid, strategic, and success-oriented. Does this success come at a heavy cost? While generating a colonial political epistemology of the personal by invoking a notion of personal identity, nowhere did Ramendra Sundar Trivedi—a cultural icon of the Bengali Indian—refer to the notion of privacy. This acts as a demonstrative proof of the actuality of the personal-first capable of being politicized and become a norm of practice in terms of its own positivity.

# II

In the second part of the conclusion, it would be instructive if we could be with Walter Benjamin who is not known for any particular sympathy for self, subject, or person-thinking in the human sciences. Therefore, when Benjamin asserts the embodiment of the personal principle in the people, those fashion-induced skeptics who think that the person and the personal are redundant and their days are over have to rethink their too quick an appraisal.

> "Corporeal substance is one of the realities that stand within the historical process itself." Pain, pleasure, touch. ... The difficult problem that now emerges is that the "nature" whose adherence to our corporeal substance has been asserted nevertheless strongly points to the limitation and individuality of the living being. That limited reality which is constituted by the establishment of a spiritual nature in a corporeal substance is called the "person." The person is limited ... by their maximum extension, the people.[3]

---

[3] Walter Benjamin, "Outline of the Psychophysical Problem," in *Selected Writings: Vol. 1, 1913–26,* eds. M. Bullock and M. W. Jennings (Cambridge: Harvard University Press, 1996), 393–401.

And when this maximum extension withdraws, what happens, where does it end? Having begun from the body of the monarch, it ought not to end; therefore, the petrification of history or pornographic scatologies we've discussed is hardly successful with the body of the monarch. Now, consider again, when Foucault said he was trying to do away with the philosophy of the subject, he meant constructing a genealogy of the subject: "I have tried to get out from the philosophy of the subject through a genealogy of this subject, by studying the constitution of the subject across history that has led us up to the modern concept of the self."[4] But this would entail—even in a weak manner—the structuralist orthodoxy where the subject is shown to have been constituted by discourses, rather than being the self-conscious, representative rallying point of discourses. But the structuralist maneuver is done away with when the "across history" tenor is brought in as an interruption; structuralism admits of no history. But where is our genealogy lurking?

One of the (proven) assumptions of this book has been that the person, the way we go about it, was (as if) the discovery of the neo-Hegelians, and the genealogy must end with them, for the moment. Here, it is exactly the case inasmuch as subsequent to the Haldar–Mctaggart debate and the inference that the absolute could be a person like a cricket club could be a person—in terms of juridical/artificial personality—and the rest of the work expands on the theme. Even as late as the 1940s (?) when D. P. Mukherjee—one of the founders of Indian sociology—wrote *Personality in the Social Sciences*, his major observations were all in all derived, and were made, under the shadows of Haldar.[5]

It is necessary, however, to hint at the obvious interrogation as to how the person is, then, different from the subject, individual, self—those other interchangeables, even if not intended, correspondences (besides the private) that haunt the notion of the person. It is true that the present work bearing the fundamental weight of the personal-private mix up was dominantly focused on it, expectedly. But the results of this study must address the distinction among the above; otherwise, while having cleared a particular confusion, inadvertently, it will be made responsible for sanctioning the substitutable use value of the person as the other name of the self, subject, individual, or a human being—that will be most unfortunate.

---

[4] Michel Foucault, "Subjectivity and Truth," in *The Politics of Truth*, eds. Sylvere Lotringer and Lysa Hochroth (New York, NY: Semiotext(e), 1997), 171–98.

[5] I discuss this in a separate paper.

To begin with, the person temporally has been prior to the individual, self, or subject. A look at the classic studies on individualism by Mcpherson or Charles Taylor on the sources of the self, and by Foucault on the subject, are ample testimonies.

The person is not an individual: this distinction, in fact, is the easiest. The person could be an individual person but as well could be a group or a collective person. The emergence and the tortuous march of the individual has been historically wedded to individualism and opposed to collectivism.[6]

The person is not the self. The self is always the self-same. It is identitarian in essence and plots itself only in opposition to the other. But when Levinas construes the relation to the other itself as personal—in fact that is the only ethical possibility—it cannot be the standpoint of the self; the self-less positioning, elsewhere, could not be, unless otherwise as a distortion, theorized as a selfish text.

The person is not the subject. The latter is mired in the subject/object, subjectivity/objectivity distinction. In the traditional reading, as we've had it, subjectivity is inwardness or the power of representation where it means the acumen to represent others as well as (self)representation. In contrast and difference, Hegels' objective ethical spirit is norms institutionalized, or externalized, from which emerges the personality of organizations that was much deliberated upon in Chapter 5.

It should have been clear by now that the personal grasps and straddles both the individual and the collective, the self and the other, and the subject and the object; it has been doing the same with the private and the public—the theme of this work.

---

[6] This has already been noticed in certain brands of personalism, particularly in Jacques Maritain and "also encountered in the personalism of Mournier," where a distinction between the individual and the person is available in some form. Individuals "as in bourgeois individualism ... [are] emphasized as distinct particulars, neglecting the universal." See Frederick Copleston, *A History of Philosophy, Vol. IX (Maine De Biran to Sartre)* (London: Search Press, 1975), 260. Moreover, an individual, while valorizing "the narrowness of the ego, [is] forever threatened and forever eager to grasp for itself" (cited in page 260).

Our study will not agree with this fully, except for its main intent. The personal particularity was disparaged in the Hegelian discourse (in Chapter 5); in fact, in the individualistic discourse, the universal is grasped as the particular and not neglected, as reiterated in Mournier.

# III

The second part of the present work is significant in many aspects; one is, of course, because the discussion of impersonal modernity in the Hegelian version (the first philosopher of modernity) finally veers toward, and is incomplete without, the inclusion of helping forms, and one is struck by the fact that even in Hegel's *Natural Law* he cannot escape the bidding that helping the poor if universalized as a maxim abolishes itself,[7] and, thereby, the arbitrary, whimsical forms of personal helping follows. We show in Chapter 5, in the instance of colonial modernity, how the impersonal principle to found civil social modernity (in Hegel, it is instituted by "positive law" as a part of the objective ethical spirit) fails and, contextually speaking, one can see—as our paradigmatic examples endorse (Sister Nivedita and B. R. Ambedkar), and it is possible to add onto them—how it is an unintended journey from the natural personal to moral or legal group personality or legal fiction. Alexandre Kojeve, in his phenomenology of law and right, perfectly names these associations or institutions as collective moral persons (more can be found in the main text) because "they reduce to a charitable, intellectual, or benevolent undertaking, endowed with a material organization, and graced with a personality" where the will of the institution is autonomously separated from its founder, or members.[8] Within this trajectory, it is possible to interpret, inclusively all the more, the arrival of charity endowments, trust deeds, and even the registered voluntary groups, who—to the great German jurist Otto Gierke—had historically paraded themselves as (an)other personalities besides the state; the latter by then had been reduced or claimed to have been reduced to just one among many associations.

But an examination of the nearly universalistic claims made by Kant to Hegel, to Brajen Seal, and to Benoy Sarkar—our philosophical and historically pitched moments—as to the deeply personal forms of helping—from charity, alms, altruism, philanthropy, and similar structures of helping to the impersonal modern niche of social work—showed their foregrounding in multimodal meaning forms but everything stitched in the personal color, that too in the affinal forms of emotional kinship— love, agape or friendship, and fellowship. Could social work in its own

---

[7] G. W. F Hegel, *Natural Law,* trans. T. M. Knox (Philadelphia: University of Pennsylvania Press, 1975), 80.
[8] Bonnecase cited in Alexandre Kojeve, *Outline of a Phenomenology of Right,* trans. B. P. Frost and R. Howse (Lanham, MD: Rowman & Littlefield Publishers Inc., 2007), 56.

temporality disavow this radical inheritance? The welfare state in its mooring is tied to citizens irrespective of identities, and citizens are objects of state provisions, not subjects. Our strenuous reading in Chapter 6 proved, tied to the personal contingencies of life, it rarely could live up to this acclaimed universal objectivity. Contemporary emphasis and immensely popular, transterritorial dissemination of microcredit programs based on family, friendly, or neighborly relational, network chains is a case in point. Similarly, social work has had its origins in friendly societies in early 19th and 20th centuries—which ran amok and infected even the Anglo-Indian charities in colonial India—where societies modeled upon friendly fellowship had sprung up and continue to this day—though at a much larger remove from their first forms. The nonrights of recipients of personal charity in ancient and medieval times became social rights in the welfare state in the 20th century, but that the welfare state itself is trapped in a self-referential, indeterminate circularity, banishes the claim of determinate, impersonal welfarism—even professionalism. Mocked by the personal, as we have seen, these are laughable ideals.

# IV

But will this reading stand the test of contemporary scrutiny, or does it generate just the joy of maverick interpretive ability?

Let us begin with two micro-examples. In a review of a recently published book on personal social services, the reviewer in 2013 celebrates (the author) "Needham's particular stance ... that personalization can best be understood as a narrative containing a string of elements, and as a response to the perceived failings of other policy approaches, including 'bureau-professional control, outsourcing, performance management and market choice.'"[9] And second, how the English local authorities, through "personal care budgets," are actualizing the current "personalization agenda."[10] These tendencies, as evident, are not an upshot of the privatization drive and is specific and positive, that is, personal in orientation.

---

[9] Mark Lymbery, "Review of Catherine Needham," *Personalising Public Services: Understanding the Personalisation Narrative* (Bristol: Policy Press, 2011)," *Critical Social Policy* 33, no. 1 (2013), 187–89.

[10] Sally Jacobs, Jessica Abell, Martin Stevens, et al., "The Personalization of Care Services and the Early Impact on Staff Activity Patterns," *Journal of Social Work* 13, no. 2 (2011), 141–63.

Finally, to illustrate the result of this intervention, I shall examine two robust case studies. The first one would be a legal one, the second a theoretical one.

Let me document here, first, how our proposed grid could appropriate and intervene, or post absolutely different interpretive registers for the "right to privacy" debate that is going on in India currently with the Indian Supreme Court first constituting a bench (K. Puttaswamy vs. Union of India) to hear the petition and then judging that the right to privacy is a fundamental right (2017).

This search for relevance and categorical adequacy is a bit extended, but burning with contemporaneity. The recent spurt of debates in India (beginning in the year 2015 and reaching a landmark in 2017) around whether privacy is a fundamental right or not could be easily interpreted through the sieve of the grid proposed in this book. We shall show how the fundamental mistake of inter-equating and conflating the personal and the private (or the person and the individual) has been reiterated and repeated in the debate, and even in the judgment. The submission at the Supreme Court of India was made more relevant by the Government of India's recent pooling of biometric data of its citizens (Aadhar) and mandatorily linking them with PAN cards, notwithstanding various fuzzy pronouncements of the Supreme Court earlier. Though the request has been for declaring the right to privacy as a fundamental right, or deciding whether privacy is a "constitutionally protected value," the relevant and real aim is to inhibit the government from pooling up citizens' data. For this, the prominent argument is the vulnerability of data and the earlier cases of data theft and unintended or malafide data disclosure; however, the court has been cunning enough to set this aside.

Now, I shall not engage with or comment on the various legal-constitutional lineaments of the case. For instance the call for data security does not immediately call for the right to privacy as a fundamental right; these two are separate claims, which has been noticed by the Supreme Court bench too, Second, consider the judges saying that the right to privacy is not an absolute right as no rights are,[11] except within reasonable restrictions, etc. And with the Supreme Court having judged the right to

---

[11] In fact, this illusion in law is something of a long-standing irony. There is no absolute right!!!! As if this is a truism. But is it? No, there are rights that are absolute and they exist in human rights tracts in whatever form. I may be killed through procedures established by law but I cannot be sexually violated in any circumstance whatsoever. This is my absolute right. It is time the legal circles hear this and start using the word "absolute" without compunction.

privacy as a fundamental right, the "legal only" lineaments are clarified, but the legal–philosophical problems remain unresolved. At this cusp, I would rather limit myself to our personal/private distinction and the way it could affect or alter the originary terms of the debate.

For this, we need to take a detour to the part of the book[12] where the personal was charted as a historical and theoretical precondition of the private, and all comfortable notions of the privacy were demolished, having been helped by W. A. Parent and his landmark paper in *Philosophy and Public Affairs*. (For instance, the Supreme Court's definition of privacy as "the right to be left alone" is what Parent demolishes first.) But the problem with and within legal circles is that when considered alone, legal theory is philosophically poor or straightaway wrong—this fact is neither confessed nor mourned.

However, as narrated by Parent, "Privacy is the condition of not having undocumented personal knowledge (Parent excludes from his definition documented personal information available in public or institutional records.) about one possessed by others. A person's privacy is diminished exactly to the degree that others possess this kind of knowledge about him." He adds, "What I am defining is the condition of privacy, not the right of privacy." Let us just take hold of the word personal in this definition. What is personal here is that which is a prior condition of privacy. The personal may provide the private or privacy with a content but the personal is not the private or privacy as such.

Now, if this is correct, our intervention follows: If the identification of the technological data, or as I shall say identity data, of a person is inbuilt into the regular optic of identity governance today—of which we are a part, often a consenting part—it is hard to understand why identity-wolves would refuse to be identified, not by others but by the government (and well, government by consent); it could well be that identity politics here is suffering a retreat and a queer reversal—as if, denying a structure of recognition (is it bad because it is statist?). Therefore, even though documented, the knowledge is (and ideally) not shared with other citizens by the government and, thus, by Parent's definition, not leading to diminished privacy.[13] Clearly, this is documented personal data and one of the

---

[12] Chapters 3 and 4; specifically page 114–116 specifically.

[13] As a note of caution let us remark that though Parent's intervention could be used to harp on and sharpen the personal private divide, his endorsement of the existence of privacy and the way he deploys it is not necessarily our agenda, and our consonance with it should not be assumed.

reasons that the government has voiced—to identify fraud recipients of welfare schemes and subsidies seems to be very plausible—rememorating the days when such a demand was vociferously, and justifiably, voiced during the early days of the welfare state and its precursor poor schemes; we've spent considerable space on that in Chapters 5 and 6. Data related to a person (which is personal data) and housed by the government is not necessarily private data, or how would it be shared with the government at all. Our personal/private distinction has to be inserted here with speed and candor.

The call for privacy would be made and positioned only when this data could be interpreted as a form of (private) property. (Though for public interest/welfare reasons, it is well-known, that the property argument could be trumped by the state.) The interesting part is that the first paper in the world of received ideas, which is supposed to have flagged the issue of privacy for the first time, initially did take such a route but later abandoned it with good sense and held on to the question of an "inviolate personality;" my argument is, after private property, the justifiable abandonment of privacy hereafter is just a matter of time and would reflect very good sense. But we would require a vestige of the *private* to protect *personality* is not persuasive enough. The personal and private are opposite as we've plotted them against each other, and the conjunction is a product of capitalist accumulation and contamination.

But here is the scandal that is all the more soothing to us. Samuel D. Warren and Louis D. Brandeis in their trendsetting, landmark article start with the property register:

> Gradually the scope of … legal rights broadened; and now the right to life has come to mean the right to enjoy life; the right to be let alone; the right to liberty secures the exercise of extensive civil privileges; and the term "property" has grown to comprise every form of possession-intangible, as well as tangible.[14]

Also, "[t]he right of property in its widest sense, including all possession, including all rights and privileges, and hence embracing the right to an inviolate personality, affords alone that broad basis upon which

---

[14] Samuel D. Warren and Louis D. Brandeis, "The Right to Privacy," *Harvard Law Review* 4, no. 5 (1890): 193–220. I'm grateful to Ayushi Gupta for making available all the research done on this, and thereafter.

the protection which the individual demands can be rested."[15] The question of property readily, and serially, is made to support the claims of individualism. Till now, it is going fine. But, while realizing that the impregnable question of personality and the personal could not be side-stepped, the question of private property is finally relinquished:

> These considerations lead to the conclusion that the protection afforded to thoughts, sentiments, and emotions, expressed through the medium of writing or of the arts, so far as it consists in preventing publication, is merely an instance of the enforcement of the more general right of the individual to be let alone. It is like the right not to be assaulted or beaten, the right not to be imprisoned, the right not to be maliciously prosecuted, the right not to be defamed. In each of these rights, as indeed in all other rights recognized by the law, there inheres the quality of being owned or possessed and (as that is the distinguishing attribute of property) there may be some propriety in speaking of those rights as property. But, obviously, they bear little resemblance to what is ordinarily comprehended under that term. The principle which protects personal writings and all other personal productions, not against theft and physical appropriation, but against publication in any form, is in reality not the principle of private property, but that of an inviolate personality (p. 205).[16]

It is to be noted—with unease—that the private is made to become the personal here and hyphenated, which is absolutely unwarranted and historically mistaken. And those who want to bring in privacy to protect the personal are in reality doing the same disservice.

In fact, the moment this is shifted and geared to the question of the person, personal, and personality, given its difference with the private, the former cannot need the right to privacy. As a precondition, the person is the transcendental condition of the private—the latter comes into being by having the person as the life-communal background, but the reverse is not true. The right of privacy as an inflection of the private could only be posed when something is treated as property: one will argue, "this is my bodily data, I own my body integrally, therefore the body being my property, the biometric data is based on my property, it is (private) property data, and not personal data. Others (and the state has to be included among these insignificant others) have no right to it."

---

[15] Ibid., 211.
[16] "[T]he right to privacy, as a part of the more general right to the immunity of the person, the right to one's personality." See Samuel D. Warren and Louis D. Brandeis, "The Right to Privacy," *Harvard Law Review* 4, no. 5 (1890), 207.

But can this argument be sustained? Warren and Brandeis and a host of others—after a splendid and threatening detour in which they try to map everything from the right to withhold emotions or express them to that of right to intangible property such as art and literature—acknowledge in a lonely footnote that a friend's letter written to another friend will not ask for, or tolerate, the interference of the court. Our canonical description of friendship being the paradigm case of the personal that escapes legislation is stated here:

> The question will be whether … the court can take notice, as a case of civil property, which it is bound to protect. The injunction cannot be maintained on any principle of this sort, that if a letter has been written in the way of friendship, either the continuance or the discontinuance of the friendship affords a reason for the interference of the court.[17]

And their confession in similar cases is poignant, too:

> Not private property, unless that word be used in an extended and unusual sense. The principle which protects personal writings and any other productions of the intellect or of the emotions, is the right to privacy, and the law has no new principle to formulate when it extends this protection to the personal appearance, sayings, acts, and to personal relation, domestic or otherwise.[18]

Evidently, when property recedes, its abstract formulation "privacy" is pushed into being (and this is my canonical statement on my whole undertaking here), and Warren et al. are complicit with it. But that is sheer tautology; it is not enough on its own strength. The law including the right to privacy has not only new but no principle to promulgate when it comes to personal relations—evinced in the canonical cases we've referred to earlier (say, friendship, love)[19]—and it cannot work without a definition and designation of property. The argument acknowledges its failure but still it is not willing to do away with the wrong, and killing word "privacy." And a host of rulings and judgments could be culled from either side to justify our inference. A term that inhabits the site of the private and

---

[17] Ibid., 200.

[18] Ibid., 213.

[19] Does the uniform civil code envisage a new or a different notion of privacy in India? I'm grateful to Ayushi for attracting my attention to this question. See Ayushi Gupta, "The UCC Debate: Homely Mirage of a Reality" (Working paper no. 1A, 2017, Auro University, Surat, Gujarat) though this will not be answered here.

private property, by a shortcut, wants to relocate itself within the space of personal liberty, personal dignity, and inviolate personality. The privacy right—collectively speaking—is made up of negative rights and refers to negative liberty, while the all the *personal* three are positive and substantive. Their—and many contemporary ours—failure to incorporate them within the negative showcase of privacy has given rise to the flop connections between privacy, dignity, liberty and personality, and the judgements that have gone atrophy including the present Indian Supreme Court judgment which fails to distinguish and separate personality and privacy. To substitute these terms by just providing another chain of independent personalytic (independent of the private) terms—say, the right to inviolate personality or replacing intellectual property rights with "personal intellectual rights"—is not definitely our exercise, though interlocutors mad for a substitute could do well to receive them for a theatrical tryst.

However, a concrete example where such a right of personality—as an "other right" nearly separate from privacy—was attempted against public and private invasions and not through the sieve of property rights is here:

The BGH[20] developed a private law "right of personality" for the first time, as constitutionally guaranteed by Art. 1(1) (respect of human dignity) and Art. 2(1) GG (right to free development of the persona). The person has to be protected against the altered and unauthorised publication of his/her written expressions. Due to the Constitution, the general right of personality must be accepted as a constitutionally guaranteed fundamental right, which is not only directed against the State and its public bodies, but also against private parties (individuals, businesses) in their relations inter se. This led to the famous doctrine of "Drittwirkung" ("third party effect"/"horizontal effect").

In 1957, the general personality right was explicitly recognised as an "other right" [...]. Notwithstanding this, there is plain evidence that the "general personality right" is not an absolute property right which is regulated under § 823(1). The civil law protections of the personality were consolidated in a short period of time: through another landmark judgment in 1958, equitable monetary compensation (solatium/damages for pain and suffering/Schmerzensgeld) was made available in cases where the personality was gravely infringed; and interdictal/injunctive relief was made possible under § 1004 BGB (p. 23). Efforts to codify this new law

---

[20] Federal Court of Justice ( Bundegerichtshof or BGH)—one of the highest German courts.

on the protection of the personality had been attempted since the end of the 1950s, however these had not prospered.[21]

We must reconsider the moment and explore as to why Right of personality has not prospered. It is necessary to be cautioned not to fall in the same trap and try to make the personal falsely juridical. Our end declaration is crucial: if we decide to carry on with our clamor for privacy resting on the private and the notion of the property (privacy as "abstract private"), we go on fine, but let us not bring in the personal and forge a criminal connection. The personal is a freestanding conception and does not require the private; the private requires the personal, and in the previous chapter—particularly Chapters 3 and 4—we've discussed it enough. This exercise has been to reiterate the lessons.

But while we've described the privacy right—as being made up of negative rights and referring to negative liberty— which personality is not, and therefore, privacy fails to grasp and map the personal, and as shown earlier in the German example—those abortive attempts to legalize the personal and the personality have fallen short, too, though they are still to be credited with a historical independence from privacy as such. Then, what was historically and theoretically necessary was to allay the negativity and try and impregnate privacy with a positive content. Has it been attempted? Has it worked? Let us see for ourselves.

The second case now. To illustrate the impact of our intervention, after having examined a crucial legal case, I arrive at the second instance—a theoretical one where I document and critically inspect a failed attempt made in response to the private/public closure and the false resolution that it tries to offer.

In a significant addition to the public/private debate, Debra Morris in an otherwise illuminating essay[22] conceives rightly the crisis that governs [critical] theory today, which shelters, allegedly, a negative political theory of privacy in as much it thinks that "what is most singular, secret, ineffable, internal, that is, private" is translatable into a common language to enter the public domain of deliberation and scrutiny[23] and, thus, according to Morris, suggesting an abandonment of privacy. Morris'

---

[21] Gert Brüggemeier, Aurelia Colombi Ciacchi, and Patrick O'Callaghan, eds., *Personality Rights in European Tort Law* (Cambridge: Cambridge University Press, 2010), 23–24.
[22] Debra Morris, "Privacy, Privation, Perversity: Toward New Representations of the Personal," *Signs* 25 no. 2 (2000): 322–51.
[23] Ibid., 322.

solution is: "What is needed, then, is a positive political theory of privacy."²⁴
She argues her position through a three-pronged thicket: first, by arguing
privacy as a transitional phenomenon. Second, as against the claim that
identity movements "in politicizing the personal destroy the private,"²⁵ she
argues that they actually vindicate the private as a "higher order norm"
absolved of "a particular class of normalizing pressures and normalizing
judgments."²⁶ Third, she theorizes the private as that which ought to be a
relief from power (but not necessarily its opposite), a singular presence
("the need...for the time space and opportunity to come into one's own"),
etc. gained by resisting "systemic analysis and perfect representation."²⁷

It is not possible to engage in detail with Morris' text here since the
text of the present book itself founds and hazards the alternative, but it is
necessary to comment upon how her failure is exemplary and irreducible,
and why and how it informs our study. The first and the most formidable
objection to her oeuvre is that by suggesting an alternative vision of
privacy, she is operating well within the liberal contours of the private/
public distinction. And if privacy is theorized as a transitional phenomenon
(not conforming fully to private/public dichotomy) or as a right not to
communicate in acknowledgement that certain questions are not to be
formulated or asked—according to Morris—this alternative privacy would
signify " the necessity for a reprieve from scrutiny and public judgment."²⁸
To say the least, this is well within various legal juridical ramification
of the private all around the globe and available in various legal regimes
particularly theorized under the rubric of minority cultures, minority rights,
etc. In fact, the most delightful aspect of her oeuvre is that they reflect and
share the predicaments of discursive or deliberative democratic arguments
meant to refine public reasoning. That some participants have to be silenced
or excluded in order to keep the conversation going is well within the
communicative pragmatic dimension of deliberative, normative modes
of reasoning of communicative ethics and has nothing to with privacy
as singularity. And the right not to communicate in order to be granted as
a right first presupposes a consensus and, thus, communication.²⁹ Then

²⁴ Ibid.
²⁵ Ibid., 325.
²⁶ Ibid.
²⁷ Ibid., 326.
²⁸ Ibid., 331.
²⁹ For a verification of this view and other related debates see Seyla Benhabib and Fred
Dallmayr, ed., *The Communicative Ethics Controversy* (Cambridge, MA: The MIT
Press, 1990).

the burden to restore and maintain that right in every dimensional and situational validity also—if I may say so—"post-supposes" an ongoing communication.

Thus, with the significant failure of such attempts at discovering alternative notions of privacy and the circular detour of discovering—for instance—proletarian counter publics,[30] what we needed, thereby, was to go beyond these two categories and find the one that is in really the originary first (the pure personal-personal as against an impure private-personal) that has been there along: this work, if correct, has tried to recover and reinstate it.

# V

Therefore, we had begun recovering the personal (pace Nietzsche)—having been silenced in Greek—and now, when we've arrived, after a long and lasting detour, in 2017, then also we cannot but notice the personalization agenda being instituted through "personal care budgets". The right of privacy being mistaken to have been carrying a protective gear for inviolate personality but the personal/private difference being instituted could lead to illuminating results. The consequent implications of the personal/private distinction will have been clear by now; this is not a rarefied clarity—the consolation that might assume the semblance of an invitation: hereafter, may we be able to separate the personal and the private, the public and the *janta* (or nonpublic) for the times to come. An attempt at exploring the cultural-cognitive self-understanding of various communities will ease this process when a theoretical, universal attitude does not reap such results; that will engender a point of view from nowhere rather than simple ideologemes with or without commitment.

---

[30] An interesting acknowledgement is available with the classical public sphere theorist: (Habermas 1994, 425–30).

# Bibliography

Adam, William. *A Lecture on the Life and Labours of Rammohun Roy.* Edited by Rakhal Das Haldar. Calcutta: Sadharan Brahmo Samaj, 1977. First published in 1879.

Adorno, Theodor. "A Portrait of Walter Benjamin." In *Prisms*, translated by Samuel and Shierry Weber, 227–41. London: Neville Spearman, 1967.

———. "Letter to Walter Benjamin." In *Aesthetics and Politics*, edited by Ernst Bloch, Georg Lukacs, Bertolt Brecht, Walter Benjamin, Theodor Adorno, 110–33. London: Verso, 1980.

———. "Anti-Semitism and Fascist Propaganda." In *The Stars Down to Earth and Other Essays on the Irrational in Culture*, edited by Stephen Crook, 218–31. London: Routledge, 2002.

———. 1990. *Negative Dialectics.* Translated by E. B. Ashton. London: Routledge, 1990.

Adorno, Theodor, and Max Horkheimer. *Dialectic of Enlightenment.* Translated by J. Cumming. London: Verso, 1992.

Agamben, Giorgio. *Homo Sacer: Sovereign Power and Bare Life.* Translated by D. H. Roazen. Stanford, CA: Stanford University Press, 1998.

Agnew, Elizabeth N. *From Charity to Social Work: Mary E. Richmond and the Creation of an American Profession.* Urbana: University of Illinois Press, 2004.

Al–Azmeh, Aziz, ed. *Islamic Law: Social and Historical Contexts.* London: Routledge, 1988.

Amir Ali, 2001. "Evolution of Public Sphere in India." *Economic and Political Weekly* 36, no. 26 (2001): 2419–25.

Ambedkar, B. R. "Caste and Class." In *The Essential Writings of B. R. Ambedkar* edited by V. Rodrigues, 99–105. New Delhi: Oxford University Press, 2002.

———. "Reply to the Mahatma." In *The Essential Writings of B. R. Ambedkar*, 306–19. New Delhi: Oxford University Press, 2002.

Althusser, Louis. *Machiavelli and Us.* Translated by Gregory Eliott. London: Verso, 1999.

Applbaum, Arthur Isak. *Ethics for Adversaries: The Morality of Roles in Public and Professional Life.* Princeton, NJ: Princeton University Press, 1999.

Aristotle. *The Politics.* Translated by Benjamin Jowett. Cambridge: Cambridge University Press, 1988.

———. "Politics." In *The Basic Works of Aristotle*, edited by Richard McKeon, 1114–316. New York, NY: The Modern Library, 2001.

———. "Rhetorica." In *The Basic Works of Aristotle*, edited by Richard McKeon, 1325–451. New York, NY: The Modern Library, 2001.

Aiyar, P. Ramanath. *P. Ramanatha Aiyar's Concise Law Dictionary.* New Delhi, Wadhwa Company: 2004.

Bachelard, Gaston. "The Dialectics of Outside and Inside." In *The Continental Aesthetics Reader*, edited by Clive Cazeaux, 151–63. London: Routledge, 2000.

Bandyopadhyaya, Asit Kumar. *Bangla Sahityer Ittivritta,* Vol. IV [Bengali]. Calcutta: Modern Book Agency Pvt. Ltd, 1973.

Bandopadhyaya, Haricharan. *Bangiya Sabdakosh,* Vol. II [Bengali]. Kolkata: Sahitya Academy, 1966.

Bandyopadhyay, Sibaji. *"East" Meeting "West": A Note on Colonial Chronotopicity.* Calcutta: Jadavpur University, 1994.

Barker, Ernest. 'Introduction.' In *Natural Law and the Theory of Society 1500–1800* by Otto Gierke, edited and translated by Ernest Barker, ix–lxxxviii. Cambridge: Cambridge University Press, 1950.

———. *Political Thought in England 1848–1914.* London: Oxford University Press, 1951.

Barnes, Jonathan. *Early Greek Philosophy.* England: Penguin Books, 2001.

Basu, Pradip. ed. *Samayiki, puruno samoyik patrer prabandha samkalan,* Vol. 1 [Bengali], 1856–1901. Calcutta: Ananda Publishers, 1998.

Beckerlegge, Gwilym. "Swami Vivekananda and Seva: Taking Social Service Seriously." In *Swami Vivekananda and the Modernisation of Hinduism,* edited by William Radice, 45–58. New Delhi: Oxford University Press, 1999.

Bengtsson, Jan Olof. *The Worldview of Personalism: Origin and Early Development.* New York, NY: Oxford University Press, 2006.

Benhabib, Seyla, and Fred Dallmayr, eds. *The Communicative Ethics Controversy.* Cambridge, MA: The MIT Press, 1990.

Benjamin, Walter. "Outline of the Psychophysical Problem." In *Selected Writings: Vol 1, 1913–26,* edited by M. Bullock and M. W. Jennings, 393–401. Cambridge: Harvard University Press, 1996.

———. "Oedipus, or Rational Myth." In *Selected Writings,* Vol. 2, Part 2, 1931–34, edited and translated by R. Livingstone et al., and edited by M. W. Jennings and H. Eiland et al. Harvard University Press: Cambridge, 2005.

Bentham, Jeremy. *Bentham's Theory of Fictions.* Edited by C. K. Ogden. London: Kegan Paul, Trench, Trubner & Co., Ltd, 1932.

Benveniste, Emile. *Indo-European Language and Society.* Translated by Elizabeth Palmer. London: Faber and Faber Limited, 1973.

Berman, Marshall. *The Politics of Authenticity: Radical Individualism and the Emergence of Modern Society.* London: George Allen & Unwin Ltd, 1970.

Beistegui, Miguel de. *Heidegger & the Political.* London: Routledge, 1998.

Bellamy, Richard. 2010. "Dirty Hands and Clean Gloves: Liberal Ideals and Real Politics." *European Journal of Political Theory* 9, no. 4 (2010): 412–30.

BellHouse, Mary L. 1997. "Erotic 'Remedy' Prints and the Fall of the Aristocracy in Eighteenth Century France." *Political Theory* 25, no. 5 (1997): 680–715.

Berger, Ann. "The Popularity of Language: Rousseau and the Mother Tongue." In *The Politics of Deconstruction: Jacques Derrida and the Other of Philosophy,* edited by Martin McQuillan, 98–115. London: Pluto Press, 2007.

Beteille, Andre. *Equality and Universality: Essays in Social and Political Theory.* Delhi: Oxford University Press, 2003.

Bhabha, Homi. *The Location of Culture.* London: Routledge, 2009. First published in 1994.

Bhadra, Gautam. *Jal Rajar Katha: Bardhamaner Pratapchand* [Bengali]. *Kolkata:* Ananda Publishers, 2002.

Bhargava, Rajeev. "The Ethical Insufficiency of Egoism and Altruism: India in Transition." In *Indian Democracy: Meanings and Practices,* edited by Rajinder Vora and Suhas Palshkar, 215–32. New Delhi: SAGE Publications, 2004.

*Rammohan Samiksha* [Bengali] edited by D. K. Biswas. Kolkata: Saraswat Library, 1983.

Black, A. "The Individual and Society." In *The Cambridge History of Medieval Political Thought*, edited by J. H. Burns, 588–606. Cambridge: Cambridge University Press, 1988.

Blunt, Sir Edward, ed. *Social Service in India: An Introduction to Some Social and Economic Problems of the Indian People.* London: His Majesty's Stationery Office, 1939.

Bratsis, Peter. "The Construction of Corruption, or Rules of Separation and Illusions of Purity in Bourgeois Societies." *Social Text 77*, 21, no. 4 (2003): 9–33.

Briggs, Asa. "The Welfare State in Historical Perspective." In *The Welfare State: A Reader*, edited by Christopher Pierson and Francis G. Castles, 18–31. Cambridge: Polity Press & Blackwell Publishers, 2000.

Brüggemeier, Gert, Aurelia Colombi Ciacchi, and Patrick O'Callaghan, eds. *Personality Rights in European Tort Law.* Cambridge: Cambridge University Press, 2010.

Burnham, Douglas. "Heidegger, Kant and 'Dirty' Politics." *European Journal of Political Theory* 6, no.1 (2007): 67–86.

Butler, Judith. *Excitable Speech: A Politics of the Performative.* New York, NY: Routledge, 1997.

Calhoun, Craig. 1997. "Plurality, Promises, and Public Spaces." In *Hannah Arendt and the Meaning of Politics*, edited by Craig Calhoun and John McGrowan, 232–59. Minneapolis, MN, and London: University of Minnesota Press, 1997.

Calhoun, Craig, and John McGrowan, eds. *Hannah Arendt and the Meaning of Politics.* Minneapolis, MN, and London: University of Minnesota Press, 1997.

Calhoun, Laurie. "The Problem of 'Dirty Hands' and Corrupt Leadership." *The Independent Review* 8, no. 3 (2004): 363–85.

Caplan, Lionel. "Gifting and Receiving." In *Tradition, Pluralism and Identity: In Honour of T. N. Madan*, edited by Veena Das, Dipankar Gupta, and Patricia Uberoi, 283–305. New Delhi: SAGE Publications, 1999.

Carr, David. *Phenomenology and the Problem of History: A Study of Husserl's Transcendental Philosophy.* Evanston, IL: Northwestern University Press, 1974.

Chakraborty, Dipesh. *Habitations of Modernity: Essays in the Wake of Subaltern Studies.* New Delhi: Permanent Black, 2004.

———. *Provincializing Europe: Postcolonial Thought and Historical Difference.* Princeton, NJ: Princeton University Press, 2007.

Chatterjee, Anuradha. "Thoreau's Walden in Our Times in the Light of Transcendentalism." Unpublished PhD Dissertation. 2017.

Chatterjee (Chattopadhyaya), Arnab. 2005. "Private/Public Dwander Baire: Personal/ Byaktigoto Niye Notun Kichoo" [Bengali]. *Ababhas* 5, no. 3 (2005): 91–108.

———. "Beyond Private and Public: New Perspectives on Personal and Personalist Social Work." *The Indian Journal of Social Work* 67, no.3 (2006): 215–31.

———. Review article on Derrida. *Political Studies Review* 5, no. 1 (2007).

———. "Objective Helping, Hegel and Three Indian reformers in the Colonial Civil Society: Prefacing the Personalytical History of Social Work." *The Indian Journal of Social Work* 71, no. 2 (2010a): 145–66.

———. 2010b. "Is person/al the terrorized unity of private and public? Rethinking Gandhi, Integrationism & the Politics of Pure Means." *Sociological Bulletin: Journal of the Indian Sociological Society* 59, no. 3 (2010b): 407–22.

Chatterjee (Chattopadhyaya), Arnab. "Corporate Social Work or 'Being' Empowered and 'Doing' Empowerment: Preface to a Discourse Ethical Monitoring of the Capability Approach." *Journal of Human Values* 17, no. 2 (2011): 161–70.

———. *Categorical Blue: Personalytic Ethic in Social Work and Other Structures of Helping.* Shimla: Indian Institute of Advanced Study (IIAS), 2017.

Chatterjee, Basudev, ed. *Towards Freedom: Documents on the Movement for Independence in India, 1938, Part III,* 2417. New Delhi: Indian Council for Historical Research and Oxford University Press, 1999.

Chatterjee, Partha. 1986. "The Moment of Manoeuvre: Gandhi and the Critique of Civil Society." In *Nationalist Thought and the Colonial World: A Derivative Discourse?* 54–130. Delhi: Oxford University Press, 1986.

———. "Communities and the Nation." In *The Nation and Its Fragments.* Delhi: Oxford University Press, 1994.

———. "Democracy and the Violence of the State: A Political Negotiation of Death." Paper circulated for CSSS Cultural Studies Workshop at Bharatpur, Rajasthan, 1999.

———. Review of *Tika Tippani* by Pradyumna Bhattacharya. *Baromas* 20, no. 1 (2000): 175–77.

———. "On Civil and Political Society in Post Colonial Democracies." In *Civil Society: History and Possibilities,* edited by Sudipta Kaviraj and Sunil Khilnani, 165–78. Cambridge University Press, New Delhi: Foundation Books, 2002 (2001).

———. "Introduction: History in the Vernacular." In *History in the Vernacular,* edited by Raziuddin Aquil and Partha Chatterjee, 1–24. New Delhi: Permanent Black, 2008.

Chattopadhyay (Chatterjee), Bankimchandra. Review of *Hindudharmer Sreshthata* by Rajnarayan Basu [Bengali]. *Bankim Rachanabali* Vol. II, 6th ed. Calcutta: Sahitya Samsad, 1977.

———. *Dharmatattva.* Translated by Apratim Ray. New Delhi: Oxford University Press, (1888) 2003.

Chiesa, Lorenzo. *Subjectivity and Otherness: Philosophical Reading of Lacan.* Cambridge, MA: The MIT Press, 2007.

Cicero. "Attack on an Enemy of Freedom (The Second Philippic Against Antony)." In *Selected Works,* 101–153, translated by M. Grant. England: Penguin Books, 1981.

Cicero. "De Oratore" and "Orator." In *The Rhetorical Tradition*: Readings from Classical Times to the Present. 2nd Ed. edited by. Patricia Bizzell and Bruce Herzberg, pp. 283–343. New York: Bedford St. Martin's, 2001.

Clarke, C. L., and S. Asquith. 1985. "The Person and Moral Agency." In *Social Work and Social Philosophy: A Guide for Practice,* 6–22. Boston, MA: Routledge and Kegan Paul, 1985.

Coady, C. A. J. 1993. "Politics and the Problem of Dirty Hands." In *A Companion to Ethics,* edited by Peter Singer, 373–83. UK: Blackwell, 1993.

Cohen, Lawrence. 1999. "Holi in Banaras and the Mahaland of Modernity." *GLQ: A Journal of Gay and Lesbian Studies* 2, no. 4 (1999): 399–424.

Copleston, Frederick. *A History of Philosophy,* Vol. IX (Maine De Biran to Sartre). London: Search Press, 1975.

Cornwell, Benjamin. "The Protestant Sect Credit Machine: Social Capital and the Rise of Capitalism." *Journal of Classical Sociology* 7, no. 3 (2007): 267–90.

Crowell, Steven Galt. "Who is the Political Actor? An Existential Phenomenological Approach." In *Phenomenology of the Political,* edited by Kevin Thompson and Lester Embree, 11–28. Boston: Kluwer Academic Publishers, 2000.

Bibliography **241**

Darnton, Robert. *The Forbidden Best-sellers of Pre-revolutionary France*, New York, NY: Norton, 1995.

Dasgupta, Sugata, ed. *Towards a Philosophy of Social Work in India*. New Delhi: Popular Book Services, 1967.

Delon, Michel, ed. *Encyclopedia of Enlightenment*, Vol 1. Chicago, IL: Fitzroy Dearborn Publishers, 2001.

De Man, Paul. "Return to Philology." In *Resistance to Theory*, edited by Wlad Godzich, 21–26. Minneapolis, MN: Minnesota University Press, 1986.

Derrida, Jacques. *Spurs: Nietzsche's Styles*. Chicago: The University of Chicago Press, 1979.

———. *The Gift of Death*. Translated by David Wills. Chicago: The University of Chicago Press, 1995.

———. "Des Tours de Babel." In *Psyche, Inventions of the Other*, Vol. 1, edited by Peggy Kamuf and Elizabeth Rottenberg, 191–225. California: Stanford University Press, 2007.

Desai, Murli. *Ideologies and Social Work: Historical and Contemporary Analyses*. Jaipur: Rawat Publications, 2002.

Digester, Peter. "Forgiveness and Politics: Dirty Hands and Imperfect Procedures." *Political Theory* 26, no. 5 (1998): 700–24.

Douglas, Mary. 1990. "Foreward." In *The Gift: The Form and Reason for Exchange in Archaic Societies*, translated by W. D. Halls, vii–xviii. London: Routledge, 1990.

Drabinski, John. "The Possibility of an Ethical Politics: From Peace to Liturgy." *Philosophy and Social Criticism* 26, no.4 (2000): 49–73.

Duby, Georges. 1990. "The Diffusion of Cultural Patterns in Feudal Society." In *French Studies in History*, Vol. II, edited by Maurice Aymard and Harbans Mukhia. 214–22. Hyderabad: Orient Longman, 1988.

Dutta, Bhabatosh. 2003. "Banglar Jagorone missonarir daan." In *Unish Sataker Bangalijiban O Sanskriti*, edited by Swapan Basu and Indrajit Choudhury. Kolkata: Pustakbiponi, 2003.

Eagleton, Terry. *Trouble with Strangers: A Study of Ethics*. Sussex, UK: Wiley-Blackwell, 2008.

Elias, Norbert. *The Civilizing Process (The History of Manners)*. Translated by E. Jephcott. Oxford: Basil Blackwell, 1978.

———. "Time and Timing." In *On Civilization, Power and Knowledge: Selected Writings*, edited by S. Mennell and J. Goudsblom, 253–59. Chicago: The University of Chicago Press, 1998.

Elster, Jon. "Introduction." In *The Multiple Self*, edited by Jon Elster, 1–34. Cambridge, MA: Cambridge University Press, 1986.

Evans, Eric J., ed. *Social Policy, 1830–1914: Individualism, Collectivism and the Origins of the Welfare State*, 102–03. London: Routledge & Kegan Paul, 1978.

Farndale, Nigel. 2002. "Geoffrey Boycott." In *Flirtation Seduction Betrayal: Interviews with Heroes and Villains*, 33–41. London: Constable & Robnson Ltd, 2002.

Farris, Sara R. *Max Weber's Theory of Personality: Individuation, Politics and Orientalism in the Sociology of Religion*. Brill: Leiden, 2013.

Fischer, Karl. "Karl Fischer's Review of The Protestant Ethic, 1907." In *The Protestant Ethic Debate: Max Weber's Replies to his Critics 1907–10*, edited by David J. Chalcraft and Austin Harrington, translated by Austin Harrington and Mary Shields, 27–29. Liverpool: Liverpool University Press, 2001.

Flahault, Francois. *Malice*. Translated by Liz Heron. London: Verso, 2003.

Foucault, Michel. "A Preface to Transgression." In *Essential Works: Aesthetics, Method and Epistemology*, Vol. 2, 69–87. London: Penguin: Books, 2000.

Foucault, Michel. "Politics and Reason." In *Politics, Philosophy, Culture: Interviews and Other Writings 1977–84*, edited by Lawrence D. Kritzman, 57–85. New York: Routledge, 1990.

Foucault, Michel. "Subjectivity and Truth." In *The Politics of Truth*, edited by Sylvere Lotringer and Lysa Hochroth, 171–98. New York, NY: Semiotext(e), 1997.

Freud, Sigmund. "Group Psychology and the Analysis of the Ego." In *Civilization, Society and Religion*, Vol. 12, translated by Sigmund Freud and James Stratchey, 89–184. New Delhi: Shrijee's Book International, 2003.

Fruzzeti, Lina, Akos Ostor, and Steve Burnett. "The Cultural Construction of the Person in Bengal and Tamil Nadu." In *Concepts of Person: Kinship, Caste and Marriage in India*, edited by Akos Ostor, Lina Fruzzeti and Steve Burnett, 8–30. New Delhi: Oxford University Press, 1983.

Galanter, Marc. *Law and Society in Modern India*. Bombay: Oxford University Press, 1992.

Gandhi, M. K. *Prohibition at Any Cost*. Compiled by R. K. Prabhu. Ahmedabad: Navajivan Publishing House, 1960a.

———. *Voluntary Poverty* (Compiled by R. K Prabhu). Ahmedabad: Navajivan Publishing House, 1960b.

———. *Collected Works of Mahatma Gandhi*, Vol. 25. India: The Publications Division, Ministry of Information and Broadcasting, Government of India, 1967.

———. *The Essential Writings of Mahatma Gandhi*. Edited by Raghavan Iyer. Delhi: Oxford University Press, 1991.

———. 1996/1991. *The Essential Writings of Mahatma Gandhi* (ed. Raghavan Iyer). New Delhi: Oxford University Press.

———. *M.K. Gandhi's Hind Swaraj: A Critical Edition*. Edited by Suresh Sharma and Tridip Suhrud. New Delhi: Orient Blackswan, 2010.

Gaston, Sean. *Derrida and Disinterest*. Continuum: London, 2005.

Geras, Norman. "Seven Types of Obloquy: Travesties of Marxism." In *Socialist Register*, edited by Ralph Miliband, Leo Panitch, and John Saville, 1–34. London: The Merlin Press, 1990.

Galinsky, Judah D. "Jewish Charitable Bequests and Hekdesh Trust in Thirteenth-Century Spain." *Journal of Interdisciplinary History* 34, no. 3 (2005): 423–40.

Gellner, Ernest. *Reason and Culture: The Historic Role of Rationality and Rationalism*. UK: Blackwell, 1992.

Gifford, Terry. *Pastoral*. London: Routledge, 1999.

Goldsmith, M. M. *Private Vices, Public Benefits: Bernard Mandeville's Political Thought*. Cambridge: Cambridge University Press, 1985.

Gonda, J. 1964. *'Gifts' and 'Giving' in the Rigveda*. Hosiarpur: Vishveshvaranand Vedic Research Institute, Sadhu Ashram, 1964. (Reprinted from *Vishveshvaranand Indological Journal* 2, no. 1 (1964).

Gore, M. S. "The Professional Social Worker." In *History and Philosophy of Social Work in India*, edited by A. R. Wadia. Bombay: Allied Publishers Private Limited, 1968, 27–34.

Griffin Leslie. "The Problem of Dirty Hands." *The Journal of Religious Ethics* 17, no. 1 (1989): 31–61.

Gross, Robert A. "Giving in America: From Charity to Philanthropy." In *Charity, Philanthropy and Civility in American History*, edited by Lawrence Friedman and Mark D. McGarvie, 29–48. Cambridge University Press: Cambridge, 2002.

Guha, Ranajit. *History at the Limit of World-History*. New Delhi: Oxford University Press, 2003.

Gupta, Dipankar. "The Domesticated Public: Tradition, Modernity and the Public/Private Divide." In *The Public and the Private Issues of Democratic Citizenship*, edited by Gurpreet Mahajan, 56–73. New Delhi: SAGE Publications, 2003.

Guthrie, W. K. C. *A History of Greek Philosophy, The Earlier PreSocratics and the Pythagoreans*, Vol. 1. London: Cambridge University Press, 1962.

Habermas, Jurgen. "The Public Sphere: An Encyclopedia Article." *New German Critique* 3, no. 51 (1974): 49–55.

———. "The New Obscurity: The Crisis of the Welfare State and the Exhaustion of Utopian Energies." In *The New Conservatism: Cultural Criticism and the Historians' Debate*, translated by S. W. Nicholsen, 48–70. Cambridge: Polity Press, 1989.

———. *The Philosophical Discourse of Modernity: Twelve Lectures*. Translated by Frederick Lawrence. Cambridge, MA: MIT Press Cambridge, 1993.

———. *The Structural Transformation of the Public Sphere: An Inquiry into a Category of Bourgeois Society*. Translated by T. Berger. Great Britain: Blackwell Publishers & Polity Press, 1996a.

———. "Further Reflections on the Public Sphere's." In *Habermas and the Public Sphere*, edited by Craig Calhoun, 421–61. Cambridge, MA: The MIT Press, 1996b.

———. *The Inclusion of the Other: Studies in Political Theory*. Cambridge, MA: The MIT Press, 1998.

———. "Walter Benjamin: Consciousness-Raising or Rescuing Critique." In *On Walter Benjamin: Critical Essays and Recollections*, edited by Gary Smith, 90–128. Cambridge, MA: The MIT Press, 1999.

———. *Truth and Justification*. Edited and translated by Barbara Fultner. Cambridge, MA: The MIT Press, 2003.

Haldar, Hiralal. *Hegelianism and Human Personality*. Calcutta: University of Calcutta, 1910.

———. *Neo Hegelianism*. London: Heath Cranton Ltd, 1927.

Hamacher, Werner. "The Promise of Interpretation: Reflections on the Hermeneutical Imperative in Kant and Nietzsche." In *Looking After Nietzsche*, edited by Lawrence A. Rickels, 19–47. Albany, NY: State University of New York Press, 1990.

———. *Premises: Essays on Philosophy and Literature from Kant to Celan*. Translated by Peter Fenves. Cambridge, MA: Harvard University Press, 1990.

———. *Pleroma—Reading in Hegel: The Genesis and Structure of a Dialectical Hermeneutics in Hegel*. Translated by N. Walker and S. Jarvis. London: The Athlone Press, 1998.

Hands, A. R. *Charities and Social Aid in Greece and Rome*. Great Britain: Thames and Hudson, 1968.

Harbans Mukhia, ed. *French Studies in History*, Vol. II, 214–22. Hyderabad: Orient Longman, 1988.

Hardiman, David. *Gandhi in His Time and Ours*. Delhi: Permanent Black, 2003.

Hastings, James. "Altruism." In *Encyclopaedia of Religion and Ethics*, Vol. 1, 354–58. Edinburgh: T&T Clark, 1974 (1908).

Heidegger, Martin. *The Question of Being*. Translated by W. Kluback and J. T. Wilde. New York, NY: Twayne Publishers, 1956.

———. *Being and Time*. Translated by J. Macquarrie and E. Robinson. San Francisco, CA: Harpe, 1962.

Heidegger, Martin. What is Called Thinking? Translated by J. Glenn Gray, 62. New York, NY: Perennial, 1976.

Heidegger, Martin. *Early Greek Thinking*. Translated by D. F. Krell and F. A. Capuzzi. San Francisco, CA: Harper and Row, 1984.

Hegel, G. W. F. *Hegel's Philosophy of Mind* (Translated from *The Encyclopaedia of the Philosophical Sciences)*. Translated by William Wallace. Oxford: Clarendon Press, 1894.

———. *Lectures on the Philosophy of Religion,* Vol. II. Translated by Rev E. B. Speirs and J. Burdon Sanderson. London: Kegan Paul, Trench, Trubner & Co. Ltd, 1895.

———. *Hegel's Lectures on the History of Philosophy,* Vol. 1. Translated by E. S. Haldane. London: Routledge & Kegan Paul, 1955 (1892).

———. "Love." In *On Christianity: Early Theological Writings*. Translated by T. M. Knox. New York, NY: Harper Torchbooks, 1961, 302–08.

———. *Hegel's Philosophy of Nature*. Translated by A. V. Miller. Oxford: Clarendon Press, 1970.

———. *Natural Law*. Translated by T. M. Knox. Philadelphia: University of Pennsylvania Press, 1970.

———. *The Philosophy of Subjective Spirit,* Vol. II. Translated by M. J. Petry. Holland: D. Reidelberg Company, 1979.

———. *Lectures on the philosophy of World History, Introduction: Reason in History*. Translated by H. B. Cambridge: Cambridge University Press, 1987.

———. *Lectures on the Philosophy of Religion* (One Volume Edition, The Lectures of 1827). Edited by Peter C. Hodgson, translated by R. F. Brown, P. C. Hodgson and J. M. Stewart. Berkley, CA: University of California Press, 1988.

———. *Elements of the Philosophy of Right*. Translated by H. B. Nisbet. UK: Cambridge University Press, 1991.

———. *Phenomenology of Spirit*. Translated by A. V. Miller. Delhi: Motilal Banarasidass Publishers, 1998a.

———. "The Difference Between Fichte's and Schelling's System of Philosophy: The Need of Philosophy." In *The Hegel Reader,* edited by Stephen Houlgate, 40–43. UK: Blackwell Publishers, 1998b.

Heyd, David. *Supererogation: Its Status in Ethical Theory*. Cambridge: Cambridge University Press, 1982.

Hobbes, Thomas. *Leviathan.* New York, NY: W. W. Norton & Company, 1997.

Hocart, A. M. *Kingship*. London: Oxford University Press, 1927.

Hobbes, Thomas. *Leviathan*, 1998. Ed. J. C. A. Gaskin, Oxford, New York: Oxford University Press.

Hobbes, Thomas. (1969 edition) 2013. The *Elements of Law : Natural and Politic*. Edited by Ferdinand Tonnies, New York: Routledge.

Holland, Sir Thomas Erskine. 1924. *Elements of Jurisprudence*, Calcutta: Progressive Publishers.

Hollis, Martin. "Dirty Hands." *British Journal of Political Science* 12, no. 4 (1982): 385–98.

Horden, Peregrine. 2005. 'The Earliest Hospitals in Byzantium, Western Europe, and Islam,' *Journal of Interdisciplinary History* 34, no. 3 (2005): 361–89.

Hussey, Edward. *The Presocratics,* London: Duckworth, 1983.

Hyppolite, Jean. *Studies on Marx and Hegel*. Translated by John O'Neill. New York, NY: Harper & Row Publishers, 1969.

———. *Genesis and Structure of Hegel's Phenomenology of Spirit*. Translated by S. Cherniak and J. Heckman. Evanston, IL: Northwestern University Press, 1974.

Irwin, T. H. 1999. "Generosity and Property in Aristotle's *Politics.*" *Social Philosophy and Policy* 4, no. 2 (1999): 37–54. (In *Aristotle: Critical Assessments,* Vol. IV, edited by Lloyd P. Gerson, 164–81. London: Routledge, 1999.)

Jacobs, Sally, Jessica Abell, Martin Stevens, Mark Wilberforce, David Challis, Jill Manthorpe, Jose-Luis Fernandez, Caroline Glendinning, Karen Jones, Martin Knapp, Nicola Moran, and Ann Netten. "The Personalization of CARE Services and the Early Impact on Staff Activity Patterns." *Journal of Social Work* 13, no. 2 (2011): 141–63.

James, Henry. "The Turn of the Screw." In *The Great Short Novels of Henry James.* Mumbai, India: Jaico Publishing House, 2002, 627–748.

Jayakar, M. R. *The Story of My Life,* Vol. II. Bombay: Asia Publishing House, 1958.

Jones, Gareth Stedman. "Hegel and the Economics of Civil Society." In *Civil Society: History and Possibilities,* edited by Sudipta Kaviraj and Sunil Khilnani, 105–30. Cambridge: Cambridge University Press: Cambridge, 2002.

Kant, Immanuel. *Lectures on Ethics.* Translated by Louis Infield. New York, NY: Harper and Row: New York, 1963.

———. 'What is Enlightenment?' In *Critique of Practical Reason, and Other Writings in Moral Philosophy,* edited by Immanuel Kant, Lewis White Beck. New York, NY: Garland Publishing, 1976.

———. *Practical Philosophy.* UK: Cambridge University Press, 1999.

Keith-Lucas, Alan. 1976. "The Art and Science of Helping." In *Talking About Welfare: Readings in Philosophy and Social Policy,* edited by Noel Timms and David Watson. London: Routledge and Kegan Paul, 267–89.

Kenaan, Hagi. *The Present Personal: Philosophy and the Hidden Face of Language.* New York, NY: Columbia University Press, 2005.

Kisiel, Theodore. *The Genesis of Heidegger's Being and Time.* Berkley, CA: University of California Press, 1993.

Klain, Maurice. "'Politics': Still a Dirty Word." *The Antioch Review* 15, no. 4 (1955): 457–66.

Klossowski, Pierre. *Nietzsche and the Vicious Circle.* Translated by Daniel W. Smith. London: Continuum, 2005 (1997).

Kristol, Irving. "Machiavelli and the Profanation of Politics." In his *Reflections of a Neo Conservative: Looking Back, Looking Beyond,* 123–35. New Delhi: Allied Publishers, 1986.

Koestler, Arthur. 1969. "Darkness at Noon." In *The Political Imagination in Literature,* edited by Philip Green and Michael Walzer. New Yok, NY: The Free Press, 192–205.

Kofman, Sarah. *Nietzsche and Metaphor.* Translated by Duncan Large. Stanford, CA: Stanford University Press, 1993.

Kojeve, Alexandre. *Outline of a Phenomenology of Right.* Translated by B. P. Frost and R. Howse. Lanham, MD: Rowman & Littlefield Publishers Inc, 2007.

Kumar, Hajira. *Social Work: An Experience and Experiment in India.* New Delhi: Gitanjali Publishing House, 1994.

Lacoue-Labarthe, Philippe and Nancy Jean-Luc. *Retreating the Political,* xiv–xxviii. Edited by Simon Parks. London: Routledge, 1997.

Laclau, Ernesto and Lilian Zac. "Minding the Gap: The Subject of Politics." In *The Making of Political Identities,* edited by Ernesto Laclau, 11–39. London: Verso, 1994.

Laski, Harold J. *The Foundations of Sovereignty.* London: George Allen & Unwin Ltd, 1931 (1921).

Lefort, Claude. "The Image of the Body and Totalitarianism." In *The Political forms of Modern Society*, edited by John B. Thompson, 292–306. Delhi: Disha Publications, 1989.

Lewis, William. "Savings Banks." In *Social Policy, 1830–1914* edited by Evans, 1978.

Levinas, Emmanuel. *Totality and Infinity: An Essay on Exteriority.* Translated by Alphonso Lingis. Pittsburgh, PA: Duquesne University Press, 2000.

Levinas, Emmanuel. "A Man-God?" In *Entre Nous: Thinking-of-the-other.* Translated by Michael B. Smith and Barbara Harshav. London: Continuum, 2007, 46–52.

Levinas, Emmanuel. *Entre Nous: Thinking–of-the-Other.* Translated by Michael B. Smith and Barbara Harshav. London: Continuum, 2007.

———. "Is Ontology Fundamental." In *Entre Nous: Thinking-of-the-Other,* translated by Michael B. Smith and Barbara Harshav, 1–10. London: Continuum, 2007.

Lloyd, Vincent. "On Gillian Rose and Love." *Telos* 2008, no. 143 (2008): 47–62.

Locke, John. *Two Treatises of Government.* London: J.M Dent & Son's Ltd. (Everyman's Library), 1982 (1924).

Long, Joseph R. "Notes on Roman Law: Law of Persons, Law of Contracts." 1912. Available at: https://archive.org/stream/cu31924021206804/cu31924021206804_djvu. txt (accessed on August 11, 2017).

Luhmann, Niklas. *Political Theory in the Welfare State.* Translated by John Bednarz Jr. New York, NY: Walter De Gruyter Berlin, 1990.

Lymbery, Mark. Review of Catherine Needham, *Personalising Public Services: Understanding the Personalisation Narrative* (Bristol: Policy Press, 2013). *Critical Social Policy* 33, no. 1 (2013): 187–89.

Lyotard, Jean-Francois. "The Desire Named Marx." In *Libidinal Economy,* translated by I. H. Grant, 94–150. London: Continuum, 2005 (1993).

Machiavelli, Niccolo. *The Prince.* Translated and edited by Robert M. Adams. New York, NY: W.W. Norton & Company, 1992.

MacIntyre, Alisdair. *After Virtue: A Study in Moral Theory,* 2nd ed. Indiana: University of Notre Dame, 1984.

Macpherson, C. B. "The Theory of Property Right." In *The Political Theory of Possessive Individualism, Hobbes to Locke,* 197–221. London: Oxford University Press, 1972.

Madan, T. N. "Of the Social Categories 'Private' and 'Public': Considerations of Cultural Context." In Mahajan, 88–102, 2003.

Maitland, F. W. *State, Trust and Corporation.* Edited by D. Runciman and M. Ryan. Cambridge: Cambridge University Press, 2003.

Malatesta, Maria. *Professional Men, Professional Women: The European Professions from the Nineteenth Century until Today.* Translated by A. Belton. Los Angeles, CA: SAGE Publications, 2011.

Manning, Paul. "Owning and Belonging: A Semiotic Investigation of the Affective Categories of a Bourgeois Society." *Comparative Studies in Society and History* 46, no. 2 (2004): 300–25.

Manshardt, Clifford. "Social Work During the British Period." In *History and Philosophy of Social Work in India,* edited by A. R. Wadia, 25–35. Bombay: Allied Publishers Private Limited, 1968.

Marshall, T. H. *Social Policy.* London: Hutchinson University Library, 1965.

———. "Voluntary Action." In *Sociology at the Crossroads and other Essays*, 329–41. London: Heinemann, 1963a.

———. "The Recent History of Professionalism in Relation to Social Structure and Social Policy." In *Sociology at the Cross Roads,* 150–70. 1963b.

———. "Citizenship and Social Class." In *The Foundations of the Welfare State*, Vol. 1. Edited by Robert E. Goodin and Deborah Mitchell. UK: Edward Elgar Publishing Ltd, 2000.

Marx, Karl. *Selected Writings in Sociology and Social Philosophy.* Edited by T. B. Bottomore and M. Rubel. Harmondsworth: Penguin Books, 1961.

———. *"A Contribution to the Critique of Hegel's 'Philosophy of Right' (1843)."* In *The Young Hegelians: An Anthology,* edited by L. S. Stepelevich, 310–22. Cambridge: Cambridge University Press, 1983.

Martinich, A. P. *A Hobbes Dictionary*, Cambridge: Blackwell, 1995.

Mathews, John H. *Treatise on the Doctrine of Presumption and Presumptive Evidence as Affecting the Title to Real and Personal Property.* London: Joseph Butterworth and Son, Law Booksellers, 1827.

Max Mueller, F. "Keshub Chunder Sen." In *Keshub Chunder Sen,* edited by Nanda Mukherjee, Calcutta: F. Max Mueller, 1976.

McCalman, Iain. *Radical Underworld, Prophets, revolutionaries, and Pornographers in London, 1795–1840.* Oxford: Clarendon Press, 1993.

McIntosh, Marjorie K. "Poverty, Charity, and Coercion in Elizabethan England." *Journal of Interdisciplinary History* 34, no. 3 (2005): 423–40.

McTaggart, J. E. "The Personality of the Absolute." In *Studies in Hegelian Cosmology.* Available at: http://www.marxists.org/reference/archive/mctaggart/cosmology/ch03. htm, para 70 (accessed on July 13, 2008).

McTaggart, J. E., and Ellis McTagart. *Studies in Hegelian Cosmology.* Cambridge: Cambridge University Press, 1918 (1901).

Mead, George H. *Mind, Self, and Society, From the Standpoint of a Social Behaviorist.* Edited by Charles W. Morris. Chicago, IL: The University of Chicago Press, 1972 (1934).

Mill, John Stuart. "On Liberty." In *Utilitarianism, Liberty and Representative Government.* New York, NY: J. M. Dent and Sons Ltd, 1936 (1910).

Molesworth, W. N. "Co-operation." In *Social Policy, 1830–1914: Individualism, Collectivism and the Origins of the Welfare State*, edited by Eric J. Evans. London: Routledge & Kegan Paul, 1978.

Monahan, Arthur. *From Personal Duties towards Personal Rights: Late Medieval and Early Modern Political thought, 1300–1600.* Montreal: McGill Queens University Press, 1994.

Montefiore, Alan. "Identity and Integrity." In *Multiculturalism, Liberalism and Democracy,* edited by Rajeev Bhargava, Amiya Bagchi and R. Sudarshan, 58–79. New Delhi: Oxford University Press, 1999.

Morales, Armado T., and Bradford W. Sheafor. *Social Work: A Profession of Many Faces.* Boston: Allyn and Bacon, 1998 (1977).

Morris, Debra. 2000. "Privacy, Privation, Perversity: Toward New Representations of the Personal." *Signs* 25, no. 2 (2000): 322–51.

Morris, Meaghan. *The Pirate's Fiancee.* London: Verso, 1988.

Mukhopadhyaya, Bhudeb. *Samajik Probondho* in *Bhuudeb Rachanasambhar*, 1–263. Edited by Pramathanath Bishi. Kolkata: Mitra O Ghosh, 1968.

Nagel, Thomas. *The Possibility of Altruism.* Princeton, NJ: Princeton University Press, 1978.

Nair, Janaki. "Beauty by Banning." *The Telegraph*, Kolkata, October 23, 2003.

Nancy, Jean Luc. "Shattered Love." In *A Finite Thinking*, edited by Simon Parks, 245–74. Stanford, CA: Stanford University Press, 2003.

Nandy, Ashis. *The Illegitimacy of Nationalism: Rabindranath Tagore and the Politics of Self*, in his *Return from Exile*, 1–94. New Delhi: Oxford University Press, 2001 (1998).

Nehru, Motilal. *Selected Works of Motilal Nehru,* Vol. 3. Edited by Ravinder Kumar and D. N. Panigrahi. New Delhi: Vikas Publishing House Pvt. Limited, 1984.

Nickel, James W. *Making Sense of Human Rights: Philosophical Reflections on the Universal Declaration of Human Rights.* Berkeley, CA: University of California Press, 1987.

Nietzsche, Friedrich. "Philosophy During the Tragic Age of the Greeks (1873)." In *Early Greek Philosophy and other Essays,* translated by Maximilian A. Mugge, 71–170. London: T. N. Foulis, 1911.

Nietzsche, Friedrich. *The Will to Power*. Translated by Walter Kaufmann and R. J. Hollingdale. New York, NY: Vintage Books, 1968.

———. *On the Genealogy of Morals and Ecce Homo*. Translated by Walter Kaufman and R. J. Hollingdale. New York, NY: Vintage Books, 1989.

———. *Basic Writings of Nietzsche*. Translated by Walter Kaufmann. New York, NY: The Modern Library, 2000.

———. *On the Genealogy of Morals* in *Basic Writings of Nietzsche*, 437–599. Translated by Walter Kaufmann. New York: The Modern Library, 2000.

———. *Beyond Good and Evil: Prelude to a Philosophy of the Future* in Walter Kaufmann (transl. & ed.) *Basic Writings of Nietzsche*, 179–436. New York: The Modern Library, 2000.

———. *Writings from the Late Notebooks*. Translated by Kate Sturge. Cambridge: Cambridge University Press, 2003.

———. *The Anti-Christ, Ecce Homo, Twilight of the Idols, and Other Writings*, 69–151. Translated by Judith Norman. UK: Cambridge University Press, 2006.

———. "Homer and Classical Philology." In *The Complete Works of Friedrich Nietzsche*, Vol. III, edited by Oscar Levy, translated by J. M. Kennedy, 1910. Available as Project Gutenberg E-Book #18188, Released on April 17, 2006 (accessed on October 8, 2008).

———. *Nietzsche: Selected Stories*. New Delhi: Mahaveer Publishers, 2011.

Nivedita Sister. "The Civic Ideal." In *Civic Ideal and Indian Nationality in The Complete works of Sister Nivedita*, Vol. IV, 205–325. Calcutta: Advaita Ashrama, 1996.

Nivedita, Sister. "The Civic Ideal." *The Modern Review* 3, no. 1 (1908): 1–4.

Oosterhout, J. Van. *The Quest for Legitimacy: On Authority and Responsibility in Governance*. Rotterdam: Erasmus Research Institute of Management (ERIM), Erasmus University, 2000.

Owen, David. *Maturity and Modernity: Nietzsche, Weber, Foucault and the Ambivalence of Reason*. New York, NY: Routledge, 1994.

Parent, W. A. "Privacy, Morality, and the Law." *Philosophy and Public Affairs* 12, no. 4 (2003): 269–88.

Parfit, Derek. *Reasons and Persons*, Oxford: Clarendon Press, 1986.

Pateman, Carole. "Hegel, Marriage, and the Standpoint of Contract." In *Feminist Interpretations of G. W. F. Hegel*, edited by Patricia Jagentowicz Mills, 209–23. University Park: The Pennsylvania State University Press, 1996.

Perlman, Harris Helen. "The Person." In *Social Case Work: A Problem Solving Process*, 6–26. Chicago, IL: The University of Chicago Press, 1957.

Pierce, Charles Sanders. "The Principles of Phenomenology." In *Philosophical Writings of Pierce*, edited by Justus Buchler, 75–97. New York, NY: Dover Publications, 1955.

Plato. "Apology." In *The Trial and Death of Socrates*, translated by G. M. A. Grube, 21–42. Cambridge, MA: Hackett Publishing Company Inc, 1975.

Pollock, Sir Frederick, and Frederic William Maitland. *The History of English Law*, Vol. 1. Cambridge: Cambridge University Press, 1952.

Pratt, J. Tidd. "The Principles of Friendly Societies." In *Social Policy, 1830–1914: Individualism, Collectivism and the Origins of the welfare state*, edited by Eric J. Evans, 104 London: Routledge & Kegan Paul, 1978.

Rawls, John. *A Theory of Justice*. Oxford: Oxford University Press, 1999.

Ray, Rajat Kanta. *The Felt Community, Commonality and Mentality Before the Emergence of Indian Nationalism*. New Delhi: Oxford University Press, 2003.

Reamer, Frederic. *Social Work Values and Ethics*. Jaipur: Rawat Publications, 2005.

Reeve, Andrew. *Property*. London: Macmillan, 1986.

Rojek, Chris, Geraldine Peacock, and Stewart Collins. *Social Work and Received Ideas*. London: Routledge, 1988.

Rose, Gillian. *Hegel Contra Sociology*. London: Athlone, 1981.

———. *Dialectic of Nihilism: Post-structuralism and Law*. England: Basil Blackwell, 1984.

Rousseau, Jean Jacques. *The Social Contract*. Translated by Maurice Cranston. Harmondsworth: Penguin, 1984.

———. *The Social Contract and the First and Second Discourses*. Edited by Susan Dunn. New Haven, CT: Yale University Pres, 2002.

Roy, Motilal. *Bharatiya Samgha Tatva* [Bengali]. Prabartak Publishing House: Kolkata, 1932.

Ruben, David-Hill. "Review of *The Reality of Social Groups* by Paul Sheehy." *Mind* 117, no. 467 (2008): 731–35.

Runciman, David. *Pluralism and the Personality of the State*. Cambridge, UK: Cambridge University Press, 2003.

Ruud, Arild Engelsen. *Poetics of Village Politics, The Making of West Bengal's Rural Communism*. New Delhi: Oxford University Press, 2003.

Sacks, David. *Encyclopedia of the Ancient Greek World*. New York, NY: Facts on File, Inc, 1995.

Said, Edward. *Orientalism*. New Delhi: Penguin Books, 2001 (1978).

Sarbagananda, Swami. *Bhavprachar O Samgathan*, [Bengali]. Kolkata: Udbodhon Karyalaya, 2003.

Sarkar, Benoy Kumar. *The Political Institutions and Theories of the Hindus: A Study in Comparative Politics*. Leipzig: Verlag Von Markert & Petter, 1922.

———. *The Positive Background of Hindu Sociology, Introduction to Hindu Positivism*. Delhi: Motilal Banarasidas, 1985.

———. "Daridranarayner Samaj-shastra." In *Samaj Vijnan*, 59–80. Calcutta: Chakraborty Chatterjee Company Limited, 1938.

Sartre, Jean Paul. "Dirty Hands." In *The Political Imagination in Literature*, edited by Philip Green and Michael Walzer, 206–19. New York, NY: The Free Press, 1969.

Scheler, Max. *Philosophical Perspectives*. Translated by Oscar A. Haac. Boston, MA: Beacon Press, 1958.

———. *Formalism in Ethics and Non-Formal Ethics of Values*. Translated by Manfred S. Frings and Roger L. Funk. Evanston, IL: Northwestern University Press, 1973.

Schelling, F. W. J. *Historico-critical Introduction to the Philosophy of Mythology*. Translated by M. Richey and M. Zisselsberger. Albany, NY: State University of New York Press, 2007.

Schmitt, Carl. *Political Theology: Four Chapters on the Concept of Sovereignty*. Translated by George Schwab. Cambridge, MA: The MIT Press, 1985.

Schneck, Stephen Frederick. *Person and Polis: Max Scheler's Personalism as Political Theory*. Albany, NY: State University of New York Press, 1987.

Schoeman, Ferdinand. "Privacy: Philosophical Dimensions of the Literature." In *Philosophical Dimensions of Privacy*, edited by Ferdinand Schoeman, 1–33. Cambridge: Cambridge University Press, Cambridge, 1984.

Seal, Brajendranath. "The Neo Romantic Movement in Literature (1890–91)." In *New Essays in Criticism*. Calcutta: Papyrus, 1994 (1903).

———. *Rammohun Roy: The Universal Man*. Calcutta: Sadharan Brahmo Samaj, 1933.

———. *Bangla Rachana* [Bengali]. Edited by Tapankumar Ghosh. Kolkata: Patralekha, 2013.

Sealander, Judith. "Curing Evils at Their Source: The Arrival of Scientific Giving." In *Charity, Philanthropy and Civility in American History*, edited by Friedman and McGarvie, 217–39. Cambridge: Cambridge University Press, 2002.

Sen, Amartya. *The Argumentative Indian: Writings on Indian History, Culture and Identity.* London: Penguin Books, 2005.

Sen, Keshub Chandra. "The Brahmo Samaj, or Theism in India." In *The Golden Book of Rammohun Roy,* edited by Saroj Mohan Mitra. Calcutta: Rammohun Library & Free Reading Room, 1997.

———. "Keshab Chandra Sen defends his conduct in regard to Cooch Behar Marriage." In *Keshub Chunder Sen by F. Max Mueller,* edited by Nanda Mukherjee, Appendix-III, 69–73. Calcutta: S. Gupta and Brothers, 1976.

———. "Asia's Message to Europe." In *Keshub Chunder Sen* by *F. Max Mueller,* edited by Nanda Mukherjee, Appendix VIII, 103–17. Calcutta: S. Gupta and Brothers, 1976.

Sengupta, Shuddhabrata, "Discussing the Public Domain." In *Sarai Reader 01,* 1–9. New Delhi: Sarai-CSDS, 2001.

Sen, Samita. "Offences Against marriage: Negotiating Custom in Colonial Bengal." In *A Question of Silence: The Sexual Economics of Modern India*, edited by Mary E. John and Janaki Nair, 77–110. New Delhi: Kali for Women, 1998.

Sennett, Richard. *The Fall of Public Man.* Cambridge: Cambridge University Press, 1976.

Seth, Andrew. *Hegelianism and Personality* (1887). In *G. W. F. Hegel: Critical Assessments* Vol. II, edited by Robert Stern, 20–40. London: Routledge, 1998.

Sharma, Sanjay. *Famine, Philanthropy and the Colonial State: North India in the Early Nineteenth Century,* New Delhi: Oxford University Press, 2001.

Shiffman, Gary. "Construing Disagreement: Consensus and Invective in 'Constitutional' Debate." *Political Theory* 30, no. 2 (2002): 175–203.

Simmel, Georg. *The Philosophy of Money.* Translated by Tom Bottomore and David Frisby. London: Routledge, 1990.

———. "The Poor Person." In *Sociology: Inquiries into the Construction of Social Forms,* Vol. 2, 409–42. Translated by A. J. Blasi, A. K. Jacobs, and Mathew Kanjirathinkal. Leiden, The Netherlands: Brill, 2009.

———. *Sociology: Inquiries into the Construction of Social Forms,* Vol. 1. Translated by A. J. Blasi, A. K. Jacobs, and Mathew Kanjirathinkal. Leiden, The Netherlands: Brill, 2009.

Skinner, Quentin. *The Foundations of Modern Political Thought,* Vol. 2: The Age of Reformation. Cambridge: Cambridge University Press, 1992 (1978).

Smiles, Samuel. *Self Help.* Mumbai: Wilco Publishing House: 2004 (1986).

Smith, Gary, ed. *On Walter Benjamin: Critical Essays and Recollections.* Cambridge, MA: The MIT Press, 1988, 292–325.

Spivak, Gayatri Chakravorty. *A Critique of Postcolonial Reason: Towards a History of the Vanishing Present.* Calcutta: Seagull, 1999.

Stace, William Terence. *The Philosophy of Hegel: A Systematic Exposition.* New York, NY: Dover Publications, 1995.

Strauss, Leo. *The Political Philosophy of Hobbes: Its Basis and Its Genesis.* Translated by Elsa M. Sinclair. Chicago: The University of Chicago Press, 1963.

Sutherland, S. L. "The Problem of Dirty Hands in Politics: Peace in the Vegetable Trade." *Canadian Journal of Political Science* 28, no. 3 (1995): 479–507.

Tiwari, Surbhi, and Arnab Chatterjee "Deathly Silence." *Hindustan Times*, August 13, 2004. (Jointly Authored).

Tiwari, Surbhi. "Ashis Nandy and the Making of Critical Neo-Gandhian Discourse on Development." Paper in UGC DRS Programme' Compendium Volume, Calcutta University, 2005.

———. "The Corrupt Son of the Erupting City: Kolkata in Law and Lovely Matters Like Relationships." Fellowship paper presented at CSDS, Delhi, in October 2006 for SARAI, Centre for the Study of Developing Societies (CSDS), Delhi, October 2006.

———. "Sexy Dresses, Erotic Spaces: The Sport of Spatial Identity in an Indian Muslim Tennis Woman." Paper presented at the "Engaging Islam: Feminisms, Religiosities and Self Determinations" conference organized by the Fall Institute, University of Massachusetts, Boston, September 12–16, 2007.

———. "Whither Formalism, Fundamentalism or Feminism? Sania Mirza, 'Sexy' Dressing and the Politics of Youth Perception." Research paper commissioned by Konrad Adenauer Foundation along with *Lokniti*, Centre for the Study of Developing Societies (CSDS), New Delhi, 2007.

———. "Women's' Studies for Clothing, Feminism for Dress? An Inquiry into Gender and Genre." Working paper presented at the Indian Association of Women's Studies (IAWS) Conference, Lucknow, 2008.

Tripathi, Amalesh. *Italir Renaissence, Bangalir Sanskriti* [ Bengali]. Calcutta: Ananda Publishers, 1996.

Taylor, Charles. *Sources of the Self: The Making of the Modern Identity.* Cambridge, MA: Harvard University Press, 1989.

———. "Modern Social Imaginaries." *Public Culture* 14, no.1 (2002): 91–124.

Thakur, Rabindranath. "Shoksawbha." In *Prabandha Samagra,* Vol. II, 505–10. Kolkata: Bikas Grantha Bhavan, 2003.

———. "Gora." In *Uponyas Sangraha* [Bengali], 1–320.Kolkata: Juthika Book Stall, 2002.

———. *Prabandha Samagra,* 3 vols. Kolkata: Bikash Grantha Bhavan, 2003.

Thapar, Romila. "Dana and Daksina [Bengali]: A Form of Exchange." In *Cultural Pasts: Essays in Early Indian Genealogy,* 521–35. Delhi: Oxford University Press, 2000.

Thompson, Kevin, and Lester Esmbree, eds. *Phenomenology of the Political.* Boston: Kluwer Academic Publishers, 2000.

Titmuss, Richard. M. "Who Is My Stranger?" In *Talking about Welfare: Readings in Philosophy and Social Policy,* edited by Noel Timms and David Watson, 207–36. London: Routledge and Kegan Paul, 1976.

Tonnies, Ferdinand. *Community and Civil Society.* Translated by Joe Harris and Margaret Hollis. Cambridge: Cambridge University Press, 2001. First published in 1887.

Trivedi, Ramendra Sundar. "Mukti." In *Jiggasa,* 171–209. Kolkata: Granthamala, 1982.

Vora, Rajinder, and Suhas Palshkar, eds. *Indian Democracy: Meanings and Practices,* 215–32. New Delhi: SAGE Publications, 2004.

Wadia, A. R., ed. *History and Philosophy of Social Work in India.* Bombay: Allied Publishers Private Limited, 1968.

Walzer, Michael. "Political Action: The Problem of Dirty Hands." *Philosophy and Public Affairs* 2, no. 2 (1973): 160–80.

Walzer, Michael and Philip Green, eds. *The Political Imagination in Literature.* New York, NY: The Free Press, 1969.

Walzer, Michael, and Philip Green, eds. "The Problem of Choice." In *The Political Imagination in Literature,* 206–19. New York, NY: The Free Press, 1969.

Warren, Samuel D., and Louis D. Brandeis. "The Right to Privacy." *Harvard Law Review* 4, no. 5 (1890): 193–220.

Waterfield, Robin, trans. *The First Philosophers: The Presocratics and the Sophists*. Oxford: Oxford University Press, 2009.

Weber, Max. *Economy and Society: An Outline of Interpretive Sociology*, Vol. II. Edited by Guenther Roth and Claus Wittich. Berkley, CA: University of California Press, 1978.

———. "Intermediate Reflections on the Economic Ethics of the World Religions: Theory of the Stages and Directions of Religious Rejection of the World." In *The Essential Weber: A Reader,* edited by Sam Whimster, 215–44. London: Routledge: London, 2004.

———. "Science as a Vocation." In *Max Weber's Complete Writings on Academics and Political Vocations,* translated by Gordon C. Wells, 25–42. New York, NY: Algora Publishing, 2008.

Wijze, Stephen De. "Tragic Remorse—The Anguish of Dirty Hands." *Ethical Theory and Moral Practice* 7, no. 5 (2005): 453–47.

Williams, Raymond. *Keywords: A Vocabulary of Culture and Society*. London: Fontana, Croom Helm, 1976.

Woodroofe, Kathleen. *From Charity to Social Work: In England and the United States*. London: Routledge and Kegan Paul, 1962.

Bernard Yack. "Rhetoric and Public Reasoning: An Aristotelian Understanding of Political Deliberation." *Political Theory* 34, no. 4 (2006): 417–38.

Zaretsky, Eli. "Hannah Arendt and the Meaning of the Public/Private Distinction." in *Hannah Arendt and the Meaning of Politics,*edited by Calhoun and Mc Growan, 207–31. Minneapolis, MN and London: University of Minnesota Press, 1997.

Zizek, Slavoj. *The Plague of Fantasies*. London: Verso, 1997.

# Index

# About the Author

**Dr Arnab Chatterjee** is former Associate Professor in Humanities and Social Sciences at the School of Law at Auro University, Surat, Gujarat. Previously he was a Fellow in social and political philosophy at the Indian Institute of Advanced Study (IIAS), Shimla, India. With diverse departmental affiliations and degrees in political science, social work, sociology, history and philosophy, he has been a faculty in pluri-disciplinary social sciences at various institutes and universities across India and West Bengal, including Yashwant Rao Chavan Academy of Development Administration (YASHADA), Pune; Jadavpur University, Kolkata; Vidyasagar University, West Bengal University of Technology etc. teaching social philosophy, applied sociology, social work, jurisprudence, political thought, engineering ethics, and more. He has held Ford Foundation and Enreca (the Netherlands) research fellowships from the Centre for Studies in Social Sciences (CSSSC), Kolkata, and the SARAI initiative of the Centre for the Study of Developing Societies (CSDS), New Delhi. His first book *Categorical Blue: Personalytic Ethics in Social Work and Other Structures of Helping* was published in 2017.